PIDGIN AND CREOLE TENSE-MOOD-ASPECT SYSTEMS

CREOLE LANGUAGE LIBRARY (CLL)

A companion series to the
"JOURNAL OF PIDGIN & CREOLE LANGUAGES"

Editor: Pieter Muysken (Amsterdam)

Volumes in this series will present descriptive and theoretical studies designed to add significantly to our insight in Pidgin and Creole languages.

Volume 6

John Victor Singler (ed.)

Pidgin and Creole Tense-Mood-Aspect Systems

PIDGIN AND CREOLE
TENSE-MOOD-ASPECT SYSTEMS

Edited by

JOHN VICTOR SINGLER
New York University

JOHN BENJAMINS PUBLISHING COMPANY
Amsterdam/Philadelphia

1990

Library of Congress Cataloging-in-Publication Data

Pidgin and creole tense-mood-aspect systems / edited by John V. Singler.
    p.   cm. -- (Creole language library, ISSN 0920-9026; v. 6)
Includes bibliographical references.
1. Pidgin languages -- Verb. 2. Creole dialects -- Verb. I. Singler, John Victor. II. Series.
PM7803.P53   1990
417'.22 -- dc20   90-32192
ISBN 90 272 5226 2 (Eur.) / 1-55619-102-2 (US) (alk. paper)   CIP

Contents

Introduction: Pidgins and Creoles and Tense-Mood-Aspect   vii
    John Victor Singler

On the Adequacy of Natural Languages: I. The Development of
    Tense   1
    William Labov

Papiamentu Tense-Aspect, with Special Attention to Discourse   59
    Roger W. Andersen

Time Reference in Kikongo-Kituba   97
    Salikoko S. Mufwene

Tense, Mood, and Aspect in the Haitian Creole Preverbal Marker
    System   119
    Arthur K. Spears

Tense and Aspect in Capeverdean Crioulo   143
    Izione S. Silva

The Tense-Mood-Aspect System of Berbice Dutch   169
    Ian E. Robertson

Nigerian Pidgin English in Old Calabar in the Eighteenth and
    Nineteenth Centuries   185
    Joan M. Fayer

The Impact of Decreolization upon T-M-A: Tenselessness, Mood,
    and Aspect in Kru Pidgin English   203
    John Victor Singler

Author Index   231

Language Index   235

Subject Index   237

Introduction:
Pidgins and Creoles and Tense-Mood-Aspect

John Victor Singler
New York University

The shared properties of creoles lie at the heart of contemporary creole studies. Strictly speaking, the question of creole genesis is paramount. But no hypothesis of creole genesis is seriously considered that fails to account for the phenomenon of shared properties.

One area of the grammar of creoles where shared properties have long been noted is in the expression of tense, mood, and aspect (TMA). Van Name (1869-70) and Schuchardt (1882) both comment on TMA particulars that are shared by creoles with different lexical bases. In the mid-twentieth century, Thompson (1961) and Taylor (1971) also draw attention to TMA. In particular, as summarized by Muysken (1981), they observe the following about the preverbal TMA particles characteristic of creoles:

(a) each Creole language tends to have three of them: a past tense marker; a potential mood marker; and a durative aspect marker.

(b) when we find more than one particle accompanying a verb, the particles always occupy a fixed order: tense, mood, aspect, main verb. The combinations of the particles are interpreted in fixed, and rather complex ways (1981:183).

William Labov, in a 1971 manuscript, also notes the shared properties of creoles with regard to tense. In his manuscript (published in this volume), Labov observes that highly rudimentary pidgins are able to express time relations by the use of temporal adverbs. He then addresses the question of **why** creole languages develop a grammatical mechanism for marking tense. In his answer Labov moves away from the monogenetic explanation of shared properties that underlies Thompson's and Taylor's work to one grounded in functional universals.

In 1974 Derek Bickerton published "Creolization, Linguistic Universals, Natural Semantax and the Brain". (Originally published in the *University of Hawaii Working Papers*, the article was republished in Day 1980. The references that follow are to the version that appeared in Day's volume.) With the distribution of Labov's manuscript and especially with the publication of Bickerton's article, TMA became the pre-eminent site for the discussion of the phenomenon of the shared properties of creoles and for the debate about its explanation.

Bickerton's article compares the TMA systems of Sranan, Guyanese, Haitian Creole French, and Hawaiian Creole English. The languages are alike in that in each "the zero form marks simple past for action verbs and nonpast for state verbs" (1980:5). There are three preverbal markers, occurring in the order noted above, i.e. tense, mood, aspect. The three preverbal markers express anterior tense, irrealis mood, and nonpunctual aspect. Further, the collocations of the preverbal markers have fixed meanings.

Clearly Bickerton's analysis of the TMA system falls within the tradition of Taylor and Thompson. From a TMA perspective, his most important departure from their work is his identification of what he calls an Anterior — rather than a Past — tense. He links this to the action/state distinction and asserts that a marker of anteriority "indicates past-before-past for action verbs and simple past for state verbs" (1980:5). The effect of an action/state distinction upon tense had been noticed before for West African languages (cf. Welmers and Welmers 1968, Welmers 1973) but not applied to creoles.

Bickerton uses the similarities in TMA as evidence for a linguistic-universals explanation of creole genesis. He develops his theory further in subsequent work, especially Bickerton (1981, 1984a, 1984b), positing the language bioprogram hypothesis (LBH). Bickerton's view holds that the setting in which creole genesis occurs is characterized by linguistic chaos and insufficient access for the learner to the target language; in an atmosphere in which linguistic transmission has been disrupted, child language learners fall back on the language bioprogram.

Particularly in *Roots of Language* (1981) but in subsequent works as well, Bickerton has continued to use TMA as evidence for the LBH. Further, he has argued that, inasmuch as not all social settings led equally to the strongest type of creolization, it is not appropriate to assign equal weight to the evidence from all creoles. (In Bickerton 1984a he proposes an implicational scale for the degree of "radicalness" of creoles.)

If Bickerton's theory of creole genesis is fundamentally correct, then it does follow that it is necessary to restrict the type of creoles whose evidence can be considered. Thus, it would be appropriate to exclude "fort creoles" (Chaudenson's 1979 "*créoles endogènes*"), since the continued presence of another language for the community would have precluded the existence of the linguistic void that is a precondition for the fullest operation of the bioprogram. For that reason it would be appropriate to concentrate on "plantation creoles" (Chaudenson's "*créoles exogènes*"). Even within the group of plantation creoles, it would be necessary to recognize that the degree of linguistic deprivation, hence degree of reliance upon the bioprogram, would vary.

This attention to the cultural matrix of creole genesis (the term comes from Alleyne 1971) has shaped the examination of creole TMA in the post-1974 period. Thus, for example, when Muysken (1981) presents data from six languages as evidence for his assertion of the inadequacy of Bickerton's (1974) account, Bickerton (1981) dismisses evidence from three of the languages out of hand because of their social history. As noted, this rejection is consistent with the larger theory of the language bioprogram.

However, creolists have in general rejected the LBH, at least in its strongest form, as the principal means of accounting for the shared properties of creoles. One of the problems with the hypothesis lies in the implausibility of the version of history that it requires (cf. Singler 1986 for a discussion of this with respect to the Caribbean). If the LBH becomes untenable as an explanatory device for the shared properties of creoles, then it follows that the exclusion from consideration of all but the most radical creoles is also untenable.

Even if the LBH were itself fully tenable, there would be problems with Bickerton's assertion that the creole TMA system, especially as described in Bickerton (1974), represents the unmarked case. To begin with, Bickerton's prototypical creole TMA system is based solely on creoles whose superstrate languages are Indo-European. (The LBH does acknowledge the role of the superstrate in creole genesis; it is the role of the substrate that it explicitly denies.) A broader spectrum of creoles is needed in order to see if the shared properties in question are to be found when the superstrate languages are non-Indo-European. Further, even the original four creoles whose shared properties form the basis for the prototypical creole TMA system do not, upon further examination, entirely conform to that system: in the present volume, the article by Spears shows that Haitian Creole departs from the prototype in significant ways.

The primary alternative to the LBH has been a theory of creole genesis that acknowledges the role of the substrate and that views substratal influence as interactive with influence from the lexifier language (the superstrate) and with linguistic universals. Such a view differs from the LBH not only in its inclusion of the substrate as a contributor to creole genesis but also in its emphasis on pragmatic as well as grammatical universals. If the communicative circumstances in which creoles arose highly favored certain linguistic strategies, recognition of this contributes to an understanding both of creole genesis and the shared properties of creoles. While Bickerton does not claim "that the LBH specifies the **only** means through which novel linguistic structures can arise" (1984b:174, emphasis Bickerton's), the more that pragmatic universals can explain, the less necessary and less likely a strong form of the LBH becomes. Further, a theory of creole genesis that accounts for the shared-properties phenomenon must also acknowledge the diversity of pidgin and creole linguistic behavior. This diversity may itself be principled, arising for example from differences among pidgins and creoles in the nature of the social setting in which they evolved and/or differences between them in the degree of homogeneity of their substratal input. (And differences between them may also be explained by differences in their respective substrates or superstrates.) In this light, the examination of a wide — rather than a narrow — range of pidgins and creoles becomes crucial.

A separate issue with regard to TMA and its impact on theories of creole genesis involves the degree to which creole TMA systems have changed over time, i.e. since genesis. It is implicit in Bickerton (1984a, 1984b) that the creoles under study have not changed significantly since genesis. On the other hand, Bickerton acknowledges in *Roots of Language* that "once you turn a completive loose in a classic creole TMA system, the only consequence must be a drastic remodeling of that system" (1981:94). An ongoing issue, then, not only for Bickerton but for all creolists is the relation of the contemporary TMA system in a particular language to the TMA system of an earlier time.

With the caveats noted and whatever the explanation of creole genesis, in a book about pidgin and creole TMA systems it is appropriate to return to Bickerton's 1974 article: as a study of creole TMA, it remains seminal. The articles in the present volume are testimony to its importance. In them and in almost all studies of individual pidgin and creole TMA systems since 1974, comparison with Bickerton's prototypical creole TMA system is the diagnostic, the starting point from which further analysis proceeds.

The present volume contains Labov's 1971 article "On the Adequacy of Natural Languages: I. The Development of Tense", followed by seven articles on TMA in individual pidgins and creoles. The languages under discussion form a diverse group. Their lexifying languages are English, French, Dutch, Portuguese, Spanish, and the Bantu language Kikongo. Geographically, the range includes West and Central Africa, the Caribbean, and the Pacific. The social histories of the languages in question vary as well. There are the *créoles exogènes*: in each case a massive displacement of diverse peoples gave rise to the setting in which the creole arose. These are Haitian Creole (represented here by the article by Spears), Papiamentu (Andersen), Berbice Dutch (Robertson), Hawaiian Creole English (Labov), and Capeverdean Crioulo (Silva).[1] In the case of Kituba (Mufwene), there has been no massive displacement; it arose from a Kikongo-based lingua franca. As such, Kituba represents a type of *créole endogène*.[2]

Finally, three pidgins are discussed in the volume: Tok Pisin (Labov), Kru Pidgin English (Singler), and Eighteenth Century Nigerian Pidgin English (Fayer). The three have very different histories: Tok Pisin is in the process of undergoing nativization, while Kru Pidgin English has existed as a pidgin for almost two centuries without nativizing. The Eighteenth Century Nigerian Pidgin is that of a diary kept in pidgin by an Efik merchant who did not speak (or write) English.[3]

The way in which the individual pidgins and creoles of the present volume conform to and depart from Bickerton's prototypical creole system can be illustrated by looking at each of them with regard to anteriority. As noted above, Bickerton's identification of the Anterior tense is one of the most important contributions of his 1974 study. Unlike the tense systems of their Western European lexifier languages, those of the creoles that he examined do not mark **absolute** tense. That is, Comrie (1985:1) defines tense as "the grammaticalisation of location in time" of a situation. (**Situation** is Comrie's cover term for events, states, processes, and the like.) In a system of absolute tense, tense locates a situation with reference to the moment of speaking. Thus, the English Past tense locates a situation as occurring prior to the moment of speech. In contrast to systems of absolute tense are ones of **relative** tense. A "pure" relative tense is one in which a situation is located vis-a-vis a reference point, which in turn is ordinarily established within the discourse. These "pure" relative tenses, ones that make no reference whatever to the moment of speaking, are apparently rare in main clauses cross-linguistically; they seem to be most often restricted to non-finite verbs and/or subordinate clauses. More common than the "pure" relative tenses are ones that relate a situation to a reference point that is in turn established relative to the moment of speech. These are not "pure" relative tenses (Comrie calls then "absolute-relative" tenses), but they have ordinarily been designated as relative (and are considered so here): Bickerton's Anterior is a case in point, at least for nonstative verbs. He defines it as "past-before-past" for actions. That is, the Anterior tense in his prototypical system locates an action as occurring prior to some reference point, this reference point in turn having occurred prior to the moment of speaking.

Of the seven individual languages under study in this volume, Haitian Creole and Eighteenth Century Nigerian Pidgin conform to Bickerton's characterization, Haitian Creole with *te* and Eighteenth Century Nigerian Pidgin with *was*.[4] Capeverdean Crioulo also has a marker of Anterior tense, one that corresponds to Bickerton's semantic characterization; however, it is a verb suffix, *-ba*, rather than a preverbal marker.

If the prototypical creole Anterior were a "pure" relative tense, it would show up on simple past events in those instances where the moment of speaking is the reference point. This is not the case in Bickerton's system (the zero verb obtaining here) nor in the languages noted — Haitian Creole, Eighteenth Century Nigerian Pidgin, or Capeverdean Crioulo. It is, however, what obtains in Kituba. There the Anterior marker (as in Capeverdean, a suffix) is present when the event occurs prior to the reference point, regardless of whether the reference point is in the past or is the moment of speaking itself. In other words, for Kituba and for Bickerton's creole prototype alike, when the reference point is in the past, the Anterior tense is used. But when the reference point is the moment of speech, the creole prototype uses the zero verb while Kituba uses the Anterior form.

Finally, the remaining three languages — Berbice Dutch, Papiamentu, and Kru Pidgin English — do not have a special Anterior tense. Instead, Berbice Dutch has a Past AUX (as well as a Completive AUX and a Perfect suffix); Papiamentu has a marker of Perfective aspect (*a*) and a marker of Past Imperfective (*tabata*); and Kru Pidgin English has neither Past nor Anterior tense.

These seven languages, then, provide a spectrum: they range from the languages that express creole anteriority with a preverbal marker to those that do not mark anteriority at all. (For those that do not mark anteriority at all, the question arises as to whether they **no longer** mark it or whether they **never** marked it.)

With regard to mood and aspect, certain terms ought to be clarified. **Irrealis** mood, according to Bickerton, refers to "'unreal time' (= futures, conditionals, subjectives, etc.)" (1980:6). In fact, the usual focus of studies of mood in creole languages — especially as part of tense-mood-aspect — has been on futures and conditionals alone. (In the present volume, Spears sets out an **indicative:subjunctive** opposition in Haitian Creole and Robertson discusses the broader range of modality in Berbice Dutch.)

With regard to what Bickerton and, following him, creolists generally term nonpunctual: in terms of the study of aspect more generally, the term **imperfective** is more widely used. That is, Bickerton's punctual:nonpunctual opposition is usually (if not invariably) a perfective:imperfective opposition. Perfectivity, according to Comrie,

> . . . presents the totality of the situation without reference to its internal temporal constituency: the whole of the situation is present as a single unanalysable whole, with beginning, middle, and end rolled into one . . . (1976:3)

Imperfectivity, then, views the internal temporal constituency of a situation. In Comrie's framework the basic division is between **habitual** and **continuous**. The latter then divides into **progressives** (nonstates) and **nonprogressives** (states). Because states are inherently (rather than variably) imperfective, the perfective:imperfective opposition does not apply to them; and they are not normally marked for imperfectivity. Thus, the fundamental types of imperfective aspect subject to overt marking are habitual and progressive, and it is Bickerton's claim that a single preverbal AUX marks both.[5]

A crucial feature of Bickerton's system is the neat compartmentalization of tense, mood, and aspect; they are presented as three discrete entities. However, as Chung and Timberlake note:

> The different temporal locations of an event — past, present, and future — are inherently correlated with differences in mood and aspect. Hence there is a correlation between future tense and non-actual potential mood [Bickerton's irrealis] and, by implication, between non-future tense and actual mood. An event that is ongoing at the speech moment has not been com-

pleted. Hence there is a correlation between present tense and incompletive . . . aspect and, by implication, between past tense and completive . .
. aspect (1985:206).

For the European-lexifier pidgins and creoles at least, it is the interaction of
these three constituents — specifically, tense and aspect but also aspect and
mood — that has given rise to the pidgin and creole TMA systems furthest
from Bickerton's prototype. The articles that follow make this point in
diverse ways.

In concluding, it is appropriate to make directly a point that has been
implicit in the discussion of how individual pidgin and creole languages
treat the Anterior tense and how they react to the interaction of tense,
mood, and aspect. This point is implicit as well in the articles that follow,
particularly when those articles are taken as a whole. Namely, while pidgin
and creole systems share critical properties, they also show a farreaching
diversity. Thus, to relate creole TMA to issues of creole genesis and issues
of TMA theory, it is necessary to take into account not only the unity but
also the diversity of tense-mood-aspect in pidgin and creole languages.

Notes

*   I wish to express my gratitude to the following:
        William Labov, for his permission to publish "On the Adequacy of Natural Languages:
        I. The Development of Tense";
        Pieter Muysken, for his helpful suggestions;
        Jane Martin of the United States Educational and Cultural Foundation in Liberia and
        David Krecke of the United States Information Service in Liberia, for logistical support;
        and
        Bob Carter, Sally Deitz, Richard Krawetz, and Steve Lynch, for their encouragement.

1.   As Silva notes, Cape Verde had no native population prior to its discovery by the Por-
        tuguese. However, the nature of Portuguese-African interaction there seems to have dif-
        fered in crucial ways from that which occurred in the Caribbean and Hawaii; con-
        sequently, Capeverdean Crioulo's history appears to resemble more nearly the history of
        créoles endogènes than is true of the other créoles exogènes.

2.   For formal evidence of pidginization/creolization in Kituba, the reader is referred to Muf-
        wene 1988.

3.   A further point about the languages under study is that two of them — Berbice Dutch and
        Kru Pidgin English — are characterized by unusually homogeneous substrates. Eastern
        Ijọ is the dominant substrate language for Berbice Dutch, and Western Kru languages,
        particularly Klao and Grebo, are dominant for Kru Pidgin English. In each case there has
        been a recent study of the impact of substratal homogeneity on the speech variety (Smith,
        Robertson, and Williamson 1987; Singler 1988).

4.   The discussion that follows is of the seven languages described in individual chapters and does not inlcude Labov's treatment of tense in Hawaiian Creole English and Tok Pisin.

5.   **Iterative** is distinct from **habitual** and **durative** from **progressive** (cf. Comrie 1976), as the following sentences from Spears's article illustrate:
   (i)   *He is sitting motionless in the living room right now.* (progressive, durative)
   (ii)   *He is hitting the nail with the hammer.* (progressive, iterative)
   (iii) *This statue used to stand in Central Park.* (habitual, durative)
   (iv)   *He used to hit the bullseye.* (habitual, iterative)
   However, creolists' tendency to equate and/or twin habitual with iterative and progressive with durative reflects the fact that these distinctions are not ones ordinarily utilized in pidgins or creoles and, therefore, not ones crucial to an understanding of creole TMA.

References

Alleyne, Mervyn C. 1971. "Acculturation and the Cultural Matrix of Creolization". *Pidginization and Creolization of Languages* ed. by Dell Hymes, 169-86. Cambridge: University Press.

Bickerton, Derek. 1974. "Creolization, Linguistic Universals, Natural Semantax and the Brain". *University of Hawaii Working Papers in Linguistics* 6(3).125-41. (Reprinted in *Issues in English Creoles: Papers from the 1975 Hawaii conference* ed. by Richard Day, 1-18. Heidelberg:Groos.)

––––––. 1981. *Roots of Language.* Ann Arbor: Karoma.

––––––. 1984a. "Creoles and Universal Grammar: The unmarked case?" Colloquium paper presented at the Annual Meeting of the Linguistic Society of America, Baltimore.

––––––. 1984b. "The Language Bioprogram Hypothesis". *The Behavioral and Brain Sciences* 7.173-221.

Chaudenson, Robert. 1979. *Les créoles français.* Evreux: Nathan.

Chung, Sandra, and Alan Timberlake. 1985. "Tense, Aspect, and Mood". *Grammatical Categories and the Lexicon, Vol. 3: Language typology and syntactic description* ed. by Timothy Shopen, 202-58. Cambridge: University Press.

Comrie, Bernard. 1976. *Aspect: An introduction to the study of verbal aspect and related problems.* Cambridge: University Press.

––––––. 1985. *Tense.* Cambridge: University Press.

Mufwene, Salikoko S. 1988. "Formal Evidence of Pidginization/Creolization in Kituba". *Journal of African Languages and Linguistics* 10.33-51.

Muysken, Pieter. 1981. "Creole Tense/Mood/Aspect Systems: The unmarked case?" *Generative Studies on Creole Language* ed. by Pieter Muysken, 181-99. Dordrecht: Foris.

Schuchardt, Hugo. 1882. "Kreolen Studien. I. Über das Negerportugiesische von S. Thomé (Westafrika). *Sitzungsberichte der kaiserlichen Akademie der Wissenschaften zu Wien* 101(2).889-917.

Singler, John Victor. 1986. "Short Note". *Journal of Pidgin and Creole Languages* 1.141-45.

———. 1988. "The Homogeneity of the Substrate as a Factor in Pidgin/Creole Genesis". *Lg* 64.27-51.

Smith, Norval, Ian E. Robertson, and Kay Williamson. 1987. "The Ịjọ Element in Berbice Dutch". *Language in Society* 16.49-89.

Taylor, Douglas. 1971. "Grammatical and Lexical Affinities of Creoles". *Pidginization and Creolization of Languages* ed. by Dell Hymes, 293-296. Cambridge: University Press.

Thompson, R. W. 1961. "A Note on Some Possible Affinities Between Creole Dialects of the Old World and Those of the New". *Proceedings of the 1959 Conference on Creole Language Studies* ed. by Robert B. LePage, 107-113. London: Macmillan.

Van Name, Addison. 1869-70. "Contributions to Creole Grammar". *Transactions of the American Philological Association* 1:123-67.

Welmers, William E. 1973. *African Language Structures*. Berkeley: University of California Press.

Welmers, William E., and Beatrice Welmers. 1968. *Igbo: A learner's manual*. Los Angeles: William E. Welmers.

On the Adequacy of Natural Languages:
I. The Development of Tense[1]

William Labov

The University of Pennsylvania

[Editor's note: William Labov wrote the article that is presented below in 1971. After writing it, he circulated the manuscript in draft form. The article has never before been published, yet it has been and continues to be an important and oft-cited document in creole studies. Except for very minor corrections (primarily of typographical errors) and the updating of the bibliography, the article appears here as it did in 1971.]

0. The Association of Language with Intelligence

For at least three decades, linguists have been aware of the harm that was being done in our schools by a wrong view of the relations between language and logic. Children have traditionally been taught that the difference between non-standard dialects and standard grammar is that the standard is logical but non-standard is not. It is easy enough for us to demonstrate that this is not so on the basis of the usual grammatical shibboleths. In recent papers on negative attraction and concord (1972b) and on contraction and deletion of the copula (1969a), I felt that the logical equivalence of standard and non-standard rules was too obvious to mention. It is of course not so obvious to teachers and educational psychologists. Some progress has been made in modifying the schools' approach to these issues for white dialects: we find that recent high school text-books discuss negative concord as a difference in rules rather than a failure of logic. But as far as Black English is concerned, the normal ethnocentric view has taken over with a vengeance.

Pre-school intervention programs have been dominated by the theory that inner city children are verbally deprived, and one of the most successful — that of Bereiter and Engelmann (1966) — begins by teaching the children a "new" standard language on the grounds that theirs is inadequate for the expression of logical thought.[2] The evidence put forward for this claim is transparently wrong, as linguists unanimously agree (Labov 1969b, Alatis 1969, Williams 1970). We have the responsibility of summarizing linguistic evidence on this question for those making educational policy; that is one responsibility that the Linguistic Society of America has recently considered. But that does not mean that we have the answers on how the vernacular and the standard are to be related in the classroom. Nobody questions the fact that the schools should teach the standard. Our own research shows almost unanimous agreement in the adult community, Black and white, on this point, and the research and experience of others all show that the community wants standard English taught in the schools. But when should standard grammar be taught? In the early grades, as a necessary tool for learning other things, or later on, when the child has already bought into the educational system, as a form of social adjustment for the job market?

We do observe an association of middle-class, standard English language with success in school. But there are three possible reasons for this: (1) standard grammar may be necessary to understand the language used by teachers and the writers of examinations; (2) standard grammar may be necessary to convince teachers that the student is intelligent and will succeed, and to demonstrate allegiance to the moral standards of the school — that is, to trigger the correct self-fulfilling prophecy;[3] (3) standard grammar is necessary or helpful in attaining the concepts of equality and inequality, assertion and negation, or for the logical analysis of complex propositions using these primitives, or for the formation of other conjunctively defined concepts like animate, concrete, human, and so on. We can refer to these three arguments for the advantages of standard grammar as its **translational**, **social**, and **logical** claims.

The translational claim is a weak argument by itself for early training in standard grammar. It is true enough that teachers and testers now demand that children be able to handle the highly specialized style developed for problems, instructions and examinations. For example, the W.I.S.C. intelligence test asks:

At seven cents each, how much do three pencils cost?

In this construction, we have backwards pronominalization of the distributive which can certainly give pause to children not used to it. It is not too much to imagine that a child familiar only with vernacular grammar might find that the language stands between him and the arithmetic. Of course those who constructed the question wanted it to discriminate sharply among the students, and the language helps them do it. But if the translational claim of standard were its only advantage, we could easily dispense with this discrimination by translating such complex forms back into more analytic language:

   Each pencil costs seven cents. What do three pencils cost?

As far as the social claim of the standard is concerned, we might be able to locate teachers whose response to children is not governed by the social values of standard grammar, who would not be manipulated by a child with super-correct enunciation: "The boy is walk-ing down the street".[4] We could then proceed directly to the subject matter of education in the early grades, using the vernacular as our basic means of communication. But if the third, logical claim for standard grammar has any weight, we would have to think twice. It might then follow that children would profit by being taught some standard grammar before anything else — possibly before they even begin to read.

It is easy enough to reject the logical claim of the standard on an emotional or ideological basis. We might say as some linguists have that all languages or dialects are adequate for any purpose — just borrow a few lexical items, and your problems are solved. I do not think that such a dogma can be defended. As we will see, there is evidence that some languages — pidgins — are relatively inadequate for some purposes. The rule systems of some two-year-olds appear to be inadequate to express their cognitive intent (Bloom 1970). And the logical claim for standard English is equivalent to saying that some dialects are relatively inadequate for logical analysis or concept formation. The fact that science or linguistic analysis is done with standard, literary grammar may merely be a matter of fashion — or there may be a cognitive advantage for the individual doing it. Before we take up valuable time and energy teaching standard grammar to pre-school children, and risk alienating them further by imposing our own style upon them, we should find out what part of our complex syntax offers a cognitive advantage, if any, and what part is merely fashionable or even dysfunctional.

1.   Strategies for Studying the Relations of Language and Thought

The moment we mention the relation of language and thought, we inevitably conjure up the Whorfian hypothesis in its strong form — the idea that our grasp of reality is heavily influenced by our grammar. For most lin-

guists, this notion has now been relegated to the category of unproven or
even wrong-headed ideas which retain their fascination but have lost their
urgency as a basis for research. But I think the urgency is still there, and
that we can profit by the problems encountered in assembling decisive evidence. There are many strategies which we can follow besides the classical
method of cross-cultural testing of native speakers from widely different
cultures. On the one hand, it is easy enough to establish that a language
lacks a given grammatical category, like the perfect or progressive, or a
transformation like the passive. But there seem to be many alternative ways
of talking about the past or its effect on the present or of focusing on the
object of an action; and no doubt many of these alternatives still escape our
notice. We usually cannot obtain any agreement among ourselves as to
what the "meaning" or the "function" of the grammatical category is. It is
very difficult, then, to argue that one language is more adequate than
another for a given purpose (e.g. explaining the theory of relativity)
because we do not know all of the alternative means available to each.

Sub-cultural studies are more promising because we can make comparisons more easily when the languages differ in more limited ways. The
most obvious and important subculture is that of children. As Lois Bloom
has shown (1970), there is a stage for many children when they cannot construct sentences with more than two lexical items, even when it seems they
have more to say. At an early stage in grammatical development, children
use negation only to express "non-existence" (*no more juice*), but not the
meanings of "rejection" or "denial". There is no question that the language
of young children is inadequate from an adult point of view. But these
observations do not always answer the classic question: is their language
inadequate for **their** cognitive needs? We are faced with the complex situation of two systems — cognitive and linguistic — developing at the same
time but not always in coordination.

It also appears that children do not follow a uniform path in this
development of language and cognition. There is a great deal of individual
variation in the strategies used to learn language, and so the detailed study
of any one case may show us idiosyncratic — not social — solutions to a
given problem.

Let us consider the case of a six-year-old girl in Harlem being studied
by Jane Torrey.[5] Shown a picture of a fence, she said,

(1)   *To keep the cow . . . don't go out of the field.*

Here she did not control the POS-ING participial construction *from getting out of the field*. But can we point to any cognitive or communicative defect inherent to the construction of (1)? Its only failing is that it is not the socially approved model for embedding sentences as complements of *keep*. In general, we find ourselves puzzled when asked to suggest — even in speculation — the cognitive correlates of failure to grasp certain standard rules. There are children whose language shows the case distinction for *he* and *him*, but not for *she* and *her*. Torrey's performance tests show that they understand the difference between the two pronouns in the speech of others.[6] Can we reasonably imagine any cognitive correlate of the failure to use the form *she* before a verb?

As another possible source of information on the differential adequacy of linguistic systems, we can turn to differences in closely related class dialects. One can, for example, ask both working class children and middle-class children to express their ideas on the same subject, as Bernstein and his students have done (Bernstein 1961). Typical results are the essays given in (2) and (3). These are cited by Lawton (1968:112-13) as examples of "restricted" and "elaborated" codes respectively.

(2)   Working-class fifteen-year-old boy's essay on
          My Life in Ten Years' Time
      I hope to be a carpenter just about married and like to live in a modern house and do a ton on the Sidcup by-pass with a motorbike and also drinking in the Local pub.
          My hobby will be breeding dogs and spare time running a pet shop. And I will be wearing the latest styles of clothes.
          I hope my in ten years time will be a happy life without a worry and I have a good blance behide me. I am going to have a gay and happy life. I am going to work hard to get somewhere in the world.
          One thing I will not do in my life is to bring disgrace and unhappiness to my family.

(3)   Middle-class fifteen-year-old boy's essay on
          My Life in Ten Years' Time
      As I look around me and see the wonders of modern science and all the fantastic new developments I feel a slight feeling of despondency. This is because I am beginning to wonder who will be in control of the world in ten years time, the machine or man.

Already men are being shot round earth in rockets and already machines are being built that will travel faster and faster than the one before. I wonder if the world will be a gigantic nut-house by the time I'm ten years older. . . Men say we will have just one or two more luxuries and it never stops. I enjoy the luxuries of to-day, but in my opinion there is a limit. But who decides what the limit will be. No one knows its just a lot of men all relaying on someone to stop this happening, but no-one is going to. We're doomed. No prayers can save us now, we'll become slaves to great walking monstrosities. Powerless in the hands of something we helped to create. I'm worried about "my life in ten years time".

Lawton's discussion seems to imply that the second essay is superior, since it does show the longer sentences, more subordination, greater use of the passive, etc., which are the quantitative measures that identify the "elaborated code". But many of us would say on the contrary that (2) is a better essay than (3) in style and expressive power — that (3) suffers from elaboration with no clear cognitive advantage. There are tests of verbal skill which are based on less subjective criteria, but even here the interpretation of the results involves a whole series of problems concerning motivation and acculturation to the test situation (see Labov 1969b), factors which insure that children with middle-class orientation and style will satisfy the examiners better on a wide range of tests.

To avoid this bias, we can search for speakers who are truly bi-dialectal, and test the adequacy of their two dialects for comparable purposes. Unfortunately, we rarely find speakers fully competent in two opposing class dialects, no matter what their claims may be. Closely related rule systems seem to interfere with each other even more than distantly related ones; if we are to judge by the problems encountered by Black English speakers in our school system where one of these dialects is subordinated to the other, we will encounter the same problems of comparing their adequacy in a given situation as when we are testing two different speakers.

Recognizing the problems of interference in closely related dialects, we might turn to co-existent systems in bilingual individuals, where the cultural settings of the two languages are similar, but the linguistic systems are distinct. Here we would have more control of the background variables than in the cross-cultural studies of Hopi and English. And people do report that they find German or Spanish useful for one task, English for another.

There is good evidence to show that bilinguals find one language more adequate than another for different topics and in different settings (Ervin-Tripp 1964). One difficulty in doing serious research with individual, displaced bilinguals is that the functional differentiation of the two languages is highly idiosyncratic, dependent on the personal history of the speaker and his degree of control over each language. On the other hand, stable bilingual communities show a different problem: two languages may be different only in surface formatives. As Gumperz and Wilson have shown in their study of Marathi and Kannada of Kupwar (1971), the two languages may actually have converged in their semantics, phrase structure, and grammatical categories until they are in effect the same language and useless for any study of the differential adequacy of languages to express thought.

With proper forethought and ingenuity, the difficulties I have just outlined can be overcome. I am sure that any of the strategies suggested can be used to throw light on the relation between linguistic forms and cognitive advantages. But this paper will be devoted to one other strategy which seems to me eminently favorable for studying the relative adequacy of languages for particular uses. That is the naturalistic observation and analysis of pidgins, their development to creoles, de-creolization in the post-creole continuum,[7] and further development of the colloquial and literary standards.

To begin with, pidgins are generally admitted to be inadequate for some communicative purposes: they are often called "limited" or "marginal" languages for this reason.[8] This is not too easy to prove, because highly competent pidgin speakers can show great ingenuity in adapting the pidgin under pressure. But we have objective evidence that pidgins do not provide all of the features which native speakers seem to demand in a language. When pidgins acquire native speakers, they change. As we will see, these changes follow a regular pattern, supplying a variety of grammatical categories and syntactic devices which were missing in the pidgin. It follows that, from the standpoint of the native speaker, the pidgins are inadequate because they lack these features. We can then follow the further acquisition of grammatical categories and syntactic rules as creoles shift towards a standard or develop indigenous standard colloquial and literary forms. Within this broad development, we should be able to detect any major trends which would support the logical claim of the standard grammars.

In this discussion, I will be drawing most heavily on tape recordings made in 1968 and 1970 of Hawaiian pidgins and creoles in actual use. The great majority of the materials were gathered in the course of a sociolinguistic study with members of the Department of Linguistics of the University of Hawaii in the summer of 1970. I would particularly like to acknowledge the assistance and insights of Michael Forman, Richard Day, Carol Odo, Ruth Watanabe, William Peet and William Powell.[9] I will also be referring to important observations of Gillian and David Sankoff of current developments in the Neo-Melanesian spoken among the Buang in New Guinea. Briefer reference will be made to less fully documented descriptions of creoles with English, French, Dutch, Spanish and Portuguese lexicons, as spoken in the Caribbean and West Africa. Black English is relevant here primarily as one of the non-standard grammars of English. If it has evolved from a creole spoken generally in the South, it is now very far along on the post-creole continuum, and does not show any of the creole features I will be dealing with here. Finally, it may be noted that the general statements made here about the developments of pidgins and creoles seem to be well supported in the literature, but they are not intended as universals.

Creole studies rest on a long tradition of excellent scholarship and field work, extending back over a century. I do not think that there is any other field of linguistics where we can find so much information on the speech community or so deep a knowledge of vernacular language. But the data actually reported by creolists is still very far from the speech of every-day life. The texts are often folk tales, reminiscences of old times, or manufactured compositions. Occasional remarks are quoted from house boys addressing Europeans. Most often, examples are given without any documentation at all. Since the interests of most creolists have centered on historical problems, it has seemed possible to avoid the questions as to whether these grammars account for the language used in every-day life. But any discussion of the adequacy of creoles for communication must face this question. We must include recordings of conversation between equals and samples of speech from extended participant-observation in the speech community. Formal interviews are essential, but even the best face-to-face interviews must be correlated with group recordings in which speech is controlled by the factors which operate when the linguist is no longer there. This paper will accordingly rely most heavily upon field work of this sort, and interpret other secondary material in the light of primary observations.

My aim is to show how data on creoles and pidgins can illuminate the theoretical problems raised above, and encourage further research with primary data of this kind.

2. Bilingual Idiolects Vs. Pidgin Grammars

A pidgin community is by definition multilingual. The term **pidgin** is generally applied to a contact language formed when speakers of a socially subordinate language have to communicate with a superordinate, exploiting culture — more or less in its own terms.[10] Those who join or direct such a labor force, or those who bargain in a mercantile community, need some generalized medium of communication that is independent of the ingenuity or personal skill of particular bilingual speakers.[11] The pressure for a stable grammar is even greater when speakers of many subordinate languages arrive on the scene. This has been the case in Hawaii: plantations have employed workers with a wide variety of native languages: Portuguese, Japanese, Chinese, Ilocano, Tagalog, Bisayan, Spanish, and many others (Reinecke 1969). Though the pidgins will show considerable variation in pronunciation, reflecting the native luage of the speaker, it is easy to show that they have regular, socially sanctioned grammars. Such grammars are shaped by a very large number of cross-cutting individual transactions. Pidgins are thus social rather than individual solutions to the problem of cross-cultural communication.

On the other hand, there are isolated individuals who never learn this social pattern, but work out their own form of cross-linguistic expression. They may be old people isolated at home, talking only to their children and grandchildren; or wives working on isolated farms, with only a few neighbors to talk to. These individuals often work out a very ingenious and original mode of expression, combining their perfect knowledge of their native vernacular with an imperfect grasp of the several other languages spoken in this new environment. We may even be able to write grammars for their multilingual idiolect. But whatever regularity their rules show, these idioms are far less regular than pidgins — and much harder to understand. The particular devices used are usually very different from the rules of the pidgin grammar; they show that pidgins are not the automatic consequence of language mixture. Before we consider the general nature of pidgins, it may be illuminating to examine one such individual effort — a case studied by Hamilton van Buren of the University of Hawaii. Let us consider the language which Obasan, a Japanese woman in her seventies, uses in speaking to her non-Japanese neighbors in Hawaii.

Obasan was born in Hiroshima about the turn of the century, and came to Hawaii when she was eighteen. She spent most of her life working on a small farm and was never part of a plantation community. The idiom which she has developed seems to be understood by one close friend, an English speaker, but it is extremely difficult for others to decipher. As analyzed by at least van Buren, this idiom turns out to show a predominantly Japanese syntax with lexical items supplied by English, Japanese and pidgin. Thus Obasan conveys the meaning of "Soon it ended" by

(4)   *Baimbai pau ni natteta.*[12]

The first word is the standard pidgin adverbial marker of the future. *Pau* is Hawaiian for "finished", widely used in all forms of Hawaiian English; the Japanese particle *ni* is normally attached to adjectives. Finally, the verb is the strictly Japanese past tense of *naru* "become". Obasan's sentence structure normally follows Japanese in having the verb at the end. But the negative is a particle preceding the verb, as in pidgin, rather than a final verb itself (*-nai*) as in Japanese; thus where a pidgin speaker would say *I no like meat*, Obasan says

(5)   *Me wa niku ga no riku.*

Here English *me* is followed by the topicalizer *wa* and the Japanese word for "meat", *niku*. The Japanese verb would have been *sukinai*, with the negating verb *nai* at the end. Instead we have pidgin *no like*, with Japanese phonology, $l \rightarrow r$ and $\emptyset \rightarrow u/k\_\#$. With these small adjustments, Obasan seems to be following the pidginizing process of re-lexifying a well-formed Japanese grammar with words from another source. But Obasan also says

(6)   *I think water ga no more.*

Here English subject and verb appear at the beginning, followed by *water* with topicalizing *ga* and the pidgin predicator *no more*. The use of the English tag *I think* commits her to a basically English word order, though she ends with the pidgin equivalent of the Japanese verb — quite distinct from the standard English "I don't think there was any water". There is no telling when Obasan will hit upon an English verb or modal early in the sentence; when she does so, the normal drive to end each sentence with a Japanese verb and tense marker is partially blocked. As an example of the complications that this bilingual idiom can get into, consider Obasan's version of "I could not go and return".

(7)   *I can nai go cómebàck.*

The meaning seems to come across in a straightforward fashion, but the formal details are strange. We have the Japanese negative verb *nai* instead of *no*, and *come back* pronounced as a single word. These forms become more comprehensible when we observe that the Japanese verb which would have ended the sentence if *can . . . go* had not intervened would be *kaerarenai*, from *kaer*, "return" or "come-back", -*are*-, "to be able", and -*nai*, the negative. Thus Obasan seems to have been aiming at the Japanese model

(7')   *Watakusi wa itta kaerarenai.*

But she could not construct a full parallel because her use of English *I can* involved her in an inversion of the preferred Japanese order, and she wound up with a syntax which is, remarkably enough, half English and half Japanese.

We can contrast the bilingual idiolect of Obasan with an example of Hawaiian pidgin under Japanese influence. This is the speech of O-san, a Japanese working man of about the same age from Kaimuki, Oahu. O-san was present when I was interviewing a group of men raised on Hawaii, speakers of the post-creole Hawaiian English. He spoke very little until we got involved with wild pig hunting: then he began a long speech about what happens when the pig is roused by the dogs. Here is a sample of his grammar.

(8)   *Go bark bark bark. All right. He go. . . He stop see. Go for the dog. Go for the dog. He no go for you, the man. He no care for man. He go for the dog.*

Though O-san's phonology shows a strong Japanese influence, his grammar is Hawaiian pidgin. The reduplication of *bark bark bark* is a common pidgin device to express continued or iterative action. There are no inflections, and the verbs appear in their invariant stem form. Negation is shown by *no* in preverbal position. The basic preposition *for* appears freely. Most sentences are short independent clauses. *He stop see* is not reduced from English "He stops to see", but rather a use of the pidgin progressive auxiliary and copula *stop* (older form of current *stay*), translated best as "he's looking" or "he takes a look".

O-san occasionally abandons pidgin grammar to borrow from Japanese syntax, as in *six over*, for "six or more". But in the main, he uses the same Hawaiian pidgin grammar that native speakers of Ilocano, Portuguese or Chinese have used for a hundred years. He continues.

(9)   *He kill dog. And then after brought all down. Then the man can-*
      not find but. Can hear, where bark. All over here, he go over
      there. He knock him down.

The syntax departs markedly from standard English grammar, but it is not
a reflection of an idiosyncratic lack of grammatical competence on the part
of O-san. Again we see him using regular pidgin constructions. *But* normally follows its clause in Hawaiian pidgin, and any object noun phrase can
be deleted; *then the man cannot find but* may be translated as "But then the
man cannot find them". The subject of *Can hear* is not dropped by any
whim of O-san: in Hawaiian pidgin, subject pronouns are regularly deleted,
so that this sentence may be translated as "He can hear where they are
barking".

Hawaiian pidgin has co-existed with Hawaiian Creole for some time,
and the grammatical characteristics just shown are quite stable. Some are
general pidgin features, but others are specifically Hawaiian. The earliest
records of Hawaiian pidgin give only a sketchy view of the grammar, but
the similarity to O-san can be quite startling. Here are examples cited by
Reinecke of "broken English" used by Hawaiians about 1874, given from
memory by a visitor many years later (Isabella Bishop, *The Hawaiian
Archipelago*, 1893, cited in Reinecke 1969:200)

(9)   a. *But can't go back, we no stay here, water higher all minutes,*
          spur horse, think we come through. . . Think we get through;
          if horses give out, we let go; I swim save you.

A more recent example of Hawaiian pidgin of the 1930's, quoted by
Reinecke, has essentially the same grammar. This is an extract from the life
history of a Chinese immigrant as recorded by her daughter "as nearly as
possible in her own words". The grammar shows a normally unmarked present and past, negative marker *no*, and other pidgin features along with a
number of Hawaiian loan words like *kau-kau* "food" and *hana-hana*
"work" and pidgin idioms such as *junk kind*.

(9)   b. *My husband house kau-kau no good — cheap kind and too li-*
          li. I kau-kau junk kind den keep good kind kau-kau for my
          mada-in-law and all da man. . . By-'m-bye my husband he go
          Honolulu. Sometime he send letta, sometime he send money. I
          no can lead, so I take da letta to my fliend and my fliend he
          lead to me. One time, da letta, he speak for me come Hon-

olulu. I come Honolulu with one friend. Dis fust time I see boat and I li-li scared da water. But I no sick one day. Maybe because I too happy.

We can observe Chinese phonological influence in this transcription, in the regular rule that all prevocalic /r/ is realized as /l/. But otherwise, we see specifically Hawaiian pidgin lexicon and grammar. When true Chinese pidgin shows up, it is immediately apparent, as in the following example cited by Reinecke (1969:203) from an advertisement of 1933:

(9)   c. *Me P.Y. Chong numba one China cook, allsame Big Boss Waikiki Lau Lee Chai, sabe anything me business — cook, waita, dishwashy, no can foolem. Me P.Y. Chong got system.*

If the ad man was faithful to the speech of a particular Chinese speaker in Honolulu, as he claimed, it was a Chinese completely isolated from the main currents of Hawaiian life. This "Chinese pidgin" is almost as remote from Hawaiian pidgin as the Japanese/English of Obasan. But there is a striking similarity between the Chinese-influenced Hawaiian pidgin of (9b), the Japanese-influenced pidgin of (9), the older Hawaiian pidgin of (9a), and the Filippine-influenced and Punti-influenced pidgins to be cited below. All of this points to the existence of a well-formed grammar which is far from Reinecke's original conception of a "makeshift" language.

Obasan's bilingual idiolect is very hard to follow: a linguist with good knowledge of Japanese, English and Hawaiian pidgin can decipher it only after careful study of the tapes. But O-san's speech is immediately accessible to anyone who has a basic knowledge of Hawaiian pidgin. Since O-san does not feel that he really speaks English, he was slow to enter the conversation between myself and the speakers of post-creole Hawaiian English. But when he did speak up, he was understood perfectly by the others, and was answered in a modified pidgin:

(10)   *But O-san. The dog bite bite bite. But when you cut the pig. The bruise, you have to throw away all that. Is best to keep the dogs from.*

O-san's Hawaiian pidgin is thus a socially recognized form of language which is adequate for some purposes, inadequate for others. There are many topics and situations where speakers like O-san will not use pidgin: they switch instead to their rapid and fluent Japanese. Thus we know that the limitations of the pidgin grammar do not represent real limitations on

O-san's basic cognitive or linguistic ability. Full competence in a pidgin grammar is still less than competence in one's native grammar. If we know the full capacity of the pidgin, and of its creole successor, we are then in a position to ask the basic questions: "what ideas, notions, distinctions can be expressed in a native language which cannot be expressed in a pidgin? what thoughts are the pidgins inadequate to express?"

The general characteristics of pidgins are well known: inflections are eliminated, grammatical categories are sharply reduced, and adverbial phrases are used to express some of the equivalent meanings. Vocabulary is very much reduced as well, and considerable analytical ingenuity is exhibited in the periphrastic forms required. The Neo-Melanesian term for "ashes" is *shit belong fire*; for "knuckle", *screw belong finger*; for "rabbit", *pussy belong Australia*.[13] But perfectly competent pidgin speakers can give the listener the impression that they are having trouble expressing themselves. The speech of O-san just cited in (8) and (9) is a good example. We know that this pidgin fails to show the full linguistic competence of the speaker, because the same man controls a fluent Japanese which contrasts sharply in speed and complexity with the pidgin.

When pidgins become creoles, and acquire native speakers, they are spoken with much greater speed and fluency. The speech of O-san is slow and deliberate; the creole used by native Hawaiians is very fast. The Hawaiian Creole spoken by adolescents in the rural Oahu town of Nanakuli is extremely fast — so that native speakers of other forms of Hawaiian English find it hard to understand. In Nanakuli, "good speech" is fast speech and if someone is thought to be expressing himself poorly, he is said to be "talking too slow".[14] Verbal skill is shown by saying what must be said quickly and concisely. For example, Raymond Makahi of Nanakuli was once telling me that a certain game was good fun when you were a kid, but that he was too old for it now — it was strictly kid stuff. What he said was

(11)   *For other guys stuff; for me, it pau.*
       [fɔadəgɑɪstɑf fɔmiɪtpɑʊ]

One of the oldest and best-established pidgins is Neo-Melanesian, which has been used as a second language in New Guinea for a hundred years. Yet Neo-Melanesian pidgin is still spoken markedly slower than the native languages. Here is a striking example of code switching by a Buang speaker, about forty years old, as observed by G. and D. Sankoff at a village meeting in Mambump.

(12) *Am͡ ùukwàmiñ͡ vo͡ ken, alòk, kek͡ ùkwang͡ iñ͡ vo͡ gángk͡ ungwe:* **yú yét sìndáun, bái͡ yu páinim sìk.**
"You think about it, but now I've thought of something else: you're the only one sitting down, you will take sick".

The first half is in rapid Buang, with only one main stress to the sentence. There are eleven words, in three phonological phrases, with eight close junctures as indicated. The pidgin half has seven words, with five main stresses, and only one juncture. It takes the speaker just as long to say these seven words as the preceding eleven. It may seem as if the content dictates a more deliberate style for the second half, but we can contrast this with another sentence in which the speaker repeats in pidgin what he has just said in Buang.

(13) *Ngàu ti͡ ngmndó,* **bái ol͡ ikòt strét lòng͡ yú.**
"You're the only one sitting down, they'll take you straight to court".

The differences in tempo should not be exaggerated: Neo-Melanesian as used by this speaker is a much more fluent medium that the halting Hawaiian pidgin of O-san. It has function words (*bai, ol, long*) and inflections (*i-*) of its own. But it still has more main heavy stresses, shorter phonological phrases, and fewer close junctures than the native language. Over-all speed is not the issue: it takes about the same length of time to say *ngau ti ngmndo* as *yu yet sindaun*. Yet the Buang has a smoother style and a more even flow, which is achieved with a more complex set of morphophonemic rules. The development of such sandhi rules and other rules of morphophonemic condensation plays an important part in the grammatical histories of creoles, as we will see later.

At first glance such developments may seem quite superficial. If our ultimate interest is the relations of language and thought, we should turn our attention to the fundamental grammatical categories of pidgins and creoles, or to their logical connectives, or to their syntactic organization. As far as the basic logical elements are concerned, we find little difference between pidgins and creoles. Neo-Melanesian has *sapos* for "if", *na* for "and", and *o* for "or". Hawaiian pidgins use *if*, *an'*, and *o'* for these three particles. Pidgins are of course analytic in their structure, and are particularly well suited for breaking down complex propositions into their elements. Expressions for "because" and "why" are not difficult to locate in pidgins; in Neo-Melanesian we find *long wonem* and *watpo* for these meanings along with other expressions. But pidgins **are** deficient in most of the basic grammatical categories and syntactic operations typical of more developed languages. In this paper I will focus on the development of one such category — tense. A second paper will examine the development of the complex operations which shift theme and focus through changes in word order: considering first the passive and allied transformations, and then in greater detail embedding of relative clauses. These are of course only a few of the many areas of grammar which might be considered, but I hope that they will show that this is a fertile field for the study of the relations of linguistic forms and cognitive representations.

3.   Time Relations in Pidgin Grammars

One of the most striking characteristics of most pidgins is that they have no tense marker and therefore no grammatical category of tense. By that I mean not only the absence of the inflectional ending, English *-ed* or French *-ais*, but also the absence of **any** obligatory element in the verb phrases to identify the time reference of each predication. Past, present and future are unmarked. Time relations are expressed by **optional** adverbial phrases. In O-san's speech (8) and (9) and in (9a) and (9b) we saw only invariant verb forms. The treatment of time relations can be seen more clearly in a past tense narrative such as (14). This is Hawaiian Pidgin as used by Max, a man of about the same age as O-san but born in the Philippines and a native speaker of Ilocano. In this passage he was giving me an account of a man who died and came back to life.

> (14)   *Well . . . in the Philippine, this now . . . you see, he die in three hours . . . and then he come back a — **live** again. . . Three hours die, after three hours, come back live, he talk — tell the story about.*
>
> *(Why'd he come back?) . . . that guy, he got — books, like — book, like that. He say, "How come you come inside here?" Say, "Ah, somebody send me down here". So, they open the book. Open the book. "Ah, you no more name. You go back". So he go, but he come back. He heal, a's why he get up.*

Max shows the same deliberate pidgin tempo as O-san, and uses essentially the same grammar. He establishes the over-all time reference at the beginning with *In the Philippine*[15] and this holds for the entire passage. A more specific time relation is shown by *after three hours*. Other than this, time relations are shown by the basic narrative sequencing rule.[16]

Hawaiian pidgin frequently refers to the past with adverbials such as *olden time, young time, small boy time*, etc.[17] Another narrative by a 70-year-old woman of Chinese (Punti) background begins with *Olden time*:

> (15) *Olden time those people they are so poor they staying on the village on the valley.*

This speaker has acquired a good many standard English forms in her careful style — e.g., the copula *are*. But her tense system remains that of the pidgin grammar: the adverbial *olden time* governs the tense of the next dozen sentences. Neo-Melanesian pidgin has a wide range of such adverbs for past time: *bipo, long bipo, asde* "yesterday", etc. To see how this works, consider (16), from a translation of Antony's funeral oration from *Julius Caesar* into Neo-Melanesian (from Murphy 1966:20).

> (16) *Taim bilong Lupercal, yu yet lukim me, mi laik mekim King long Kaesar.*

That is, "You all did see that on the Lupercal [i.e., the Lupercalia, Feb. 15th] I tried to make Caesar king". Here *Taim bilong Lupercal* comes first, and governs the whole following paragraph.

> (17) *Long taim bipo, yupela hamamas tumas long Kaesar. Em i stret. Watpo yu noken sori longen nau?*

That is, "You all did love him once. He was honest. Why do you not mourn now?" Again the time adverbial *long taim bipo* comes first, and governs until we encounter *longen nau* in the second most favored position, which controls the second sentence.

As a third example, we may consider the pidgin French spoken in Vietnam, *Tây Bôi*, as recently described by Reinecke (1971). This is a stable pidgin with a long history, first noted by Schuchardt in 1888. It never acquired any native speakers, and is now expiring as the French depart from Vietnam. The verb is invariant, and there is no tense.

> No restructured system of auxiliaries was developed as in the French Creole dialects. Time and aspect are inferred from the context or indicated only by the adverbs of time. (Reinecke 1968)

Thus we have *mwa buve te* "I drink tea", *mwa buve te suə avɛŋ* "I drank tea yesterday", and *dəmən mwa buve te awɛk ami* "tomorrow I will drink tea with my friends". Note that these adverbs are in first or last position, rather than next to the verb.

This system may seem primitive, but it is hard to prove that it is inadequate. If time is expressed with optional adverbs, then it is only necessary to signal the time once at the beginning of a narrative or for as long as we are in the same sequence of events. But with a tense system, we have to use the tense marker over and over again. In their recent discussion of "Indigenous Pidgins and Koinés", Nida and Fehderau say that "the use of independent adverbial particles, rather than inflectional forms, to denote various tenses and aspects points in the same direction of greater redundancy" (1970:150). But they fail to consider that the tense markers are obligatory, the free adverbs optional.[18] It is the tense system of the standard languages that is normally redundant. The pidgin system can be cumbersome, but in most discourse situations it proves to be quite efficient to designate time relations: specifically when called for, otherwise not.

4.   The Development of Tense in Neo-Melanesian

It is not at all obvious that a pidgin will develop obligatory tense markers when it becomes a native language. Yet this has happened in case after case. These developments are not imitations of the model colonial languages, nor are they forms borrowed from a universal creole grammar. When pidgins become creoles, the system of optional adverbs gives way to an obligatory tense marker next to the verb. (In most cases, the pidgin verb phrase has no "auxiliary" in the conventional sense, and this may represent the first in a long series of steps re-constructing an elaborate auxiliary apparatus.) The particular forms used are idiosyncratic to that language; there is usually a long period of experimentation with various likely candidates for auxiliary status until one wins out.

We can observe this process taking place in Neo-Melanesian where a first generation of native speakers is beginning to appear in many areas of New Guinea. The most striking example is the future, which was traditionally indicated with the adverb *baimbai*. As Cassidy has noted (1971), this item has a very broad distribution, obviously by diffusion through various trading operations. We find it variously spelled as an archaic feature in a number of creole and post-creole situations, in the Caribbean (Sranan, Jamaica, cf. Uncle Remus *bimeby*) and the Pacific (Beach-la-Mar, Pitcairnese, Hawaii). The English model *by and by* indicating immediate future is obvious.[19] Despite the wide distribution of *baimbai*, it has not generally

served as the basis for a future auxiliary: forms of *go* are much more generally used.[20] But in Neo-Melanesian *baimbai* is now in the process of becoming the future auxiliary.

The traditional representation of the future is given by Mihalic
(1957:29) as *Baimbai mi go*, "I will go". There are a number of other competing forms for the expression of the future: the adverb *bihain* "later,
then" is often used, as well as specific adverbs like *tumara* "tomorrow".
There are also concatenative verbs that have been shifted to simple future
meaning in some contexts, *laik* and *ken* (see below). But *baimbai* has
apparently won out as the normal way of indicating future time, and is now
becoming a tense marker. We can observe this shift through the valuable
observations of Gillian and David Sankoff of Neo-Melanesian in actual use
among the Buang in Mambump village. Instead of the usual handbook data
based on the normative observations of a few informants, we have accurate
observations of what speakers actually say in social interaction with other
users of the language. First of all, we find that *baimbai* is obsolete: it has
been shortened to *bai*.[21] Secondly, it can now appear after the subject preverbal position, just before the third-singular marker *i-*.

(18)   *General miting bilong Sake bai ikirap long Chimbuluk.*
       "The Sake general meeting will be held at Chimbuluk".
                                   — Simu Bel, 50, Sake meeting 8/26/68

(19)   *Mani bilong stua, bai ibekim ologeta ples.*
       "The money from the store will pay back all the villages".
                                   — Savil, 35, village meeting 1/23/67

We also find that *bai* will be inserted after the pronoun *em*, "him" third person pronoun, but precedes the other persons. (See also [12].)[22]

(20)   a. *Naim bilong en, Masta Kol. Em bai ikam kisim ples bilong
          John ToVue.*
          "His name is Mr. Cole. He will come to take the place of
          John ToVue".
                                   — Simu Bel, 50, Sake meeting 8/26/68
       b. *Na bai yu go wok wonem, w, long Trinde ia?*
          "Now what work are you going to do, uh, on Wednesday"?
                                   — Unidentified Mambump man, village meeting 8/16/68

We can of course have zero or implicit futures, as in most standard languages. But the obligatory character of the *bai* marker is beginning to be
felt as it is used redundantly with *klostu* "soon".

(21) *Dispela pik nau, igat sik ikamap long en, na bikpela gras ikamap pinis — klostu bai idai.*
"Now this pig has become sick, and has grown a lot of hair — he'll die soon".

— Gu Sege, ca. 50, church sermon

The church sermon cited here also gives us the best evidence of the change in progress. It was delivered in an archaic style by a Lutheran evangelist home on leave. Mixed with the normal future forms like (21) were the only examples of *baimbai* noted by the Sankoffs in several years' work in this village.

(22) *Baimbai, ologeta wok bilong yumi, iken kamap.*
"All our work will flourish".

The condensation of *baimbai* to *bai* is now accomplished, and the shift to preverbal position is underway. Most importantly, *bai* no longer requires stress and is becoming a normally unstressed particle which can enter into the typical morphophonemic reduction rules of the auxiliary.

Further confirmation of the movement of *bai* can be seen in the large body of Neo-Melanesian letters written to the Sankoffs from residents of Mambump. In these materials there are many uses of the future, sometimes in close conjunction with other tenses.

(23) *Orait na mi bin istap wan taem Masta Kol long Mumeng na mi tokem em olsem, bai mi kirapim conpaon long Bapuong long dispela geraon em mi bin list long em.*
"Now I was there with Mr. Cole in Mumeng and I told him that I'm going to start a compound at Bapuong, on this land I'm registered for".

The future particle is always *bai*, never *baimbai*. Its position is largely determined, but there is some variation as Table 1 shows:

Table 1

Position of *Bai* in Neo-Melanesian Correspondence
Proportion of Cases Following the Subject

Pronoun subjects

1st sg.	*mi* 2/28		1st exc.	*mipela* 0/1
2nd sg.	*yu* 0/13		1st inc.	*mitupela* 0/4
3rd sg.	*em* 3/3		2nd pl.	*yutupela* 0/2
			3rd pl.	*ol* 0/4

Other NP subjects 13/17

The general pattern is that *bai* follows the third singular pronoun and full noun phrases, but we find two cases of *mi* preceding *bai* and a few cases of *bai* preceding long noun phrases like *yunion sosaiti*. All this indicates change in progress, but exactly how it will be resolved we cannot be sure.

We also find further evidence that this obligatory *bai* is no longer regarded as an adverb. It cooccurs with one of the earlier adverbs of time, *bihain*, a future marker itself.

(24) *Na nau dispela tok ikamap long Sam olsem bipo yumi lukim long Mambump na bihain bai ikam bek gen long Buang.*
"And now this discussion came up at the Sam, like the one we attended at Mambump, and in the future, it'll come back to the Buang again".

There are a number of verbs in Neo-Melanesian which we might classify in English as **quasi-modals**. They are often found in constructions with other verbs, and sometimes display a full lexical meaning: in other constructions, they take on more abstract meanings, as markers of tense or aspect. In this way, they behave like the concatenative verbs of other South-East Asian languages. As noted above, both *ken* and *laik* often carry a future meaning. In their lexical use we have

(25) *Bai igat askim, sapos yupela laik wanem yupela iken tol, "Orait, mipela iken kisim dispela wok, iorait".*
"There will be questions — whatever you people like, you can say, 'All right, we can take on this job; it's O.K.'"
— meeting of cooperative society 8/26/68

Note that the predicate marker *i-* precedes the verb *ken* and *laik*, but is usually not attached to the following verb. There is some oscillation on this, however.

(26) *Sapos mama bilong pik, iken lukautim gut pikinini bilong en, baimbai iken istap, pikinini bilong en iken stop.*
"If the pig's mother took care of him properly, the pig would live, this baby of hers could live".
— same as (23-24)

This development shows another route for the development of tense markers, more common than the shifting of adverbs: the reduction of full verbs to auxiliaries. The morphophonemic alternation shown above *iken istap/iken stap* is the beginning of more complex reductions which would operate in a fully native language. In (26) *ken* carries a future implication as part of its meaning, but in (22) above, it has only future force. The Sankoff letters contain many uses of *ken* co-occurring with *bai*, where *ken* has the meaning "will be able to" and also a number of cases where it simply means "will". As an example of each case:

> (27) a. . . . *bai yunion sosaiti i ken givim*
>   "the Union Society will be able to give . . ."
>   b. *bai pas iken kamap*
>   "a letter will arrive"

It is interesting to note that three of the four exceptional cases of *bai* preceding a full noun phrase subject in Table 1 have *iken* preceding the verb. Here it seems that *ken* takes over the modal function, and *bai* retrogresses to its adverbial position. The competition between *ken* and *bai* as future tense markers is not entirely resolved therefore, but it seems clear that *bai*, which has no other meaning, is now the dominant form. There is some indication that *laik* was a strong contender for a future auxiliary thirty years ago, but it does not appear at all in this data.[23]

5.   The Selection of Tense Markers in Pitcairnese

The general tendency in the marking of tenses is for the present to be unmarked in contrast to the past and future. However, creoles do not always follow this principle in the reconstruction of auxiliaries. The case of Pitcairnese is a striking one. This is the English-based creole which was developed by the descendants of the Bounty mutineers and their Tahitian wives. As described by Ross and Moverly (1964), this creole had obviously passed through a stage in which all inflections except *-ing* disappeared. The past is unmarked. In the following example, a Pitcairnese girl is telling how a house was built:[24]

> (28) *We saw em stick f'a frame down tedside. I get em stick f'a beam
>   out a ship. We put on em pine fa a wall.*
>   "We sawed the timber for the frame down at the other side of the
>   island. I got the timber for the beams out of a ship. We put on
>   imported boards for the walls".

These invariant verb forms would mark the habitual present in standard English, but they ambiguously signal the past in Pitcairnese. The habitual present is marked with the auxiliary *usa*.

(29) *Hem usa about a weko. Hem usa lehu a brefut an lupu a miti. An usa get a mutepele, an usa hiwe a popoi, an usa about a teate on a jola, and us' stil a pea soup, an usa soak em bean.*
"They busy themselves with the food. They scrape the bread-fruit, and mix up the coconut cream sauce, and get out the coconut meat, and throw away the waste . . . and do the sweet potatoes on the grater, and stir the pea soup, and soak the beans".

It seems fairly clear that this *usa* [jusə] is a back-formation from the habitual past *used to* [justə].[25] There is no past tense meaning associated with it at all, as we can see in the following answer to the question, "Do you like chocolate?"

(30) *I usa like it. I too like it.*
"I do like it. I like it very much".

The other tense markers of Pitcairnese are also typically derived from English quasi-modals or auxiliaries. There is an optional past marker *bin* which may have a perfective meaning, and a future *gwen*, derived like so many creole future markers, from the periphrastic future with *go*. But in *usa* Pitcairnese again indicates that creoles take their own paths in reconstructing the system of tense markers.

6. The Past Tense in Hawaiian Creole

We can now return to Hawaiian Creole (HC) and examine the rebuilding of the tense system out of the tense-less Hawaiian Pidgin. Although English was always present as a possible model, standard English *-ed* and *will* did not form the basis of the Hawaiian Creole system. The future is regularly *gon* [gon], with a syllabic [n].[26] There was considerable experimentation with various past tense auxiliaries in the early stages: we find *been*, *had*, *was* and *wen*, but *wen* became the almost universal form.[27] The development of this past tense *wen* will be our major concern in the following discussion.

Older speakers of Hawaiian Creole use *wen* regularly with all non-copular verbs. The pattern is shown in the formal equivalents provided by an extremely knowledgeable and talented informant of the older generation, Lippy Espinda:[28]

(31)   Standard English (SE)   Hawaiian Creole (HC)
  a. *I picked it up.*   *Oh, I wen grab em up.*
  b. *He lived for twenty*   *Oh, he wen live over*
     years longer.   *twenty years, boy.*
  c. *We liked him.*   *Eh, we wen enjoy em, boy.*
  d. *He began to work*   *Yesterday he wen start*
     yesterday.   *work.*
  e. *They showed us*   *They wen show us all*
     everything.   *over the place.*
  f. *I asked him to go*   *I wen tell im for go with me.*
     with me.
  g. *But he had drunk*   *But he wen drink too much.*
     too much.
  h. *Then his wife came*   *But then — the wife wen come.*
     along.

Lippy uses *wen* as a past tense marker with verbs that take *-ed* in SE, as *pick, live, enjoy,* and *show* above, as well as *ask, look, check up, beg, kill, roll,* etc.; and with the stems of verbs that show ablaut and other vowel change in SE, as *tell, drink,* and *come* above, as well as *eat, meet, go, see, keep, bring,* and *do.* Note that the same form — *wen* + Vb — is given as equivalent of the past perfect in (31g) above, and we find in fact that there is no distinct past perfect in HC.[29]

The negative has an entirely different auxiliary in the preterit:

(32)   SE   HC
  a. *We didn't eat there.*   *We never eat there.*
  b. *I didn't tell him.*   *I never tell him.*
  c. *They haven't done it.*   *They never do em.*

Never has no indefinite feature in this use, but is simply the preterit negative. Again, no distinction is made between the perfect and the preterit.

This is the system generally recognized as characteristic of Hawaiian Creole, as reported in the literature. It seems quite clear that *wen*, borrowed from English *went*, was adopted as the past tense marker at the expense of *been* and other competing forms earlier in the century. It is the further development of this system in current Hawaiian Creole which is of interest to us: such on-going evolution should give us some clue as to what the system of auxiliaries does for native speakers, which a pidgin system would not.

7. The Problem of What Data for What Grammar

Most observations of current creole developments are confined to assertions that they are losing their original creole character under the pressure of education in the schools and of the standard language. The real creole is always in the process of receding over the horizon, and creole grammars tend to be normalized descriptions of an earlier phase of the language that no one is quite sure was ever spoken by anyone. Thus Beryl Bailey says of her own description of Jamaican Creole that it is merely an idealized construct of all those forms that are most different from English.

> Jamaican Creole (JC) is, therefore, in my frame of reference, that form of language used in Jamaica which is syntactically, phonologically, and lexically farthest removed from the Jamaican standard (1971:342).

There is no question of documenting the grammar with forms actually used by native speakers to each other. The creole grammars of the literature do not even represent any one speaker's intuitions about his own language. Bailey continues:

> The speakers of unadulterated JC are rare indeed, but the pedagogue or the text-book writer must deal with maximal situations, and it would seem that optimal effects will be achieved only when all possible divergencies are taken into consideration (1971:342).

In other words, the description of a non-standard language is to be a kind of *grammaire des fautes*, a pedagogical caricature of the language rather than a portrait of it. Whatever value such constructions have for the teachers or learners, they cannot contribute anything to our study of the adequacy of languages. If such "pure" creoles are not used, they are not used for some good reason. We can only argue from grammars that are used for the serious purpose of communication in every-day life.

It would of course be even more deceiving to write a grammar incorporating everything that informants say. The data given in formal elicitation by Lippy Espinda in (31) and (32) does not give us a direct view of the grammar of Hawaiian Creole at any stage of development. His responses show many inconsistencies — some representing an oscillation between *been* and *had*, some switching to the zero forms of the historical present, some showing an inconsistent importation of standard forms. The same is true of the formal speech of most older Hawaiians and students in school situations, who have provided most of the data for earlier descriptions.

There are regular tendencies in the various mixtures of the basic vernacular and superposed varieties; but none of these transitional forms are as regular as the basic vernacular which is used when the minimal attention is paid to speech, based on the deeply rooted rules learned in the pre-adolescent years.

It is this situation which has led some observers of the Hawaiian situation to share the doubts of Caribbean creolists as to whether the object of their grammatical description actually exists. In an important paper on "Coexistent Systems in Language Variation," Tsuzaki provides a convincing argument that there are at least four grammatical systems within Hawaiian English (HE).

> . . . the basic systems of HE consist of (1) an English-based pidgin, (2) an English-based creole, and (3) a dialect of English, which in turn is divisible into (a) a non-standard, and (b) a standard variety. (1971:330)

This analysis has been fully justified by recent sociolinguistic studies of Hawaiian English, and it provides the basic framework for all of my remarks so far about Hawaiian Pidgin and Creole. Though Tsuzaki's analysis represents a great advance over earlier treatments, we might modify it further to account for the actual variability we find. He cannot find empirical justification for four co-existent systems in "pure" or "unadulterated" form, and therefore suggests that they be formally portrayed as "overlapping". If each system is portrayed as an invariant, homogeneous one, then each variation must be defined as a borrowing from another system, and that leads to great difficulties. We must challenge the construction of such homogeneous models on the ground that homogeneity is itself dysfunctional. There is a growing body of evidence to show that natural linguistic systems show inherent internal variation, and that it is necessary to abandon the identification of structure with homogeneity (Weinreich, Labov and Herzog 1968). We have argued that a native-like command of heterogeneous structures is not a matter of multidialectalism, but rather a part of unilingual linguistic competence. Our task is therefore to distinguish (1) the invariant rules of a linguistic system, (2) the variable rules of that system, (3) borrowings from other systems, and (4) idiosyncratic mistakes. All four phenomena can be found in any extended body of language behavior, and no analysis can be considered adequate which does not have the means to distinguish among them. A study of the development of the tense system in Hawaiian English must begin with the isolation of the most consistent vernacular, embodying invariant and variant rules, and fully account for shifts out of that system in terms of the interaction of socially located speakers.

8.   The Tense System of Hawaiian Creole in Actual Use

At this time, a consistent Hawaiian Creole is the every-day language of a large segment of the population of the islands. We now know that it is used consistently by children from an early age to late adolescence in many rural areas and lower working class sections of Honolulu. A form of non-standard Hawaiian English (Tsuzaki's third system) is used by youth in upper-working class urban areas, and by older speakers with a wide range of class and ethnic backgrounds. Many older speakers frequently use quotations from earlier pidgin and creole grammars, borrowing forms from their Hawaiian English for various humorous and affective purposes. We do not know as yet which if any of the older speakers use their original creole vernacular in given social contexts: traditional lore, expert judgments, introspection and current research are all faulty on this question.

Our best data on current Hawaiian Creole stems from research done in 1970 in Hauula on the windward side of Oahu, in Nanakuli on the leeward side, and in Pauoa and Kalihi in the Honolulu sections of Oahu.[30] The grammars used by pre-adolescents, adolescents and older youth in these areas are all essentially the same, although there are small differences. Most of the speakers have in their background mixtures of Hawaiian, Portuguese, Philippine and Chinese ethnic groups; they are considered "Hawaiian" as opposed to "haole" or white. The parents are creole speakers themselves in most cases. The sizeable group of recent immigrants from Samoa do not speak this creole grammar. Predominantly Japanese communities seem to show much more switching to Hawaiian English, even among the youth, and provide much less reliable evidence on the basic creole grammar.

The data to be cited here is drawn from the interaction of natural peer groups of creole speakers, or from group interviews under conditions which minimize the effect of observation and maximize interaction among peer group members.[31] Let us consider first a long narrative — a ghost story from an evening session at Nanakuli. The speaker is Gregory Wang, 16.

(33) *See that lady over there? She see — she said she was walking up*
       this third road, uh, right here. The lights was all off. So she was
       walking. So she seen one cigarette, you know, the fire of the

cigarette, like this . . . seen that and she was walking. So she wen
pass . . . she never know who was. She was gon say "Hi" but she
donno who was, so she wen pas'. She wen turn around for look .
. . seen the cigarette. She said she wen smoke em from over there,
home. And she wen run right to her mother and she just holding
on.

At first glance, this passage shows an inconsistent use of the *wen* marker.
But if we align the verbs with *wen* as against the verbs with other preterit
forms, a regular pattern emerges.

said	*wen pass*	*never know*
seen	*wen pass*	*never see*
seen	*wen turn*	
	wen smoke	
	wen run	

This is the system now in general use throughout Hawaii by younger speakers. *Wen* is used obligatorily with regular verbs which take *-ed* in SE, and
the verbs that are irregular in SE — strong verbs and shortened weak verbs
— follow the English model.[32] For the negative preterit, *never* is used with
both classes.

Another story by the same speaker shows a switch to historical present
in the middle, not uncommon in this grammar.

(34)   *So my auntie and the guy was walking. So they heard, you know,*
        horses, eh, like that. Get one horse, yeah, was galloping, was
        coming, coming closer and closer. So she like look around, eh,
        but he tol' em, "No, no! No look back! No look back!"
        But she was curious, eh. Just wen rip herself away from the
        guy. She wen turn back. She seen one black horse coming up, eh,
        with red eyes . . . was coming. And had, you know, smoke, eh,
        coming. And that thing was coming and something black on top
        the horse, riding, never have head. So she wen go hug him like
        that. Horse wen go pass them, eh. So like the thing was coming
        back for them. So he had — the guy had one cross. Rip off the
        cross and wen go show em and he started swearing, eh. Thing
        come smaller and wen started disintegrate. So she wen faint right
        there. So he wen go carry — wen carry and then wen take her
        home. . . So they took her home.

If we take this long narrative as a whole, certain further complications begin to appear. The past tense forms are:

heard (2)	*wen walk*	*wen go hug*	*never have*
told	*wen rip*	*wen go pass*	*never get*
seen (3)	*wen turn*	*wen go show*	
took	*wen faint*	*wen go sleep*	
said	*wen carry*	*wen go lie*	
wen(t)	*wen take*	*wen go open*	
	wen go	*wen go carry*	
	wen get up		
	wen look		
	wen faint		
	wen wake up		
	wen started		
	started		

Note that *wen* appears with all regular verbs, with the exception of *started*. This is not a single accident: we regularly find only two verbs with *-ed* in current HC: *wanted* and *started*. The first is used in place of the older *wen like*, since *like* is the normal form of "want" in the present. It is interesting to note that *start* and *want* are the two quasi-modals that occur most frequently in ordinary narrative in other dialects of English.[33] Obviously the *-ed* cannot carry very much past tense signification, because it co-occurs with *wen* in *wen started*.

We also note that the class of SE-irregular verbs can occur either in the regular paradigm of *wen + stem* or in the various irregular forms. *Take* and *go* appear in both columns.

A third complication appears with the *wen go* forms. This is a common alternant of *wen*, used more often in Nanakuli than in Hauula. We have of course searched for a difference in meaning between *wen* and *wen go*, but no clear answer has been found. The search for a difference in meaning between *wen* and *wen go* deserves a paper in itself. Several hypotheses have been clearly eliminated: it does **not** mean continued action; nor is there a special class of nonstative verbs which take *wen go*. We do have some indication that *wen go* can imply a more deliberate action, equivalent to SE "He went and ____". But any difference in meaning is a subtle one, a matter of implication rather than meaning, and there is no clear case of a *wen go* construction which could not also be *wen*.[34] It should be noted that *go* also occurs as an auxiliary in the present. Here is an example of historical present with *go* in a story told in a younger group of Nanakuli boys:

(35) *An' I see in my dream about again . . . a thing come up from . . . I get up quick. Spooky! I dream I stay walking, somebody following me, ah. I look behind, standin' over there. I soon go fall down. Nah, one time I go wake up, I wake up fast.*

These boys are heavy *wen go* users.

(36) *(How come you were in the hospital three months?) Because, da kine. You know the coconut tree? I wen go climb up when I was one baby. . . I wen go climb all the way up, an' I wen go* **chop** *[single gesture], an' I missed em, an' I wen go . . . right down in the mud.*

Yet *wen* is always a possible equivalent of *wen go*. In addition to *wen go chop*, we also have *wen chop* for the same event:

(37) *(How did you land?) . . . feet firs', then on my back. I wen chop em an' den I was right in the pool of mud.*

We know that speakers faced with synonymous alternatives have a strong tendency to find some difference in meaning. Yet *wen go* is still barely differentiated from *wen*. It seems likely that *wen go* originated through a purely formal re-analysis of the paradigm, such as:

	Past	Present	Future
a.	*wen pass*	*pass*	*gon pass*
b.	*wen pass*	*go pass*	*gon pass*
c.	*wen go pass*	*go pass*	*gon pass*

In an early version of the HC tense system (a), the existence of the auxiliary *gon* in the future reinforced the selection of *wen* as the past tense marker. A slight re-analysis would lead to stage (b), where *go* would be considered an underlying morpheme for temporally specified predications; the past and future features added to *go* naturally give *wen* and *gon* respectively. But this analysis depends upon the recognition of the suppletive relation of *wen* to *go* in English. Stage (c) shows another formal device for adding tense marks to *go* which disregards this relation: the past tense marker *wen-* is prefixed to *go* and the future marker *-n* is suffixed to it. This solution is particularly neat because, as we will see, morphophonemic rules reduce *wen* to a simple nasal, and the past and future are then symmetrically (and iconically) realized as prefixation and suffixation of a nasal to the carrier *go*.

This reconstruction is admittedly speculative. Whether or not it is correct, the fact remains that the elaboration of *wen* to *wen go* carries HC further away from SE, not closer to it. We raised the question at the outset: why do creoles develop obligatory tense markers? No immediate conceptual advantage appeared; indeed, there was no obvious change in the semantic system. The time relations of "before" and "after" the time of speaking seem to be marked efficiently and adequately by optional adverbs, along with discourse rules for the scope of these adverbs and the ordering of narrative clauses. The same adverbs and the same discourse rules exist in the creole system. What then is the advantage of the obligatory tense marker?

We know that the time relations signalled by the adverbs *today*, *tomorrow*, *then*, *now* and *later* are not automatic and obvious acquisitions of language learners. A child almost three years old may respond like this:

(38) — *Did you play with me tomorrow?*
       — *Yes.*
       — *Yes? Will you play with me yesterday?*
       — *Yes. Last yesterday.* (Bloom 1970:229)

If the concepts of *tomorrow*, *yesterday*, *before* or *after* were clearer in the tense system of HC than they were in the tense-less system of HP, we would have a rational explanation for this development. But no such advantage appears; and even if we could account for the importance of *wen* in this way, it is clear that some other factor is promoting the elaboration of the auxiliary to produce *wen go*. Insofar as tense markers serve conceptual purposes, the distinctive features of time relations would be involved: yet *olden time*, *wen* and *wen go* do not seem to vary along that set of dimensions.

It would be pointless to argue that the conceptual advantage of the tense system lies in more complex relations which require two reference points in time. It is true that the past perfect and future perfect which embody such complexity seem to have no simple equivalent in an adverbial system. But the development of a tense system occurs without direct reference to such compound tenses: in HC there is backward reference but no backward reference from some past point.

The development of tense markers has a general historical interest in the light of the usual portrayal of linguistic change as the cross-product of mechanical sound change and analogical restoration. Whether or not we recognize that grammatical requirements can directly affect the course of sound change in progress, it is clear that grammatical innovations are usually conceived as responses to conceptual needs. Yet here in the elaboration of creole auxiliaries we see a grammatical process with the same compulsive, automatic character that we recognize in sound change.

The tense system we have outlined so far is extremely regular and widespread. We can represent the current HC rule for the past as follows:

$$(39) \quad \text{Past} \rightarrow \begin{cases} \text{a.} \quad never & / \quad \begin{bmatrix} \underline{\quad\quad} \\ +\text{neg} \end{bmatrix} \\ \text{b.} \quad was & / \quad \begin{cases} \underline{\quad}[+\text{prog}] \\ \underline{\quad}\text{Pred} \end{cases} \\ \text{c.} \quad had & / \quad \underline{\quad\quad}\text{NP} \\ \text{d.} \quad <wen\ (go)> & / \quad \underline{\quad\quad}<\text{*weak}> \end{cases}$$

This rule can best be understood by taking the four ordered cases in sequence. Case (a) is categorical: the past is always signalled by *never* when a negative is present. This includes the existential *get* (=SE *there is*), past *had* (=SE *there was*), and negative past *never have*. Case (b) is also perfectly regular for positive forms: the past progressive is quite common (see [33-4] above) with *was . . . -ing*; *was* is also the past form of the copula, identified here as the verb inserted before *Predicate*. Case (c) concerns the past tense of the verb inserted before bare NP, i.e. *have*.[35] Case (d) is the major case, here shown as a variable rule in angled brackets. The optional *go* is shown in parentheses, indicating that it is in free variation.[36] The notation <*weak> in the environment indicates that this variable rule is obligatory if a weak verb follows, [+/− weak] being a category of HC which corresponds almost exactly to verbs which take *-ed* in SE and those which do not. For [−weak] verbs the rule is variable, subject to further constraints we have not fully analyzed. If case (d) does not apply, then the category *Past* is not rewritten, and becomes the relevant environment for selecting irregular past tenses in the dictionary, with an entry such as

(40) *eat* [+Vb, +__NP, +__#, [−Stative] . . . īt/Past__, ēt, . . .]

Wanted and *started* would also appear in the dictionary as irregular forms, so that *start* and *want* would here be classified as [−weak] verbs. Note that *wen* never co-occurs with an irregular past: we do not get *wen ate*.

The phrase structure rule (39) has three invariant components for special environments, and one variable rule which combines a variable and invariant case. This is the basic HC system for expressing the past tense: whenever we find expressions with *didn't* or *wasn't* or *there wasn't* or *passed* or *checked* we must recognize a different system. There is no rule of *do*-support in this grammar, in past or present, emphatic or negative, which would provide the basis for *didn't*. Nor is there any canonical form which requires a subject NP and leads to the insertion of a dummy *it* or *there*.[37] We can provide empirical support for this formulation by examining two types of texts: (1) group interaction among adolescent peers where an outside observer does not figure at all, where no formal context appears that requires code switching and (2) formal contexts where topic and style both demand code switching.

For the first type of evidence on consistent vernacular use we will consider a transcript of conversation on the "Second Trip to Ala Moana" with five members of the adolescent group from Hauula interacting with each other during a 45 minute car ride (myself driving). This was the sixth such expedition, and the culmination of a long series of participant observations and social activities in which close relations had been set up between the author and these speakers of HC.

(41) Hiram: *They go blame us and then broke the machines. And I*
              got lickins, slap on the head, punchins from the punk.
       Buli: *Only you?*
       Hiram: *Yeah, Alfred too. And these guys only laughing.*
       Buli: *Why, you guys wen go come up you guys house?*
       Hiram: *Came up Alfred's house.*
       Alfred: *No, never come my house.*

Here we see the intimate variation of *wen go come up* and *came up*, and the invariant *never come* for the negative past. But weak verbs are always found with *wen*.

(42) Alfred: *We — no — we seen the cars — we seen the guys putting*
              the people inside.
       Buli: *Fuck, even though down there boy. Four cars smash.*
              Four car. . . The Datsun wen smash bumbumbum.

The set of past tense verbs used during this trip included the invariant *had* and *was*, and for the non-copular verbs:

[+ weak]	[−weak]	
wen smash	*wen go* (3)	*ate* (3)
wen swim (3)	*wen go come up*	*came up*
died	*wen keep*	*seen* (3)
		saw (9)
		hit
		wanted

The exceptional feature here is *died*, a weak verb with *-ed*. *Died* does not fit into the system just outlined, and can be considered an importation from the parallel system of Standard Hawaiian English. It is not an accidental switch: we find that the standard *-ed* occurs fairly often in solemn, not necessarily formal, discourse. There are other speakers who follow the HC system except for the switching to *-ed* in solemn style. Here is the end of a narrative by a seventeen-year-old Hauula speaker which exemplifies this slow and solemn style.

(43) Clarence: *My Uncle Ae was looking down the other side, he sneaked right in the back and hit him on the head with the pipe wrench.*

WL: *Wow!*

Clarence: *When they took him hospital, he died.*

WL: *He did.*

Clarence: *. . . died.*

Tony: *He died.*

Clarence: *Hit it right in his forehead.*

Tony: *Broke his skull.*

Joe: *An' he could build any kind cars, eh.*

Clarence: *My uncle could build any kind cars.*

The use of standard *-ed* forms in this passage fits in with the solemn, quiet tone and careful articulation. We also see the hyper-correction typical of such code switching: *Hit it right in his forehead* for "hit him . . ." HC uses *em* for standard *it*, and here *it* is used for standard *him*. But in contrast, the same speaker uses rule (39) without any such code switching in telling the story of a fight a few minutes before:

(44) *We was playin' basketball, with my cousin. An' my cousin took*
the ball away. So I took the ball away from him. So he started to
punch me on my back; so he told me, "After school, we'll fight".
Then I told 'im, "O.K."

Then — soon pau school, I jus' wen' down to the park, for
fight. So I told 'im that if he wanted to fight, he say, "C'mon; you
throw first". I told 'im, "No, you throw".

So he never like. So I'n pick up my books and walk away.
Then he came in the back of me, he w'punch me on my back, then
I'n put down my book, then I wen' for 'im. That's when I — gave
'im lickin'. . . 'N' right there the fight wen pau.

Here we have a regular example of current HC. As noted above, *started*
and *wanted* have *-ed*; they are also followed by *to* instead of the general
creole preposition *for*. The negative of *wanted*, however, is not *didn't want*
but *never like. Tell* is used for "ask": *So I told 'im that if he wanted to fight.*
The intransitive verb *pau* "finish", a Hawaiian loan word, is used with the
auxiliary *wen* in the last line. The preterit forms in (44) thus follow the
expected pattern:

	[+weak]		[−weak]	
was playin'	*wen pick*	*wen put*	*took* (2)	*started*
	wen walk		*told* (4)	*wanted*
	wen punch		*wen'* (2)	
	wen pau		*came*	
			gave	

Even more extreme forms of code switching are found in formal speech
events: telling traditional ghost stories, reciting the plots of movies, or
responding to teachers, angry parents, or adults outside the peer group.
Here, for example is the list of past tense verbs used by Hiram of Hauula in
telling the story of Samson and Delilah:

[+weak]	[−weak]		[+neg]
wen look	*wen fall*	*came*	**didn't believe*
wen pick		*made*	*never had*
wen betray		*took*	**didn' give*
*betrayed God		*said* (2)	
wen cut (2)		*gave*	
wen blind		*went*	
wen destroy		*got*	

The three items marked with an asterisk represent switches to the standard system appropriate to this topic and situation.

9. Phonological Condensation of the Tense System

Speakers of HC are able to enlarge the stylistic resources of the creole by switching to a co-existent English system. On the other hand, natural conversation among current speakers of HC shows a further development of the tense system in the other direction: rules of morphophonemic condensation which were not used by older generations. In (44), I have indicated such condensation by writing *'n* and *w'* for reduced forms of *wen*. But this transcription gives only a faint idea of the complex set of phonological rules that are now operating in HC. Condensation of the auxiliaries is so extreme that the outside listener often does not perceive the relevant bits of sound, and thinks that he is hearing zero forms.[38] If one were listening to the narrative of (34), the auxiliary *wen* would be hard to recognize from the reduced phonetic forms such as

(34) a. *But she was curious, eh. [ʃʌsɛn] rip herself away from the guy. [šiwn] turn back. . . So he had — the guy had one cross. Rip off the cross [əwŋgošoəm]. . . Thing come smaller, [ænɛnstʌtəd] disintegrate. So [šiwɛn] faint right there. So [iŋgo] carry . . . [wɛn] carry an' 'en [wɛn] take . . .*

Alternating with the full form [wɛn] are reduced forms [wən] and [wn], [ɛn], [n] and [ŋ], [wə] and [w]. The lone nasal consonant usually assimilates its point of articulation to a following consonant. The lone glide can be particularly difficult to hear: it may be reduced to a feature of rounding on a vowel or consonant.

(45) a. *So they wen walk [dew:ɔk] pas' the bridge.*
b. *We wen looking [w:nlʊkm] for the guy Malcolm, eh.*

(46) *I wen go [aᵒŋgo] kick one of 'em.*

(47) *So I wen look [alʷ:ʊk] by the door.*

Such reduced forms can be derived by five phonological rules:

(48)

		A	B	C
		wɛn	wɛn	wɛn
1. $w \rightarrow (\emptyset) /$ __ $\begin{bmatrix} V \\ -str \end{bmatrix}$		ɛn		
2. $[V, -str, -tns] \rightarrow ə$		ən	wən	wən
3. $[+nas] \rightarrow (\emptyset) / \#\#wə$__$\#\#$			wə	
4. $ə \rightarrow (\emptyset)$		n	w	wn
5. $[+nas] \rightarrow \begin{bmatrix} αant \\ βcor \end{bmatrix} / \#\#$__$\#\# \begin{bmatrix} αant \\ βcor \end{bmatrix}$	m,n,ŋ			

There are three basic routes to reduction, variably favored by certain phonological environments, but shown here produced by five rules in their simplest form. In route A, the initial glide is lost, and the vowel may then be reduced. Rule (3) cannot apply, but the schwa may be eliminated by the contraction rule (4) and the nasal assimilated to the following point of articulation by (5), yielding the minimal nasals shown.

In route B the glide is retained, and if the vowel is reduced, the nasal can be dropped; the contraction rule (4) then gives us the long [w:] of (45), which can then be further condensed to a mere feature of rounding. The third route simply involves vowel reduction and contraction. These rules yield twelve different variants of *wen*, but exclude such forms as [ə], [wɛ], [wŋ] or [wm].

The negative also shows morphophonemic condensation in rapid speech. *Never* [nɛvʌ] loses the intervocalic [v] and the two vowels coalesce, yielding such forms as [šinɛgɛdʌp] for *she never get up*.

These reduced forms seem to undo the work of the processes which introduced the obligatory auxiliary *wen* and elaborated it to *wen go*,[39] and they make the earlier introduction and complication of the obligatory auxiliary even more of a puzzle. In the earlier forms of Hawaiian Creole, we do not seem to get such condensations: the reduction and de-nasalization of [wɛn] to [wən] and [wəd] is as much as we have observed among older speakers. The condensation of the auxiliaries seems appropriate for the rapid-fire, short bursts which are the hallmarks of good speech in Nanakuli and Hauula. But from a long range point of view, there seems to be something dysfunctional, almost self-defeating in the introduction of forms that are then so rapidly eroded. One can see the process of re-pidginization at work as new speakers entering the community fail to grasp the condensed forms and return to the zeros with which the pidgin started. We are forced to ask again, in what way is Hawaiian Creole a more adequate language than Hawaiian Pidgin because it is equipped with obligatory tense markers?

These processes are of course not unique to HC; we can observe similar developments in other new creoles. In Neo-Melanesian, we have seen the initial condensation of *baimbai* to *bai*. Jamaican and Haitian Creoles are notorious for morphophonemic condensation of the auxiliary. We cannot lean too heavily on the published materials, because the limitations mentioned above show up most severely in just this area. Yet examples of extreme condensation are not hard to find. Where Mauricien Creole has *Mo te apre manze* for "I was eating", the usual representation of the Haitian equivalent is *mtap manže* (Faine 1939). In the French creole of the Antilles, we have a future marker *ke* which seems to have been derived from the durative marker *ka* with *ale*: *ka+ale → kale → kae → ke*.

This does not mean that such morphological condensation is more characteristic of creoles than ordinary colloquial language. We can turn to English, standard and non-standard, for even more striking examples. We find a number of different routes for the condensation of *I am going to* depending upon what boundaries are dropped in what order — i.e., what lexicalization takes place in the auxiliary. The most common sequence in Northern States produces fifteen variant forms:

(49) *áɪ##ǽm##gów#ŋ##tu*
1. vowel reduction   → *áɪ##əm##gówɪ̃ŋ##tə*
2. lexicalization (1)   → *áɪ##əm##gówɪ̃ŋtə*
3. glide deletion   → *áɪ##əm##góɪ̃ŋtə*
4. nasal assimilation   → *áɪ##əm##góɪ̃ntə*
5. nasal flap formation → *áɪ##əm##góɪ̃ɾ̃ə*
6. monophthongization   → *áɪ##əm##góɪ̃ɾ̃ə*
7. flap reduction   → *áɪ##əm##gónə*
8. contraction   → *áɪ##m##gónə*
9. lexicalization (2)   → *áɪ mgonə*
10. vowel reduction   → *áɪmgənə*
11. monophthongization   → *ámgənə*
12. nasal assimilation   → *áŋgənə*
13. contraction   → *áŋgnə*
14. cluster simplification → *áŋnə*

This is as far as the process can go; there is no further step [ánə] which would express the future in English. But there are other routes in Southern States English which depart from step (9) by deleting the [g] instead of assimilating the [n] to it.

11'.   cluster simplification → *ámənə*

A dialect such as Black English takes one further step here. Contraction of the second vowel can take place despite the fact that the resulting form has no tense marker;[40] this leads to

12'.   contraction   → *ámnə*
13'.   cluster simplification → *ámə*

Southern States dialects in general often use a different form of step (9), lexicalizing with stress on *gon* instead of *I*: this leads to a completely different series of reductions, in which the final schwa drops out, the vowel nasalizes, and the [n] disappears:

9".   lexicalization (2")   → *aɪmgónə*
10". final schwa deletion   → *aɪmgón*
11". monophthongization   → *amgón*
12". vowel nasalization   → *amgṍn*
13". nasal deletion   → *amgṍ*
14". cluster simplification → *amṍ*

No further reduction of (14") seems possible. With these six, we have a total of twenty-three variants of *I am going to*. To these we can add at least five variants of *I will*: [aɪ##wɪɬ], [aɪ##ɨɬ], [aɨɬ], [aɬ] and [aᶧ]. A reasonable description of English morphophonemics would therefore have to include an account of twenty-eight ways of combining *I* with the future auxiliary, along with the phonological rules which operate to produce these. None of these are purely hypothetical intermediates: they are all attested forms which occur in recorded conversations.

The extreme condensation of HC *wen* should therefore not surprise us since the creole is providing native speakers with some of the same stylistic machinery which our own English has elaborated over a longer period of time. There is a striking parallel between the elaboration of *wen* to *wen go* and the development of English *am going to*. A traditional view of the development of periphrastic auxiliaries is that the simpler form was in danger of extinction through the operation of phonetic reduction, and the additional auxiliaries preserved the category. But that can hardly be said about English *I will* which has as firm a phonetic foundation as *They're* and *They w're*. We can say that the periphrastic form with *going to* offers a much richer variety of stylistic options than *will* and the same can be said about *wen go*. As far as we can see from our present limited data, the development of *wen* to *wen go* took place **before** the rules of phonological condensation had brought about the present reduction of *wen*.

10. The Development of Tense in Other Creoles

It is not feasible to review here the development of tense systems throughout the vast creole literature. Such a search of the literature may not in fact produce the basic vernacular, and is even less likely to provide information on creoles in actual use. Nevertheless, we can find enough evidence to suggest that the processes sketched above are generally characteristic of the development of pidgins, creoles, and the post-creole continuum.

Most creole tense markers are derived from concatenative verbs or auxiliaries of the contact language. In French Creole, the older dialectal *té* (related to standard *été*) is the dominant preterit marker (Goodman 1964). The English-based creoles often leave the preterit unmarked, or experiment with an optional *been* (with or without a perfective sense), *did* or *went*. But we also find some cases where auxiliaries are reduced from adverbs. The re-elaboration of auxiliaries and development of phonological condensation can be seen in a number of Caribbean and West African creoles which are much further developed than Neo-Melanesian or HC.

We find some remarkable parallels to HC developments in Crioulo, the Portuguese-based pidgin spoken in Guinea (Wilson 1962). The simple past and present are both normally unmarked: *i sibi* can mean "he knew" or "he knows". The post-position *ba* (from Portuguese imperfect marker *va*) is added to indicate the past perfect: *i sibi ba* "he had known". But in the crucial cases where a simple past tense marker is appropriate, Crioulo has developed uses of *bay* "go" and *bing* "come" which convey this meaning. Thus narrative sequence, "and then", is expressed by *bing* in auxiliary position: *i bay Mansoa, i bing bay Bissau, i bing bing li* "he went to Mansoa, then he went to Bissau, and then he came here". The same verb *bing* can have the literal meaning of "come and" in this position. The situation is the same for HC *wen go*, which is used as a simple past tense marker, as we have seen. There is no reason that *wen go* in narrative could not be translated as "and then". But *wen go* can also have the deliberative meaning of English *went and*, as in *He went and chopped down the tree*.[41] According to Wilson, Crioulo also uses the verb *bay* "go" as a concatenative verb, and an even more specialized form *baa* meaning "go and". Thus *i bay pa baa ben-dii-l* "he went to (go-and) sell it". It would be idle to argue here than this parallel is to be explained by the diffusion of the original Portuguese-African creole grammar, since there are a great variety of other auxiliary elaborations in the intervening creoles. But we can begin to see the outlines of the various routes which creoles can use to develop auxiliaries, based upon semantic links derived from universal experience.

In Hawaiian this process occurred once with *wen* and is apparently being repeated with *wen go*. If someone has left his usual location and traveled to a place where he performed an act, it is normally inferred (the unmarked case is) that (a) he traveled there for that purpose and (b) therefore that the action was a deliberate one. It follows that to *go and do X* may shift to "did X deliberately". A sentence such as *He went to town and bought a dog* is ambiguous in the sense that *went* is [+/− deliberate]. But in *Even after I told him to be quiet he went and sneezed*, *went* has no meaning of "motion" and is therefore only deliberate.

Without the basic meaning of "motion", *went* is open to reinterpretation as a general past tense or perfective marker. Most deliberate actions in a past context are completed ones, of the sort that occur in narrative. Many narratives are told in such a way that every action has this deliberative character: *and then he went and told Joe*. The general adoption of *wen* for the past tense, as in *The Datsun wen smash bumbumbum* would represent a weakening of this voluntary or deliberative meaning. *Wen* then signals a completed or even punctual action, as against the past progressive. Thus the derivation of *wen*, *bay* or *bing* as a past tense marker may be traced as three steps: (1) the strengthening of *went (and)* from "travel to" to "deliberately", (2) the generalization of this to all voluntary past tense predications, (3) the weakening of *went* to mean only "past" with all nonstative predications. We can envisage this process as the result of the overlapping of three sets:

1 = actions performed after traveling to a place
2 = deliberate actions
3 = completed events

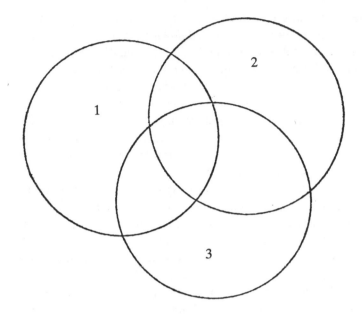

The question is certain to arise as to whether *wen* is actually a tense marker at all; perhaps it is a perfective aspect marker. This may have been true at one time, but *wen* is surely now a tense marker, opposed to present and future.

The elaboration of the auxiliary in Papiamentu as reported by Lenz (1928) shows us several striking parallels with the Hawaiian and Neo-Melanesian examples we have examined. The future in Papiamentu has been formed by the same process as that which is now taking place in Neo-Melanesian. It is expressed by *lo* placed before the subject pronouns, derived from Spanish *luego* "later, then, soon" in a manner parallel to the shift of *baimbai* to *bai*. Thus *Lo mi kanta* is equivalent to Spanish *yo cantaré*, just as Neo-Melanesian *Bai mi go* expresses "I will go". The past auxiliary is not formed from an adverb, however, but directly from the Spanish imperfect of *estar*, *estaba*. The allegro form *taba* is the one which was apparently used in Papiamentu originally, but it has since been strengthened by adding the reduced form of the present of *estar*, *está*. Thus we have the past tense auxiliary *tabata* as the equivalent of Spanish *estar* and *ser* imperfect and past progressive. Thus Lenz cites *e tabata malu* "él estaba enfermo", *bo tabata bon* "tu cras bueno", and *nis tabata kome* "estábamos comiendo, comíamos". (The simple preterit and perfect use the auxiliary *a* reduced from *haber*.) In this elaboration of *taba* → *tabata* we can see the same process operating as in Hawaiaan *wen* → *wen go*. We do not have data on rapid speech in Papiamentu, but no evidence is cited that *taba* was reduced to the point that it would be lost or confused with *a*. We can surmise that the elaboration of *taba* to *tabata* offers Papiamentu speakers rich possibilities for stylistic variation.

I have cited examples from grammatical sketches of two creoles to indicate the generality of the processes we have examined above. Even this discussion should indicate that each of the many studies of creole grammar opens the door for a deeper and more fruitful examination of linguistic evolution in progress.

11. On the "Adequacy" of Creoles

At the beginning of this discussion, it was conceded that pidgins are "inadequate" languages for some purposes. Most of our testimony on this point comes from those who have learned the pidgins as outsiders and tried to communicate with insiders. But we also have testimony from sympathetic linguists who tried to translate a variety of ideas into the pidgin with the help of sympathetic speakers. For example, Reinecke (1968) writes of his experience with Tây Bôi:

> an idea which appears very simple in Standard French was hard to express in Pidgin French (sometimes, of course, because an adequate vocabulary was lacking in Pidgin French). E.G., *Que le meilleur gagne! Il vaux mieux que vous restiez. Voici deux robes, laquelle voulez vous?* (1968)

The informants who were trying to help Reinecke reconstruct Tây Bôi were not native speakers, but were simply trying to remember the pidgin they heard spoken as children in Saigon and Hué. It is hard for us to evaluate this experience: no one would suggest that the same inadequacy is found in the French creoles of the Caribbean. Nevertheless, the traditional view of these creoles is that they too were inadequate languages. Vendryes writes:

> But in Creole these (European) languages appear shorn of their morphological peculiarities and reduced to a pulverized condition. It is like gravel from which the lime has disappeared, or stones without cement — a thin and formless substance. The necessity to carry on a conversation with foreign merchants . . . forced the natives to learn a foreign language. . . But their apprenticeship to this language was never completed. It was

limited to its superficial characteristics, to expressions representing the
ordinary objects and essential acts of life; the inner essence of the language, with its fine complexities, was never assimilated by the native
(1951:295).

In the light of this description, we should not be suprised that Vendryes
takes a straight colonialist position. He further describes Creole as "the
speech of inferior beings and of a subordinate class whose superiors have
never troubled nor desired to make them speak any language correctly".
What then is the **inner essence** which is lacking in the creoles? What are the
fine complexities which were never assimilated by the native? Here of
course we have been dealing with only one item — the expression of tense.
And in tracing the development of tense so far, it appears that the essence
is a stylistic one. There is no basis for arguing that tense markers express
the concepts of temporal relations more clearly than adverbs of time. What
then is the advantage that they offer to native speakers, the advantage
which native speakers seem to demand? The most important property
which tense markers possess, which adverbs of time do not, is their stylistic
flexibility. They can be expanded or contracted to fit in with the prosodic
requirements of allegro or lento style. Because tense markers are not
assigned stress in the normal cycles, their vowels are reduced and contracted
and the remaining consonants can be reduced to the smallest possible bits
of phonetic information. But because speakers seem to demand an ever
wider range of formal and informal styles, we find the auxiliary elaborated
to give a broader and broader base for the rules of phonological condensation.

It might be argued that tense markers can permit us to shift and contrast time relations with dramatic suddenness. The incorporation of the
negative into the auxiliary permits such pithy remarks as *He will and he
won't*; *He did and he didn't*. But similar co-ordination of different tense
markers without modifying adverbs is not as happy an effect: *I did and I
will eat*, or *I ate and I will eat*, or *I worked, work, and will work on the problem*.

A reference back to (23) will show how a new creole can juxtapose
future clauses with past and future markers in successive clauses of the
same sentence: *mi bin istap. . . mi tokim em olsem, bai mi kirapim conpaon*
"I was there . . . I told him that I will start a compound", where the
optional preterit marker *bin* is followed by the zero unmarked preterit and
the future marker *bai*. But this is only slightly more compact than the orig-

inal pidgin forms, and a long way from saying *mi bin na bai istan* "I was and will be there".

Rapid alternations of tense are rare; but the variable use of rules of condensation is common in any given text, and the forces operating in this direction obviously have far more effect on the evolution of a language than the need to make rare and subtle alternations of such questionable grammaticality.

This view must fit in with a more general notion of the function of grammar. One might say that a developing grammar serves the need of stylistic variation. But it would be more accurate to say that grammar **is** style. The deep and complex apparatus that has developed in English syntax and morphophonemics does not necessarily make the speakers wiser, more logical, or more analytical in their ways of talking. A logical analysis of propositions entails breaking down normal English syntax into the simplest kind of clause structure with a minimal amount of elegant variation. Such a calculus has no place for the kind of contraction and expansion we have just seen, with twenty-eight different ways of saying the same thing. On the whole, grammar is not a tool of logical analysis: grammar is busy with emphasis, focus, down-shifting and up-grading; it is a way of organizing information and of taking alternative points of view. Grammar allows us to see every side of every question if we so desire; or to put it another way, there is no side to any question which cannot be seen with the help of our grammatical apparatus. But as this apparatus becomes elaborated, it must be controlled. If we want to emphasize the temporal location of an action, we should be able to do so, but if we want to let this slide into the background, we must have means of packing away our grammatical tools so they will not interfere with some other focus. The accordion-like nature of the tense system, as we have seen it develop in Hawaiian Creole, is admirably suited for this purpose.

A study of the development of aspect in the same creole continuum will add another dimension to this question. While the progressive is almost always found in English-based creoles, expressions of the perfect develop much later. No English perfect with *have* is present in HC. But on the other hand, it is argued by many creolists that the French and Portuguese creoles of the Caribbean have developed a rich system of aspects, at the expense of tense, possibly on the basis of African models (Valkhoff 1966). Any difficulty we may have in discussing the cognitive advantages of a tense system is compounded many times in dealing with aspect, since we find that linguists rarely agree on the meanings of aspect particles to begin with.

12. The Treatment of Tense in English Dialects

This paper began with a consideration of questions that were raised on the adequacy of the vernacular language of children in the inner city — primarily Black children. Our final topic will therefore be an examination of the treatment of tense markers in vernacular English, with special attention to Black English.

Most English dialects use the historical present freely in narrative or in vivid descriptions of past events. Black English is much more restricted than most other dialects in this respect. Zero forms occur frequently but only as a result of the phonological processes deleting -ed. The irregular past tense forms *kept, told, lost* are used consistently in narratives of the past, and it can almost be said that Black English does not employ the historical present. We therefore have a completely obligatory tense marker, which is developed by the rule

$$
(50) \quad \text{Past} \rightarrow
\begin{cases}
\text{a.} & \begin{cases} ain't \\ didn't \end{cases} / \left[\underline{} \atop +\text{neg} \right] \\
\text{b.} & had \quad / \quad \underline{} \quad \text{Past} \\
\text{c.} & \#ed \quad / \quad \underline{} \quad [+\text{weak}]
\end{cases}
$$

There is a superficial resemblance of this rule to the Hawaiian Creole rule (39) which should not be overstressed. BE has an option of choosing *ain't* or *didn't* (in free variation) when a negative is incorporated into the tense marker. We need not write a special rule for *was*; this is simply the irregular form of *be*, to be treated as a [−weak] verb along with *have* and *do*. Hawaiian Creole needed a special rule for *was* and *had* because other [−weak] verbs could be used optionally with *wen*. The *had* of (50b) is of course the "past perfect", a common tense in Black English. Finally, there is an obligatory -ed with all [+weak] verbs. The main stylistic variation in the expression of tense in BE is the result of a variable rule:[42]

(51) $[-\text{cont}] \rightarrow <\emptyset/> \; / \; [+\text{cons}] <\emptyset> \underline{} <-\text{syl}>$

The first angled brackets around $\emptyset$ indicate that the rule is variable; the angled brackets in the environment indicate those environmental features that favor the rule. Thus the rule applies more often when there is no morpheme boundary in the cluster, more often in *old* rather than *roll#ed*, and it applies more often if a consonant follows. These variable constraints hold for every speaker and every group. Since the rule recognizes the existence of the # boundary in words like *roll#ed*, it provides strong evidence for the obligatory character of the tense marker in BE.

The second variable constraint, <−syl>, indicates that the rule applies more often when the cluster is *not* followed by a vowel or syllabic. Thus we have four possible combinations of variable constraints.

1.	2.	3.	4.
Ø__K	Ø__V	#__K	#__V
just me	*just us*	*passed me*	*passed us*

Rule (51) will apply most often for case (1) and least often for case (4); cases (2) and (3) will be intermediate in the frequency of consonant cluster simplification.

However, it would be misleading to characterize (51) as a rule of Black English. It is the rule which controls the realization of the tense marker for all English speakers. There are some few white speakers who rarely simplify past tense clusters, and never seem to do so before a vowel, so that the <Ø> constraint is simply missing. But this is rarer than most people realize. Here are some figures on working class white dialects from recent interviews in various sections of the United States.

Table 2

Consonant Cluster Simplification for Four
White Working-Class Dialects of English

		Percent Simplified			
		Ø__K	Ø__V	#__K	#__V
1.	*West Texas*				
	Bud Stokes, 79	79	29	13	00
	Sonora, Texas				
	Wade Stokes, 23	84	09	25	00
	Sonora, Texas				
2.	*St. Louis*				
	Ken Gabelman, 25	93	52	29	00
3.	*Atlanta*				
	Henry Grattons, 60	83	40	36	03
	No. Atlanta				
	Mrs. Hentry Grattons, 58	90	19	27	00
	No. Atlanta				
4.	*New York City*				
	Inwood group, 14-17	67	09	14	09

In some of these dialects, the grammatical constraint is much more power-ful than the phonological constraint. This is characteristic of middle class dialects in general, southern and northern. But in the basic vernacular of Black English, the situation is quite different:

Table 3

Consonant Cluster Simplification for Six
Groups of Black English Speakers

		Percent Simplified			
		Ø__K	Ø__V	#__K	#__V
1.	T-Birds, 9-13	97	36	91	23
2.	Cobras, 13-17	98	45	100	12
3.	Jets, 13-17	98	82	60	05
4.	Oscar Bros., 16-18	97	54	85	31
5.	Adults, Working Class Northern	90	56	84	25
6.	Adults, Working Class Southern	93	21	41	18

Here the grammatical constraint is much weaker than the phonological con-straint. We can express this difference between the Black and white rules by weighting the constraints as follows:[43]

(52) a. BE
         $[-\text{cont}] \rightarrow <\text{Ø}> / [+\text{cons}] <\text{Ø}>_2 \underline{\quad} <-\text{syl}>_1$
      b. White dialects
         $[-\text{cont}] \rightarrow <\text{Ø}> / [+\text{cons}] <\text{Ø}>_1 \underline{\quad} <-\text{syl}>_2$

It is obvious that this difference in weighting is a relatively minor element which does not reflect any of the basic relations reflected in the rule. The fact that Black speakers do not treat the grammatical boundary in *roll#ed* in the same way as white speakers in this particular rule does not say any-thing about the status of the past tense marker in BE. As we have noted, Black speakers show a more regular use of the past tense in narrative than white speakers do. What we see is that Black speakers have a little greater stylistic latitude in their use of the consonant cluster reduction rule. Whereas white speakers are severely constrained in the use of the rule with the *-ed* suffix, Black speakers are not. But the low figures in the right hand column show that all groups are aware of the existence of this suffix, which is normally salient for every group.

There are some dialects which show a much more radical reduction of the -ed suffix than Black English. BE regularly preserves the epenthetic schwa with verbs ending in t or d. But the Atlanta vernacular of Henry Grattons, for example, regularly drops this vowel. In place of the normal voicing assimilation rule, we usually have regressive assimilation, where a stem -t of the verb is voiced to [d], and we have a long [d:].

(53) a. *started to*   [stɑrd:u]
      b. *toted*   [tod:]
      c. *traded in*   [tred:ɪn]
      d. *traded it in* [tred:ɪn]

This removal of schwa is part of the general contraction rule, which operates here as in many dialects without regard to the presence of the tense marker. This is evident in (53d), where the vowel of *it* has been removed as well, leading to an over-all assimilation to a long [d:].[44] The removal of the requirement that contraction can operate only when the tense marker is present opens the door to many stylistic possibilities: *as, to, the, it* are now affected with dramatic consequences. In (54) we can see the same process operating independently of the -ed particle:

(54) [a:nuˊa:d:uɪt]   "I knew how to do it"

It follows that in some ways, this dialect has an even wider range of stylistic possibilities in handling the tense marker than Black English. There are grammarians as well as school teachers who would say that the speakers of this dialect are lazy and slovenly articulators. The full and reduced forms are of course identical in cognitive content.

The discussion of -ed in English shows that suffixes as well as separate auxiliaries are fertile material for stylistic variation. We can conclude that adequate languages must make full use of such reduced particles. The pidgins which we first discussed have only two options: insert an adverb such as *olden time* or *long bipo*, or leave the past unmarked. Dialects of English have a much wider choice, including fully stressed adverbs (*Long ago I started to do that*); a lighter treatment with a semi-auxiliary (*I once started to do that*); emphasis with an auxiliary (*I did start to do it*); a past tense suffix (*I started to do it*); or just enough phonetic substance to show that the past tense had been there ([stɑrd:uɪt]), where it is only the voicing of the consonant after [r] that tells us we are talking about the past.

In emphasizing this range of stylistic possibilities, it should be evident that control of both ends of the spectrum is necessary. Students graduating high school to look for white collar jobs will probably want to maintain firm control over the -*ed* suffix, and any student would want to have that control for writing standard English. But there is no reason to think that productive control over this rule — with the ability to produce -*ed* 100% of the time — is a necessary tool for learning. The concept of past time does not depend upon the ability to inhibit rules of consonant cluster simplification. In that sense, the logical claim of standard English finds no support in the development of tense markers.

Notes

1.   This paper is an expanded version of the first part of "On the Adequacy of Natural Languages" given at the Symposium on Language and Intelligence at the annual meeting of the Linguistic Society of America in Washington, D.C., December 1970.

2.   See "The Logic of Non-Standard English" (Labov 1969b) for some substantive comparisons between the verbal styles of working-class Black English speakers and middle-class Black speakers of standard English, as well as the implications of grammatical differences for this discussion.

3.   The particular self-fulfilling prophecy referred to here is of course that studied by Rosenthal (1968). There have been some criticisms that Rosenthal's observations are merely statistical correlations without any evidence as to how the teacher's early views of student's abilities can result in such dramatic effects in later years. Seligman, Lambert and Tucker (1971) have provided strong experimental evidence that the pupil's verbal style is the single most influential factor in determining a teacher's evaluation of his scholastic work.

4.   This is a direct quotation from tests of verbal ability typical of those utilized by educational psychologists. Children are shown a standard photograph and asked to tell a story about what they see. Those who respond well to this test in terms of volume of speech frequently use all of the formal marks of "school language" even at the age of six: articulation of final consonants with full release, exaggerated syllable junctures with special attention to morpheme boundaries, spelling pronunciation of functional words, inhibition of normal sandhi rules, and elimination of most of the stress reduction rules of the transformational cycle. Children who show signs of succeeding at school tasks thus show an early recognition of the linguistic variants that win approval from teachers; this extends in some cases to saying "Thank you" in response to teacher's standard closings. For analysis of the discourse rules involved in these forms of verbal manipulation, see "Finding Out About Children's Language" (Labov 1971b).

5.   From studies carried out in New York City in 1968-69 with children six to eight years old in South Central Harlem supported by a grant from the Public Health Service.

6.   That is, children were able to use their grammatical competence to decipher correctly utterances such as "The clown kicked she ran away" as opposed to "The clown kicked her ran away" where only the *she/her* opposition and not the intonation marks the subject.

7. The term "post-creole continuum" is from DeCamp's characterization of the Jamaican situation (1971).

8. "Marginal languages" is the term used by Reinecke in his dissertation, summarized in Reinecke (1964). There is no direct evidence of the inadequacy of pidgins, and certainly none on creoles. The traditional views of pidgins and creoles reflect primarily the political and ethnocentric limitations of traditional linguists (see section 11 below). This paper therefore relies upon the indirect evidence provided by the regular developments which take place when pidgins acquire native speakers.

9. In this undertaking, we were also fortunate in having the advice and experience of scholars who have worked with Hawaiian Pidgin and Creole for many years. I am particularly indebted to John Reinecke, who contributed a great deal to the interpretation of the data, and Stanley Tsuzaki, whose view of co-existent systems in Hawaii provides the basic framework for the investigation. The assistance and informed observations of Steve Boggs of the Department of Anthropology were of the greatest importance, and some of the data cited below were obtained with the help of Lewis Mamoa and Raymond Makahi, local research assistants associated with his Nanakuli project. The over-all initiative and planning that led to this research was that of Byron Bender and George Grace, whose interest in the sociolinguistic investigation of the Hawaiian speech community made possible the research findings cited here.

10. This definition points to one limitation of the present discussion. All of the data is derived from pidgins and creoles formed under the influence of a Western European colonizing language: English, Dutch, Portuguese, Spanish and French. The grammars and syntax of the superordinate languages are similar in many respects, just as the social contexts of the pidginizing process are similar. Further explorations of the general principles developed here will require the examination of pidginization under the influence of non-Indo-European languages, as Nida and Fehderau urge (1970), citing the cases of Police Motu and Swahili. There are also many parallels to be drawn with other kinds of contact languages — lingua francas and koines. We can also profit from a study of the deterioration of languages in emigrant situations, or their ultimate decline and decay, which will show some parallels to the process of pidginization.

11. We find many examples of spontaneous pidginization occurring on ranches in the Southwestern United States, where the efforts of foremen to communicate with laborers lead to varieties of "foreigner talk" (Ferguson 1971) interacting with "Tex-Mex". Perhaps the lower limit of linguistic competence was reported to me by an eighty-year-old horse breeder from Sonora, Texas, who had hired and bossed many Mexicans in his time. He said that he could handle the language enough to tell the men what to do. "But when it came to anything complicated," he said, "like using adjectives . . ." This kind of idiosyncratic grasp of the skeleton of a language would not fall under the category of "pidgin" as conceived here.

12. For the analysis of these examples, I am indebted to Hamilton van Buren.

13. D. Sankoff warns that the last example may be ephemeral.

14. These observations are due to Steve Boggs.

15. It is not unusual for time and space to be indicated by locatives; cf. *back on the farm* or *in the old country*.

16. The basic discourse rule which defines narratives as one means of recapitulating past experience states that: If a narrative clause with a preterit head N_i follows another narrative clause with a preterit head N_{i-j}, then it is asserted that N_i occurred after N_{i-j} in the original semantic interpretation.

17. Note the parallel in the "pleonastic" colloquial forms with *time when, place where*, and *reason because* in which the abstract temporals, locatives and reason features implicit in the adverbials are overtly realized. Pidgins make frequent use of such semi-suffixes as *-time* and *-side*. In (9b) above we see a parallel use of adverbs with *-time* to mark the time relations: *sometime, one time*, etc.

18. Among those who would reverse the perspective of Nida and Fehderau, Martin Joos has made the clearest statement on the place of redundancy in the development from pidgins to creoles. In a concise set of "Hypotheses as to the origin and modification of pidgins" delivered at the 1968 Mona conference, Joos argued that "Solidarity and redundancy tend to be in equilibrium". Among the redundancies he specifies are concord and idiomatic constructions. He then posits that "Incipient solidarity tends to convert pidgin into creole as (more) redundancies emerge and lexicon is elaborated; styles begin to differentiate and to get stratified". (Joos 1971:187)

19. Whinnom notes that *baimby* may be a re-lexification of Portuguese *logo* (cited by Cassidy 1971). In that case, the parallel noted below between Crioulo *lo* and Neo-Melanesian *bai* is the result of diffusion rather than independent adoption of an adverb of time as an auxiliary. It is even more striking then that both *logo/luego* and *baimbai* underwent parallel phonological reduction to monosyllabic unstressed auxiliaries.

20. After pointing out that *by-and-by* is found throughout the Caribbean and the Pacific, and is parallel to the future marker *logo* in Macanese, Cassidy adds "I do not know of *bimeby I come* having turned into a regular future construction, but one can see how it well might, so far as the meaning is concerned" (1971:211).

21. A recent method for learning Neo-Melanesian produced by Stephen Wurm and others (1971) shows examples with the future as *bai* but without any grammatical statements.

22. Mihalic notes that *baimbai* can be placed after the subject in some cases, so that if this was indeed the case the movement to pre-predicate position seems to overlap with the reduction to *bai*. The data from Mambump, however, indicates that the reduction to *bai* came first.

23. Murphy (1966) gives *laik* as the form for the immediate future, alternating with the general marker *baembai* (1966:12).

24. This text is from a pseudo-conversation conducted by Moverly with a Pitcairnese girl in Australia. The text represents my own rough orthography from Ross's phonetics.

25. Ross and Moverly state that *used to* must have lost its [t] by the general rule of consonant cluster simplification, and the resultant residual form was "naturally" utilized for the present. But we find that the word boundary and *-ed* in *used to* disappear in many colloquial English dialects, and the [st] cluster is then medial and not subject to simplification. It seems Pitcairnese has no problem with medial clusters (cf. *basket, ostenbird* "Austin-bird"; Ross and Moverly 1964:133,134). It therefore seems much more likely that the [t] was dropped by a grammatical process of back-formation.

26. The distribution of *gonna* in HC shows that it is a clear marker of a switch to Hawaiian English (HE), along with *don't*, *-ed*, etc. Derek Bickerton has called my attention to the connection of this fact with the *for/to* alternation. One of the most general characteristics of pidgins is the reduction of prepositions in favor of such a general marker as *for*. Though the schwa suffix on *gonna* may be taken as a part of the word, it is also possible that it implies a system with the infinitive marker *to*, and Creole speakers with consistent *for* may consistently reject *gonna* in favor of *gon*. Bickerton points out (personal communication) that the Black English alternation of *gon'* and *gonna* should be re-examined in this light.

27. There is a Jamaican parallel for this alternation. Beryl Bailey lists five geographic variants of *en*: *ben*, *bin*, *men*, *min*, and *wen* (1966:140). This strongly suggests that *en* is a reduced form of *wen*, by the same rule used in Hawaiian Creole (see Rule 1 under [48] below). But we should also bear in mind the possibility that *been* is the ultimate source of all these, through progressive lenition to a bilabial fricative, glide, approximant and finally zero. The forms used by Lippy Espinda (see below) often show such a lenition of initial *b* in *been*, and it is sometimes difficult to distinguish *been* from *wen*. Of course we must also be prepared for the possibility that the selection of *wen* is the conflation of two influences: the grammatical analog with the generalized auxiliary *go*, and the phonological approximation to *been*.

28. Lippy Espinda is a well-known citizen of Honolulu, used-car dealer and television personality. In his advertisements and television appearances he used HC as his main trademark. For example, a gasoline discount card reads "Hey BRADDA! Give us chance for Grease, Tires, Tune-up, Battery Sale". He was raised in an HC-speaking community outside of Honolulu with a strong Portuguese-Hawaiian tradition. He is an extremely sensitive and insightful informant, with an intuitive grasp of deep structure equivalents which is sometimes astonishing.

29. Lippy Espinda also uses *been* as a past tense marker. There is some evidence that *been* can have a perfective connotation, but it also varies freely with *wen*. The fact that strings of *been* and *wen* clauses tend to cluster in narrative indicates that they may be derived from separate sub-systems. Reinecke's observations of earlier Creole indicate that *been* was the more general form, and his citations from the 1930's bear this out. For example, the older pidgin speaker quoted in (9b) above uses the auxiliary *been* occasionally.

   (i) *Wen I come down boat, one man, he lock me in big loom. He ask wot for I been come Honolulu — if I come stay for hana-hana licee field. I speak "No". Den he ax me if somebody he been sell me. . . I velly glad — das ony face I sabbee — all face no see before. Dis fust time I been see kanaka.*

In these instances, *been* seems to be operating as a past perfect, even plainer in "*He know, because he been come Honolulu, one time before*". This use of an unmarked preterit with a past marker for the past perfect is similar to Crioulo (see below). It seems logical for such a specialized use of *been* to have survived in current HC, but we have no evidence of it from younger speakers.

30. The research in Kalihi was done by Ruth Watanabe, in Pauoa by Richard Day, in Nanakuli by Michael Forman and myself, and in Hauula by myself.

31. The basic principles for the observation of the vernacular used here are summarized in Labov (1970), and exemplified in some detail in Volume I of Cooperative Research Report 3288 dealing with research on Black English in South Central Harlem (Labov,

Cohen, Robins, and Lewis 1968). The work in Hawaii was exploratory in character, not as systematic as the Harlem work, but some of the basic techniques for participant-observation of peer groups were carried even further.

32. The problem here is the classic one in linguistics of distinguishing variable from invariant behavior. When certain special sub-classes are split off (*started*, *wanted*) verbs fall into two major classes: one with invariant *wen*, the other with variable *wen* alternating with irregular ablaut and shortened forms. This variation is itself subject to variable constraints which we have not explored thoroughly here.

33. The grammatical sub-class of quasi-modals is not the only factor operating here. Note that both *started* and *wanted* end in clusters with *-t* and show epenthetic schwa, which favors the retention of *-ed* in dialects such as Black English.

34. Tests carried out by Carol Odo showed that *wen go* was most likely to be used in translating from SE to HC if the English had an overtly purposive construction. *They went to chop down a mango tree* is very apt to elicit a translation with *wen go chop*: *John chopped down a coconut tree* is much less likely. *Those guys went and chopped down four trees* is intermediate in this respect. The major influence is no doubt the presence of English *go and*. But whether the variable constraints on these translations give us a direct insight into the meaning of *wen go* in HC is still an open question.

35. There is an oscillation between *never have* and *never had*, which is the only case of a redundant past tense signal in *never* and in the verb stem.

36. Systematic variation in the use of *go* would be signalled by variable constraints on the rule. In that case, *go* would appear in a nested pair of angled brackets, cross-referenced to a feature such as $<+\text{pur}>$ in the environment.

37. One of the most striking differences between HC and HE is that HC has no syntactic canonical form of the shape $S \rightarrow NP+VP$. There is no obligatory subject, so that no dummy *it* or *there* appears when there is no lexical item before the verb. Cf. *Get one policeman* and *He never knew who was*.

38. Our first recognition of the highly reduced character of these auxiliary forms was the result of a detailed phonetic transcription of a Kalihi text by Ruth Watanabe, who gradually corrected her zero transcriptions to indicate residual nasals and liquids. It is not accidental that this transcriber was closer to a native speaker of HC than any of the other linguists in the research project, and had been exposed to HC in her own extended family. We then found the same rules operating in Nanakuli and Hauula. Anthropologists working in Nanakuli for some time, in intimate association with consistent speakers of HC, were then able to observe and develop sensitivity to the presence of these auxiliaries themselves.

39. The question may be raised as to whether the elaboration of *wen* to *wen go* may not have been the result of phonological condensation, and a response to a threatened loss of this auxiliary. We do not have the solid information on the HC of speakers 30 to 60 years old which would resolve this question. But the evidence we have indicates that morphophonemic condensation followed the development of *wen go* rather than preceded it. Secondly, we must bear in mind that the contraction of *wen* is optional, like the simplification of -KD clusters in SE, which entirely eliminates the *-ed* ending when it applies. There is considerable evidence that such variable rules are compatible with a stable grammar, and it is only when the contraction and deletion rules become semi-categorial that compensating grammatical changes are called for (see Labov 1970, Labov 1971b).

40. The tense marker was present in the original contraction of step (8). It is not accidental that the development of (11') is a Southern feature. The SE condition that contraction requires the presence of a tense marker (Labov 1969a) is absent in a number of regional dialects, including the Lower South. As noted above, any function word or suffix with schwa can be contracted with many further consequences for surface structure.

41. See above under footnote 34 for some evidence on this point.

42. The conventions for variable rules are developed in Labov (1970). Angled brackets are used here instead of parentheses to indicate variable outputs and variable constraints, and the ordering of constraints is used only optionally. The most general form of such variable rules shows only the direction of each constraint, since specific ordering is characteristic of a particular stage of a dialect in space and time.

43. For a systematic approach to the weighting of environments in phonological rules, see C.-J. Bailey (1972).

44. After the contraction rule applies, a rule of voicing assimilation operates to assimilate [t]'s to [d] in the vicinity of the past tense D. This is a later rule than the progressive voicing assimilation which operates on the past tense suffix itself, and is typical of the kind of low-level condensation rule which applies after boundaries are removed. The simplification of geminates which then may follow is controlled by tempo.

References

Alatis, James E., ed. 1969. *Twentieth Annual Round Table: Linguistics and the teaching of standard English to speakers of other languages or dialects* (= *Georgetown Monograph Series on Languages and Linguistics*, 22.) Washington: Georgetown University Press.

Bailey, Beryl. 1966. *Jamaican Creole Syntax: A transformational approach.* Cambridge: Cambridge University Press.

————. 1971. "Jamaican Creole: Can dialect boundaries be defined?" Hymes 1971.341-48.

Bailey, Charles-James. 1972. "The Integration of Linguistic Theory: Internal reconstruction and the comparative method in descriptive analysis". *Linguistic Change and Generative Theory* ed. by Robert P. Stockwell and Ronald Macaulay, 22-31. Bloomington: Indiana University Press.

Bereiter, Carl, and Siegfried Engelmann. 1966. *Teaching Disadvantaged Children in the Pre-School.* Englewood Cliffs: Prentice-Hall.

Bernstein, Basil. 1961. "Aspects of Language and Learning in the Genesis of the Social Process," *Journal of Child Psychology and Psychiatry* 1.313-324. (Reprinted in *Language in Culture and Society* ed. by Dell Hymes 1964.251-63. New York: Harper and Row.)

Bloom, Lois. 1970. *Language Development: Form and function in emerging grammars*. Cambridge, MA: MIT Press.

Cassidy, Frederic G. 1971. "Tracing the Pidgin Element in Jamaican Creole (with Notes on Method and the Nature of Pidgin Vocabularies)". Hymes 1971.203-21.

DeCamp, David. 1971. "Toward a Generative Analysis of a Post-Creole Speech Continuum". Hymes 1971.349-70.

Ervin-Tripp, Susan. 1964. "An Analysis of the Interaction of Language, Topic and Listener". *The Ethnography of Communication* ed. by John Gumperz and Dell Hymes (= *American Anthropologist* 66, No. 6, Part 2), 86-102.

Faine, Jules. 1939. *Le Créole dans l'Univers: Etudes comparatives des parlers français-créoles. Tome I. Le mauricien*. Port-au-Prince: Imprimerie de l'Etat.

Ferguson, Charles A. 1971. "Absence of the Copula and the Notion of Simplicity: A study of normal speech, baby talk, foreigner talk, and pidgins". Hymes 1971.141-50.

Goodman, Morris F. *A Comparative Study of Creole French Dialects*. The Hague: Mouton.

Gumperz, John J., and Robert Wilson. 1971. "Convergence and Creolization: A case from the Indo-Aryan/Dravidian border". Hymes 1971.151-67.

Hymes, Dell, ed. 1971. *Pidginization and Creolization of Languages*. Cambridge: University Press.

Joos, Martin. 1971. "Hypotheses as to the Origin and Modification of Pidgins". Hymes 1971.187.

Labov, William. 1969a. "Contraction, Deletion, and Inherent Variation of the English Copula". *Lg* 45.715-62. (Revised version appears in Labov 1972a.65-129.

―――. 1969b. "The Logic of Non-Standard English". Alatis 1969.1-44. (Reprinted in Williams 1970.154-91 and Labov 1972a.201-40.)

―――. 1970. "The Study of Language in its Social Context". *Studium Generale* 23.30-87. (Revised version appears in Labov 1972c.183-259.)

―――. 1971a. "Finding out about Children's Language". *Working Papers in Communication* ed. by D. Steinberg. Honolulu: Pacific Speech Association.

―――. 1971b. "The Notion of 'System' in Creole Studies". Hymes 1971.447-72.

———. 1972a. *Language in the Inner City: Studies in the Black English Vernacular*. Philadelphia: University of Pennsylvania Press.

———. 1972b. "Negative Attraction and Negative Concord in English Grammar". *Lg* 48.773-818. (Reprinted in Labov 1972a.130-96.)

———. 1972c. *Sociolinguistic Patterns*. Philadelphia: University of Pennsylvania Press.

Labov, William, Paul Cohen, Clarence Robins, and John Lewis. 1968. *A Study of the Non-Standard English of Negro and Puerto Rican Speakers in New York City*. Cooperative Research Report 3288. Vols. I and II. New York: Columbia University.

Lawton, Denis. 1968. *Social Class, Language and Education*. London: Routledge and Kegan Paul.

Lenz, Rodolfo. 1928. *El Papiamento, la Lengua Criolla de Curazao (la Gramática Más Sencilla)*. Santiago de Chile: Balcells & Cia.

Mihalic, Francis. 1957. *Grammar and Dictionary of Neo-Melanesian*. Techny, IL: Mission Press.

Murphy, John J. 1966. *The Book of Pidgin English*. Revised edition. Brisbane: W.R. Smith and Paterson. (First edition, 1943.)

Nida, Eugene, and H.W. Fehderau. 1970. "Indigenous Pidgins and Koinés". *IJAL* 36.146-55.

Reinecke, John E. 1964. "Trade Jargons and Creole Dialects as Marginal Languages". *Language in Culture and Society* ed. by Dell Hymes, 534-46. New York: Harper and Row.

———. 1968. "Tây Bôi: Notes on the Pidgin French spoken in Viet Nam". Paper delivered at the Creole Conference held in Mona, Jamaica. (Revised version appears as Reinecke 1971.)

———. 1969. *Language and Dialect in Hawaii*. Honolulu: University of Hawaii Press.

———. 1971. "Tây Bôi: Notes on the Pidgin French spoken in Vietnam". Hymes 1971.47-56.

Rosenthal, Robert. 1968. *Pygmalion in the Classroom*. New York: Holt, Rinehart and Winston.

Ross, Alan S.C., and A.W. Moverly. 1964. *The Pitcairnese Language*. London: Andre Deutsch.

Schuchardt, Hugo. 1888. "Kreolische Studien. VIII. Über das Annamitofranzösische". *Sitzungsberichte der Kaiserlichen Akademie der Wissenschaften zu Wien*. 116(1). 227-234.

Seligman, C.R., G.R. Tucker and W.E. Lambert. 1972. "The Effects of

Speech Style and Other Attributes on Teachers' Attitudes Towards Pupils". *Language in Society* 1.131-42.

Tsuzaki, Stanley. 1971. "Coexistent Systems in Language Variation: The case of Hawaiian English". Hymes 1971.327-39.

Valkhoff, Marius. 1966. *Studies in Pidgins and Creoles with Special Reference to South Africa*. Johannesburg: Witwatersrand University Press.

Vendryes, J. 1951. *Language: A linguistic introduction to history*. Trans. Paul Radin. New York: Barnes and Noble.

Weinreich, Uriel, William Labov, and Marvin Herzog. 1968. "Empirical Foundations for a Theory of Language Change". *Directions for Historical Linguistics* ed. by Winfred Lehmann and Yakov Malkiel, 97-195. Austin: University of Texas Press.

Williams, Frederick, ed. 1970. *Language and Poverty: Perspectives on a theme*. Chicago: Markham.

Wilson, W.A.A. 1962. *The Crioulo of Guiné*. Johannnesburg: Witwatersrand University Press.

Wurm, Stephen A. 1971. *New Guinea Highlands Pidgin: Course materials*. Pacific Linguistics D-3.

Papiamentu Tense-Aspect, With Special Attention to Discourse

Roger W. Andersen[1]
University of California, Los Angeles

1. Introduction

The standard treatment of tense-modality-aspect (TMA) in creole languages is to focus on **position** and **meaning** of the various preverbal TMA markers.[2] The reasons for this are clear: creole languages of different lexical stock and geographical location share these features of preverbal position of free temporal morphemes and the basic meanings that they encode, and the search for an explanation for these commonalities (whether in terms of universals, relexification, or substrate or superstrate origin) requires a focus on what the creoles have in common. The present treatment of temporal reference in Papiamentu begins with this same type of exposition of form-position-meaning, but then focuses more precisely on the **function** of any given form within the total discourse context of natural speech. It also attempts to pay more than lip service to the assumption that this array of surface forms constitutes a coherent linguistic **system** (or subsystem) in which the appearance or non-appearance of any particular form (or group of forms) in a clause (embedded within meaningful discourse) takes on meaning especially because the forms contrast with each other and constitute a well-defined system.

The general approach taken here is, therefore, a functional approach. One goal of such an approach is to provide for Papiamentu a realistic and usable description of the temporal system. Realistic in that it actually fits real daily use of the language and usable in that language specialists can use such a description for basic or applied research or simply practical application. There are at least three concrete uses to which such a description can be put:

(1)   Papiamentu has been mentioned frequently as counterevidence
       for the validity of Bickerton's (1981, 1984) bioprogram.
       Although I do not intend to enter the debate on this issue in this
       article, it is clear that existing grammatical treatments of
       Papiamentu, as good as some of them are, are inadequate for
       settling the issue.

(2)   The Portuguese- and Spanish-based creoles have been neglected
       in the recent theoretical and empirical studies of pidgin and
       creole languages. Given earlier proposals that placed a Pidgin
       Portuguese in an important position in the development of the
       creole languages of the world (e.g., Whinnom 1956, 1965,
       Thompson 1961, Taylor 1971, Naro 1978, to mention a few), this
       neglect needs to be remedied. What is needed to begin with is a
       thorough comparison of all existing Portuguese- and Spanish-
       based creoles, based on primary empirical data. This article is an
       attempt to begin to provide a basis for such a comparison.[3]

(3)   Applied linguists in the Netherlands Antilles are currently pre-
       paring instructional materials for the new role that Papiamentu
       now has as a subject in the school curriculum.[4] A description of
       the temporal system of Papiamentu, in addition to serving the
       theoretical goals just discussed, must be relevant to the more
       practical concerns of native speakers of Papiamentu who must
       make sound linguistic decisions within an educational setting and
       in language planning.

Bickerton (1975, 1981) has characterized the prototypical creole TMA
system as consisting of three preverbal free morphemes, one for tense
(+anterior), one for modality (+irrealis) and a third for aspect (+nonpunc-
tual), which occur in this order if two or more occur together. Papiamentu
apparently stands out as an exception in that it has no anterior marker, the
irrealis marker (*lo*) does not keep its predicted position, and the aspectual
system is complicated by the fact that it is clearly encoded only in past time
reference and appears to mirror the Spanish perfective:imperfective opposition. In other words, the Papiamentu tense-modality-aspect markers *ta*,
tabata, *a*, and *lo* simply do not fit Bickerton's paradigm. *Ta* is usually
characterized as a "present" marker (Goilo 1972, Maurer 1985), *tabata* and
a as a past imperfective and past perfective marker, respectively, and *lo* as
a "future" marker. It is important for both theoretical and practical reasons

that it be determined empirically whether the Papiamentu temporal markers are indeed essentially tense markers and thus deviate from the prototypical creole temporal system or whether they actually match more closely the prototypical creole temporal system in being basically markers of aspect. This article is organized around these basic questions concerning the status of the various temporal markers as markers of tense, aspect, or tense plus aspect. The irrealis category is also crucial to Bickerton's bioprogram and earlier comparative studies on creole languages and is a logical part of any treatment of the complete temporal system of a creole language. For reasons of space, however, mood and modality, including irrealis, are dealt with in a separate article (Andersen 1988).

Papiamentu has been in close linguistic contact with Spanish since its apparent origin in Curaçao in the late seventeenth century.[5] While this contact has not resulted in the same type of full creole continuum found in many of the English creoles (e.g. Jamaican, Guyanese, and Hawaiian Creole English), it has had an important influence on the more formal varieties of Papiamentu. With respect to the temporal system, this influence of Spanish results in formal registers of Papiamentu acquiring a temporal system based on absolute tense, while varieties of Papiamentu not so directly influenced by modern Spanish show greater aspectual focus (and less grammaticalization of tense) than the more hispanized varieties.[6] It is beyond the scope of this article to illustrate the full range from basilectal (and thus nonhispanized) to fully hispanized varieties of Papiamentu.[7] Instead I will focus on the basilect, which is really the only lect relevant to Bickerton's bioprogram.

Table 1: Data Used for In-Depth Analysis

TEXT	TABATA INDEX	TYPE
1	0	Animated conversation between two boys, about 14 and 15 years old, in rural store.
2	24	Traditional folk tale, told by 89-year old man in his home in the country.
3	49	Relaxed interview by native speaker about the period when two men in an old folks' home were young. Text 3a: 87-year old former seaman. Text 3b: 77-year old man.
4	71	Public forum, in which four invited speakers responded to questions from audience.

Table 1 lists the data used in this in-depth analysis. This sample comes from a total corpus of over 80 hours of recorded natural speech by over 200 native speakers of Papiamentu, in Curaçao, Netherlands Antilles. Although the examples for this article come from this smaller set of texts, the analysis evolved out of detailed study of a much larger number of texts.

The *"Tabata* Index" in Table 1 is based on Andersen (1983), in which ten phonological variables were quantified in six texts ranging from the most basilectal to the most hispanized registers of Papiamentu. Texts 1-4 in Table 1 are the first four texts in the 1983 publication and the most natural, spontaneous speech of that study. The other two texts, not used here, were from radio and television news broadcasts. The *"Tabata* Index" is the percentage of usage of the full form *tabata* out of all the various forms used. The full form, *tabata*, is used in the most formal registers and "abbreviated" (and more natural) forms are used in more casual speech: *ta'ata*, a phonological variant of *tabata*, and *ta'a*, a separate form which probably originated through phonological loss of [b] in an older form, *taba*. An index of 0 means the full form *tabata* was never used; an index of 71 means the full form was used 71% of the time. This index provides a rough approximation of the degree of formality of the four texts used for this study.

2. The Semantics of Tense, Aspect, and Modality

2.1 *Aspect vs. Tense*

"Tense relates the time of the situation referred to to some other time, usually to the moment of speaking" (Comrie 1976:1). Thus, *he lied* and *he was lying* are past and *he's lying* and *he lies* are nonpast "tense". Aspect, on the other hand, refers to the internal nature of the event as viewed by the speaker or, in Comrie's (1976:4) terms, "the internal temporal constituency of the situation". The basic distinctions used in this article are past, present, and future tense for an absolute tense system, anterior and non-anterior tense for a relative tense system, and perfective and imperfective aspect. Grammatical encoding of "perfective" aspect treats the event or situation as a whole, whereas "imperfective" aspect makes "explicit reference to the internal temporal structure of the situation, viewing a situation from within" (Comrie 1976:24).

2.2 Lexical Aspect and Grammatical Aspect

The discussion in the preceding paragraph was with reference to grammatical aspect. Languages differ as to whether they have grammatical aspect (Hebrew does not, for example) and what type of grammatical aspect they have (English and Spanish both have progressive and perfect aspect, Spanish also has perfective and imperfective aspect, but English does not encode perfective and imperfective aspect as morphologically distinct grammatical categories). Separate from such morphologically conveyed aspect is what is called "lexical aspect" or "inherent semantic aspect" of verbs and predicates. Grammatical vs. lexical aspect is referred to in German as *Aspekt* vs. *Aktionsart*, and in French as *aspect* vs. *mode d'action*. (See Comrie 1976:6-7, fn. 4, and Meisel 1985:324, fn. 1.) The effect of grammatical aspect is often to override the natural semantic aspect of a verb or predicate.

Certainly the most detailed and explicit treatment of tense and aspect in creole languages is that of Bickerton (1974, 1975, 1981). Bickerton's terminology of punctual vs nonpunctual (or durative) is apparently used for both inherent semantic aspect (Aktionsart) and grammatical aspect (Aspekt). To avoid confusion I will use Comrie's terms perfective and imperfective aspect for the grammatical aspect encoded by *ta*, *a*, and *tabata* in Papiamentu and restrict the terms punctual, durative, stative, and the like to the inherent semantics of a predicate.

In the remainder of this section I will discuss the categories of inherent semantic aspect that I will use. Comrie (1976:41-51) describes three binary sets of inherent aspect: punctual vs durative, stative vs dynamic, and telic vs atelic. I follow Comrie for the first two, but Mourelatos (1981) for telicity.

(1) Punctual verbs denote momentary events of minimal duration, whereas durative verbs describe "situations that must inherently last for a certain period of time" (Comrie, p. 41). In *the ball fell to the floor and then rolled across the room*, *fall* is punctual and *rolled* durative.

(2) Stative verbs, such as *know*, *seem*, and *have*, denote physical or internal states. Dynamic verbs, i.e. all nonstative verbs, such as *run*, *push*, *drop*, and *jump*, require energy for the action or event to take place — and to continue — whereas states require no energy for them to continue, once the state has been entered. (Entering or leaving a state, however, depending on the particular circumstances, may be conceived of as "dynamic".)

(3) Telic events express "action continuing towards a goal" and "involve a product, upshot, or outcome" (Mourelatos 1981:193). Thus, *he built a house* and *he found a diamond* are both telic, whereas *he ran* and *the ball rolled* are atelic. In this regard, it is important to note that, whereas in many cases it "works" to assign the labels punctual:durative, stative:dynamic, and telic:atelic to individual verbs, very often it is a verb-plus-particle, a predicate, or a whole clause which has that attribute. Thus, as Vendler (1967:102) notes, *he ran* is different from *he ran a mile*. Both are dynamic and durative, while *ran* is atelic and *ran a mile* telic. Vendler categorizes verbs (or predicates, as the case may be) into four categories (with examples from Vendler):

STATE	ACTIVITY	ACCOMPLISHMENT	ACHIEVEMENT
have	*run*	*paint a picture*	*recognize (someone)*
possess	*walk*	*make a chair*	*realize (something)*
desire	*swim*	*build a house*	*lose (something)*
want	*push*	*write a novel*	*find (something)*
like	*pull*	*grow up*	*win the race*

In terms of the three binary oppositions discussed earlier, activities, accomplishments, and achievements are all DYNAMIC situations (vs STATES); achievements are PUNCTUAL events, while the other three categories (including states) are DURATIVE; accomplishments and achievements are TELIC, and activities and states are ATELIC. The basic difference between accomplishments and achievements is that in accomplishments the telic reaching of a goal or endpoint is preceded by a durative action or series of actions (and thus, *making a chair* is not "accomplished" until that endpoint is actually reached), whereas in achievements the event itself is the endpoint (or beginning point, as the case may be). Thus, Mourelatos's "punctual occurrences" is an equivalent term for Vendler's "achievements".[8] Since relations among these four categories were not clear in Vendler's work, Mourelatos (1981) proposes a hierarchical organization which joins accomplishments and achievements as EVENTS (or Performances). Events contrast with PROCESSES (or Activities, in Vendler's terminology). This is captured in Table 2, which maps the stative:dynamic, punctual:durative, and telic:atelic categories onto Mourelatos's hierarchy. (Decisions as to correspondences in this mapping are my own. "A" gives Mourelatos's hierarchy with Vendler's categories in parentheses, "B" maps the binary oppositions onto the hierarchy, and "C" represents these oppositions as semantic features.)

Table 2: A Re-Interpretation of the Vendler-Mourelatos Hierarchy

A:

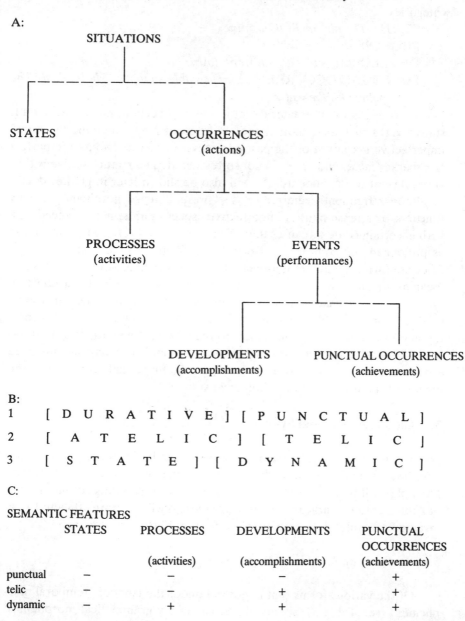

B:

1	[D U R A T I V E] [P U N C T U A L]
2	[A T E L I C] [T E L I C]
3	[S T A T E] [D Y N A M I C]

C:

SEMANTIC FEATURES	STATES	PROCESSES	DEVELOPMENTS	PUNCTUAL OCCURRENCES
		(activities)	(accomplishments)	(achievements)
punctual	−	−	−	+
telic	−	−	+	+
dynamic	−	+	+	+

Mourelatos (1981:201) provides the following examples of his categories:

STATE: *The air smells of jasmine.*

PROCESS: *It's snowing.*

DEVELOPMENT: *The sun went down.*

PUNCTUAL OCCURRENCE: *The cable snapped. He blinked. The pebble hit the water.*

As is discussed in greater detail in the next section, most (but not all) stative verbs in Papiamentu cannot be preceded by either the "present" imperfective marker *ta* or the past perfective marker *a*. The past imperfective marker *tabata*, however, is not so restricted. The feature stative is thus very relevant to Papiamentu. As will also be shown later in greater detail, *ta*, although frequently referred to as a "present" tense morpheme, actually functions as a tense-neutral imperfective aspect morpheme: *ta* preceding a verb in certain contexts causes the action depicted by verb to be interpreted as prolonged and continuous. The effect is to give to the verb a meaning associated with the inherent aspectual feature durative. And the perfective meaning of the marker *a* imparts to the verb (and predicate) a punctual interpretation. *Tabata* is clearly a tense marker, but it is also an aspect marker: *tabata*, like the tense-neutral *ta*, imposes an imperfective interpretation on the situation, again similar to the inherent semantic feature durative. This treatment of inherent semantic aspect and grammatically imposed aspect is useful as a framework to interpret the functional properties of the Papiamentu tense-aspect morphological system.

3. The Basic Temporal System

The purpose of this section is to present the basic "pieces" of the temporal system and show how they function together as a coherent system. Examples will be drawn as much as possible from recordings of natural use of Papiamentu in Curaçao. In a few instances it will be more efficient to use invented examples or examples taken from published grammars.

3.1 *Inventory of Temporal Morphemes*

Of the various forms that might fall under the label of "temporal morphemes" (see Table 3), six appear to be strictly grammatical morphemes: four tense-aspect morphemes (*ta*, *a*, *tabata*, and *sa*) and two morphemes of mood (*lo* and the "zero" morpheme).[9] The others are either modal auxiliaries (*ke, mester, por*), periphrastic temporal forms which function in a fashion similar semantically to modal auxiliaries (*ta bai, tin ku* [or *tin di*], *kaba di*), or a type of temporal adverbial, only one of which will be treated here (*kaba*). These forms are given, with invented examples and English glosses, in Table 3.

Table 3: Inventory of Temporal Morphemes

Group 1: Mood, Aspect, Tense Morphemes

FORM   MEANING

1a: Tense-Aspect

ta	imperfective	*Wan ta kome bonchi.*
		"John eats/is eating beans".
a	perfective	*Wan a kome bonchi.*
		". . . ate/has eaten/had eaten . . ."
tabata	past imperfective	*Wan tabata kome bonchi.*
		". . . was eating/used to eat . . ."
sa	habitual	*Wan sa kome bonchi.*
		". . . usually eats . . ."

1b: Mood

lo	irrealis	*Wan lo kome bonchi.*
		"John will eat beans".
0	subjunctive	*(Si) wan 0 kome bonchi . . .*
		"(If) John eats beans, . . ."

Group 2: Full Verbs with Temporal Functions

2a: Modal Auxiliaries

ke	"want"	*Wan ke kome bonchi.*
		"John wants to eat . . ."
mester	"can/may/might"	*Wan por kome bonchi.*
		". . . can/may eat . . ."

2b: Quasi-modal Auxiliaries

ta bai	"going to"	*Wan ta bai kome bonchi.*
		"John is going to eat . . ."
tin di	"have to"	*Wan tin di kome bonchi.*
		". . . has to eat . . ."
tin ku	"have to"	*Wan tin ku kome bonchi.*
		". . . has to eat . . ."
kaba di	"just"	*Wan a kaba di kome bonchi.*
		". . . just ate . . ."

2c: Completive Adverbial

kaba	completive	*Wan a kome bonchi kaba.*
		". . . has already eaten . . ."

3.2 *Tense-Aspect Morphemes*[10]

The standard description of Papiamentu tense and aspect depicts *ta* as simply a "present" marker, *a* a "past perfective" and *tabata* a "past imperfective" marker.[11] Such a description is not necessarily incorrect. First of all, the register of educated formal speech and writing fits this description fairly accurately. Users of this register, however, are bilingual or, more commonly, multilingual; and it appears that, rather than Papiamentu intrinsically having an absolute tense system (and paying rather less attention to aspect) like Spanish, Dutch, or English, the languages these speakers typically know very well, in this register Papiamentu is made to conform to the same absolute tense system they use for formal Spanish, Dutch, or English. The description also "works" in many cases in Papiamentu itself: present time reference will usually require *ta* and past time reference will require *a* and *tabata* in many cases. However, as discussed in more detail in sections 4 and 5, I argue that **basilectal** Papiamentu has a different tense-aspect system from that described in formal grammatical treatises (such as Goilo 1972).[12] In basilectal Papiamentu, I argue, there is an opposition between tense-neutral *ta* (imperfective) and *a* (perfective). Although *ta* is certainly the typical "present" marker, as traditional grammars call it, this is a consequence of its status as an imperfective marker. And perfective *a* usually has past time reference, but not because *a* is intrinsically a "past" marker. Rather, a perfective event is, by its very nature, a past event once it has occurred. Imperfective *tabata* functions as a past-marked variant of *ta* and is used in spontaneous discourse only to anchor an event clearly in the past when otherwise the use of *ta*, which is tense-neutral, would be misleading. This interpretation, which departs considerably from the standard interpretation, is based on careful study of natural recordings of Papiamentu and will be supported with excerpts from some of these recordings. This interpretation is possible only if the analyst works with continuous discourse. A sentence-level grammar is inadequate.

As shown in Table 3, *ta* typically has present time reference, either a generic time or a progressive meaning as in example (1):

(1) a. *E ta   bai ku   bus.*
        he T-A go with bus
        "He takes the bus (to school in town)".
                    (Text 1, Conversation, 66)

b. *Nan ta yora pasobra nan ta pober.*
they T-A cry because they be poor
"They are crying because they are poor".
(Text 2, Folk Tale, 29-30)

The English glosses for examples (1a) and (1b) differ only because the larger context within which they are embedded makes it clear that in (1a) reference is to a customary action (offered in response to another speaker's expression of amazement that the boy referred to attends a particular school in town, even though he lives out in the country), while in (1b) reference is to action at a particular moment in a story, which makes it clear that the meaning is similar to English "progressive". What *ta* encodes is not "present", "simple present", or "present progressive", but rather tense-neutral imperfective, which here is easily interpreted as having present reference, in contrast to perfective *a* (*el a bai* . . . "he went . . ."; *nan a yora* . . . "they cried . . .").

In example (2) *a* is used because reference is made to an action that is assumed to have occurred at some time prior to the current point of reference within the text. Depending on the particular context, this would be equivalent to English "Didn't you learn . . .?", "Haven't you learned . . . ?", or "Hadn't you learned . . . ?" In this particular case, *a* is interpreted contextually as a simple past.

(2) *Bosonan no a siña na skol?*
you-pl not T-A learn in school
"Didn't you learn (about that) in school?
(Text 1, Conversation, 534)

Tabata (including its variants *ta'ata* and *ta'a*), like *ta*, causes the action of the following verb to be interpreted as durative, whether as iterative, habitual, or progressive. In this particular case (example [3]), the man referred to was the same man who earlier was filling a bucket with water, which imposes a progressive interpretation on the form.

(3) *El a haña un hòmber sintá den port'e kamber.*
he T-A find a man seated in door-of room
"He found a man sitting in the doorway".
E hòmber ku ta'ata yena awa ku makutu
the man who T-A fill water with bucket
"The man who had been filling a bucket with water"

basha den e bari sin bòm.
empty in   the barrel without bottom
"(and) pouring (it) in the bottomless barrel".[13]
                    (Text 2, Folk Tale, 108-10)

Tabata (in the form *ta'ata*) is required in order to anchor the action of filling a bucket with water clearly in a period prior to the current point in the narration (not unlike Bickerton's anterior).[14] If *ta* had been used instead of *tabata*, the only possible meaning would be that the man sitting in the doorway was (at that moment) filling a bucket with water. This would have been expressed with a serial verb construction:

(3')   *El a   haña un hòmber sintá den port'e   kamber*
       he T-A find a   man   seated in   door-of room
       "He found a man sitting in the doorway"
       ta   yena awa . . .
       T-A fill   water
       "filling a bucket with water . . ."

Example (3') is hypothetical, but a very similar construction appears earlier in the same text:

(4)   *Antó el a   weta un hòmber yongotá ei   bou,*
       then he T-A see a   man   kneeling there below
       "Then he saw a man kneeling down below",
       ta   saka   awa ku   un makutu
       T-A remove water with a   bucket
       "taking out water with a bucket"
       basha den un bari   sin   bom.
       empty in   a   barrel without bottom
       "(and) pouring (it) in a bottomless barrel".
                    (Text 2, Folk Tale, 75-77)

(As an aside, it is worth calling attention to the fact that a single tense-aspect marker can be used once for a series of verbs within the same sentence, provided there is a continuity of action, temporal reference, and aspect across the verbs, as in examples [3] and [4]. A more rigorous formulation is possible, but this should suffice for our purposes.)

Sa is, like *ta*, a type of imperfective marker, but with much narrower meaning, the habitual (see Table 3). In example (5) the man referred to is a hunter. Since he is not used to going home empty-handed from his hunting trips, he continues further from his home in search of game in the particular episode from which the example is taken. *Sa* helps establish the motive for continuing. This difference between *ta* and *sa* is subtle, but important.

(5) *E' n ta hende ku sa keda bashí.*
he not be person who T-A remain empty
"He's not a man who is accustomed to going home empty-handed".
(Juliana 1970:28)

Sa has a different status from the other tense-aspect markers. First of all, unlike *ta*, *a*, and *tabata*, *sa* is not obligatory. Furthermore, *sa* is also an independent verb, as in *Mi sa hulandes* "I know Dutch" and, with an auxiliary function, *Mi sa landa* "I know how to swim". The two meanings, "know" and "be accustomed to", are clearly distinct; and I have chosen to include *sa* among the tense-aspect markers in spite of its more marginal status.[15]

3.3 *Lexical and Semantic Restrictions on* **Ta** *and* **A**

A small group of verbs, all statives, cannot be preceded by either *ta* or *a*.[16] These are:[17]

ta	"be"
tin	"have, exist"
por	"can, may"
sa	"know (something)"
konosé	"know (someone)"
ke	"want"
mester	"have to, must, should"
yama	"be called"

The only way to mark these verbs explicitly for past time reference is with *tabata*. For example, *Mi ke un sigá* "I want a cigar" could only be expressed as past time by *Mi tabata ke un sigá* "I wanted a cigar".[18]

A second group of verbs can occur either with or without *ta*. They too are all statives:

debe	"owe"
gusta	"like"
kosta	"cost"

bal	"be worth, cost"
stima	"love"
meresé	"deserve"
parse	"seem, look like"
nifiká	"mean"

Only a few of these verbs appear to restrict the use of *a*, however.[19] Although all the verbs in both groups are statives, as Maurer (1985) has noted, three stative verbs require the use of *ta*: *kere* "believe", *komprondé* "understand", and *pertenesé* "belong". In Bickerton's (1981) bioprogram, stative verbs cannot co-occur with the durative aspect marker precisely because they are already durative. If we wish to use separate terms for inherent and grammatical aspect, we could rephrase this as "a tense-neutral imperfective aspect marker cannot be used with a stative verb, since both 'imperfective' and 'stative' imply durative". This use of "durative", however, is different from the more general use in Table 2, where "states", "processes", and "developments" are all durative: there are no restrictions on the use of *ta* or *a* with these other categories of "durative" verbs.

The major implication of the similarity between this restriction on the use of *ta* with most stative verbs in Papiamentu and Bickerton's claims with regard to similar restrictions in all creoles is that *ta* is indeed an aspectual marker similar to Bickerton's durative (or nonpunctual) and not a tense marker.

Before concluding this section, I wish to cover two additional aspects of past time reference. First, although the negative *no* "not" occurs frequently, the most natural negative in spontaneous speech is simply *n*, as in (6):

(6) *Ni   mi ni   kola   n' por a   bira.*
     neither I   nor Kola   not can T-A become
     "Neither I nor Kola could become (government employees)".
                                    (Text 3a, Interview, 759)

In addition, when such a form would occur before perfective *a*, the *a* is deleted:[20]

(7) *Mi   n'   baña.*   (= *Mi no a baña.*)
     I   not bathe
     "I didn't take a bath".
                                    (Text 2, Folk Tale, 122)

The second detail involves the past imperfective forms of two verbs, *ta* and *tin*. Both verbs are preceded by *taba* (not *tabata*) and, orthographically, the result is written as one word: *tabata* and *tabatin*. In more spontaneous basilectal speech, the more regular forms *tabata ta* and *tabata tin* are common, although both are considered substandard.

4. Basilectal *Ta* Marks Aspect, Not Tense

As mentioned previously, almost any treatment of Papiamentu tense-aspect is framed within a traditional present-past-future paradigm of absolute tense.[21] I will support my alternative analysis of basilectal Papiamentu tense-aspect with cases of two frequent uses of *ta* which should not occur in Papiamentu if *ta* is indeed a "present-tense" marker. The first case involves the use of *ta* in embedded clauses. *Ta* very frequently occurs in such embedded clauses even though the tense-aspect morphology of the main clause is nonpresent and the reference of the entire sentence is nonpresent. The second case to be discussed has to do with *ta* embedded within past-time reference discourse, where some other form would be expected if *ta* is indeed a "present" morpheme.

4.1 *Ta* in Embedded Clauses

The example in (8) provides a straightforward context where *ta* could indeed be interpreted as a "present" marker: the gloss would be literally something like "God knows how many years they have that they run after [or are running after] doctors". Even though this certainly sounds odd in English, the presentness of the gloss is clear and logical. My interpretation is that *ta* simply encodes the meaning of imperfective and that any present time reference is inferred from the total context. Such expressions with *time frame* + *tin* + *V* always require *ta* before the verb, to indicate duration.

(8)　*Bo   ta   mira e   hende bieu nan, no?*
　　　you T-A   look the person old PL   no
　　　"You see the old people, OK"?
　　　Dios   sa
　　　God   know
　　　"God only knows"

> *ni   kuantu   aña nan tin*
> not-even how-many year they have
> "how many years they"
> *ta   kana tre'   i dokter.*
> T-A walk after of doctor
> "have been running after doctors".
> (Text 1, Conversation, 1152-55)

This interpretation is confirmed in (9). (See also the discussion of this example, presented above as [4].) The event is clearly in the past and *ta* makes the action of "removing" water imperfective, interpreted through context as continuous.

(9) *Antó el a   weta un hòmber yongotá ei   bou*
     then   he T-A see a   man   kneeling there below
     "Then he saw a man kneeling down below"
     ta   saka   awa   ku   un makutu . . .
     T-A remove water with a   bucket
     "taking out water with a bucket . . ."
     (Text 2, Folk Tale, 75-76)

Similarly, in (10), "treating [two people] badly" is expressed as an imperfective. It happens to have a future time reference, but in (11) a similar expression can only be interpreted as having past time reference. In (11) the *ta* marks a repeated action.

(10) *El a   bira   poko ku   idea*
      he T-A become little with idea
      "He became a little conceited (and consequently began)"
      ta   trata e   dos nan aya   malu.
      T-A treat the two PL   there bad
      "treating the two back there badly".
      (Text 2, Folk Tale, 184-85)

(11) *El a   stop nan.*
      he T-A stop them
      "He stopped them".
      El a   bin   ta   trata nan   malu.
      he T-A come T-A treat them bad
      "He started treating them badly".
      (Text 2, Folk Tale, 191-92)

The particular type of imperfective notion that the listener (or the reader in this case) gets from these uses of *ta* in embedded past-reference clauses depends on the context of each situation. In (12) the man squeezed a lemon on a lemon tree. Real-world knowledge about liquids and seeping causes us to interpret *ta lek* as a sort of progressive or continuous event.

(12) *El   a   bolbe   tros'   é di dos   be.*
he T-A return squeeze it of two time
"He again squeezed it the second time".
awa   a   kuminsa ta   lek fe'i   d' e   pal' i   lamunchi.
water T-A begin   T-A seep from of the tree of lemon
"Water started to seep from the lemon tree".

(Text 2, Folk Tale, 560-61)

In (13), on the other hand, the two actions marked by *ta* are inherently of shorter duration, only because "starting to hit" someone with a hatchet and "asking God" to prevent something are perceived as shorter than water dripping.

(13) *M'   a   haña un hombru yen   di kabei*
I   T-A find a   man   full of hair
"I found a man full of hair"
ku   su hacha   na man ta   bai kap un mucha mané ami
with his hatchet in hand T-A go cut a   boy   like me
"with his hatchet in his hand going to hit a boy like me"
antó un hombu mané swa   na rudia ta   pidi dios
then a   man   like brother-in-law on knee T-A ask God
"and a man like you, on his knees asking God"
p'   e n' kap e.
for he not cut him
"for him not to hit him".

(Text 2, Folk Tale, 729-30)

(14) is similar to (13): the speaker in (14) unexpectedly found himself on his way from the U.S. to France on a boat. What *ta* encodes is only that the event is not perceived as perfective. The duration of *ta bai* is simply relative to the punctuality of *a haña mi*.

(14) *E   guera a   kohe nos na merka.*
the war   T-A catch us   in America
"The war caught us in the United States".

M' a   haña mi ta   bai konvoi di binti   barku
I   T-A find me T-A go convoy of twenty ship
"I found myself going on a convoy of twenty ships"
fo'i   merka   pa fransha.
from the U.S. for France
"from the U.S. to France".

(Text 3a, Interview, 875-76)

It is not the case, however, that only *ta* can be used in such embedded clauses. (15), (16), and (17) are examples of other markers. In (15) *ta'ata*, like *ta*, encodes the notion of imperfective, but in addition is an explicit marker of "prior to the current time of reference" in the discourse. If *ta* had been used in place of *ta'ata*, the reference would have been simply imperfective with no explicit encoding of pastness. We can infer from the final clause in (15) that the object no longer is hurting the man's eye. Besides the knowledge that the object is in a bottle, this information is encoded in *ta'ata*.[22]

(15) *El a   bai Colombia bin*
      he T-A go Colombia come
      "He went to Colombia and came back"
      k'   un d' e   kos   ku ta'tin   den su wowo
      with one of the thing that T-A-have in   his eye
      "with one of the things that (there) had been in his eye"
      ta'ta daña su   wowo, den un bòter . . .
      T-A harm his eye   in   a   bottle
      "(that) had been harming his eye, in a bottle . . ."

(Text 1, Conversation, 1254-57)

Similarly, in (16) *tabata* clearly encodes a past habitual notion. *Ta* instead of *tabata* would still allow such an interpretation, but by way of contextual inference, whereas *tabata* explicitly anchors the activity in the past.

(16) *Hasi ku   mi*
      do   with me
      "Do with me"
      manera nos a   lanta   na kas
      like   we T-A grow-up in house
      "as we grew up at home"

tabata hasi.
T-A   do
"doing".

(Text 2, Folk Tale, 366-68)

Unless this is due simply to a chance bias in the samples on which I have based this article, it appears that there are many more occasions to use *ta* in embedded clauses than either *tabata* or *a*. Perhaps this is because many events (especially those which are expressed by an inherently punctual verb) would be interpreted as perfective without explicit marking of the event as imperfective and thus there is greater need for *ta* to be used. In (17) we seem to have the mirror image of this situation: *a* is used in two embedded clauses to force a punctual interpretation. In clause 761 the intention seems to be to make clear that the man speaking was waiting for the point in time when he could place the other man's sister in safe hands and be finished with the matter. This same interpretation applies to clause 765: *a* makes clear that the man disappeared almost instantaneously. These clauses appear at the very end of the story and such an ending is appropriate.

(17) 760 *Ma mi no por a   haña un hende*
           but I not can T-A find a   person
           "But I couldn't find a person"
           ku   situasion manero abo
           with situation like   you
           "with a situation like you have"
      761 *pa mi a   entregá bo bo   shishi,*
           for I T-A turn-over you your sister
           "for me to turn your sister over to you".

           . . .

      764 *El a   weta*
           he T-A watch
           "He watched"
      765 *e   hòmber a   flektu bai.*[23]
           the man   T-A flee   go
           "the man vanish in an instant".

(Text 2, Folk Tale, 760-65)

These several examples of embedded tense-aspect markers provide further evidence that in basilectal Papiamentu *ta* and *a* are tense-neutral aspect markers and that *tabata* is an anterior-imperfective tense-aspect marker, the presence of which is determined by discourse and pragmatic factors, not solely sentence-level semantics and syntax.

4.2 *Ta in Past-Reference Main Clauses*

The same interpretation offered in the previous section applies to the use of *ta* in main clauses in clear past-reference discourse. In (18) temporal adverbial constructions (clauses 91, 93, 97, 99, 103, adverbial in capitals) inform the listener whether the time reference is now or then. *Ta* does not have this function. In clauses 93, 94, 108, 110, 113, 114, and 117, *ta* or *0* provides an imperfective interpretation, with time reference established, maintained, and switched with adverbials. It is interesting to note that *a* in clause 97 is within a present frame of reference. English would use the perfect *have changed*, which bridges present and recent past. This does not make *a*, however, a perfect or even a past marker. Notice also that *ta* in clause 99 is interpretable as present reference, not because of *ta* itself, but because *awó* switches the time reference to the present.

    (18) FIRST COMMUNION
         OLD MAN

        91   *TEMPUNAN DI NOS* **ta'ata** *tempu*
            time-PL   of we   was   time
            "Our time was the time"

        92   *ku*   *dios* **ta'ata** *aki* *bou* *huntu* *ku* *nos.*
            that God was   here below together with us
            "God was down here with us".

        93   *TEMPUNAN EI*   *bo* **ta** *bai* . . .
            time-PL   there you T-A go
            "Those days you would go . . ."

      94-5 *Bo* **0** *tin* *ku* *risibí* *ku* *djesdos aña, no promé.*
            you T-A have that receive with twelve   year   not before
            "You had to receive (first communion) at the age of twelve, not before".

INTERVIEWER
97 *Ai, ta   AWOR AKI nan a   but' e seis, shete aña.*
oh FOCUS now   here they T-A put it six   seven year
"Oh, yeah, they have only recently changed it to six or seven".

OLD MAN
99 *Nan ta   pon'é ku   seis ku   shete AWÓ.*
they T-A put it with six   with seven now
"They make it six or seven now".

INTERVIEWER
101 *Shete aña, sí, sí.*
seven year yes yes
"Seven, yes, yes".

OLD MAN
103 *TEMPUNAN AYA, no.*
time-pl   there no
"But not in those days".

INTERVIEWER
105 *Djesdos aña.*
twelve   year
"Twelve".

OLD MAN
107 *Djesdos aña.*
twelve   year
"Twelve".
108 *Bo n' 0   por 0   risibí   promé ku   djesdos aña.*
you not T-A can T-A receive before than twelve year
"You couldn't receive communion before you were twelve".

INTERVIEWER
110 *Antó, ta   konformá mesora   tambe?*
then T-A confirm   same-time too
"Then, would you be confirmed at the same time, too"?

OLD MAN
112 *No, no.*
no   no
"No, no".

113 *Konformashon, sí, 0   tin   bia*
    confirmation   yes T-A have time
    "Confirmation, oh, yes, there were times"

114-5 *bo 0   tin   ku warda te ora   ku . . .*
    you T-A have that wait   'til time that
    "you had to wait until . . ."

116 *N' **tabatin**   obispo, no . . .*
    no T-A-have bishop no
    "There was no bishop, you know . . ."

117 *Mester 0   warda*
    must   T-A wait
    "You had to wait"

118 *te   ora ku unu **a**   bira   obispu.*
    'til time that one T-A become bishop
    "until someone became bishop".

              (Text 3a, Interview 91-118)

(19) and (20) each show *ta* used in similar fashion: as a descriptive statement that applies over an indefinite span of time, one that happens to refer to past time because of the total frame of reference of the discourse in which the *ta* form is embedded.

(19) BRINGING ICE TO CURAÇAO FROM THE U.S.
    El a   bai merka.
    he T-A go America
    "He went to the U.S."
    Eis ta'ata bini na bloki grandi fei   merka korsou,
    ice T-A   come in block large   from U.S.   Curaçao
    "Ice would come in large blocks from the U.S. to Curaçao",
    nan ta   deskarg'é aki,
    they T-A unload   it here
    "they would unload it here",
    para deskargá eis.
    stop unload   ice
    "they'd stop and unload ice".
    Seis, shete dia e   barku ta   deskargá eis.
    six   seven day the ship T-A unload   ice
    "For six or seven days the ship would unload ice".

antó eis tabata un plaka pa liber.
then ice was   one plaka for pound
"So ice was one 'plaka' for a pound".

(Text 3a, Interview, 176-81)

In (20) we can again see how clear reference to two time frames, one present and the other past, is made with adverbials of place and time. Any listener knows that the big plantations of big landowners belong to the remote past.[24]

(20) WAGES THEN AND NOW
      DEN KUNUKUNAN DI E   SHONNAN,
      in   plantation-PL   of the gentleman-PL
      "On the plantations of the big landowners",
      nan ta   pag'é   trinta sens.
      they T-A pay him thirty cents
      "they'd pay him thirty cents".
      Nan ta   dun' é   un kan'i   ariña
      they T-A give him a tin of flour
      "They'd give him a tin of flour"
      of un kana di maishi chikitu.
      or a   tin   of corn   little
      "or a tin of 'wild corn'".
      Esei ta e   tempunan
      that is the time-PL
      "Those were the days"
      ku   nan ta'ata traha maishi chikitu,
      that they T-A work corn little
      "when they would make 'wild corn'".
      tin maishi na pipita k' e   kosnan ei.
      have corn in bud with the thing-PL there
      "They had wild corn and things like that".
      Nan ta   dun' é   un kos   ei, un kan'i maishi.
      they T-A give him a thing there a tin of corn
      "They would give him one of those things, a tin of corn".
      E ta   haña su   trinta sens.
      he T-A find his thirty cents
      "He'd get his thirty cents".

Mas ku   e   trinta sens ei,
but   with the thirty cents there
"But with those thirty cents",
AWOR AKI e   trinta sen ei   no ta   yega
now   here the thirty cent there not T-A reach
"nowadays those thirty cents aren't enough"
pa bo   bebe un kòp'i kòfi.
for you drink a   cup coffee
"for you to get a cup of coffee".
. . .

Pero E   TEMPU AYA ku e   trinta sens   ei,
but   the time   there with the thirty cents there
"But in those days with those thirty cents",
nan   ta   kumpra tres plaka di buní . . .
they T-A buy   three plaka of tuna
"they would buy three "plakas'" worth of tuna . . ."
(Text 3b, Interview, 439-50)

I conclude with an example which contains an alternation of the "sub-junctive" zero morpheme for unrealized (irrealis) events in subordinate clauses and *ta* in main clauses, all within a past reference episode.

(21) *El a   haña un chuchubi   meimei di dos palu grandi.*
he T-A find   a   mockingbird between of two tree large
"He found a mockingbird between two large trees".
Ora e   chuchubi   0   lanta
when the mockingbird T-A rise
"Every time the mocking bird would fly"
for di e   palu di-pa riba,[25]
out of the tree of-for up
"off of the higher tree",
ku e   0   baha na esun   di pa bou,
if   he T-A lower on that-one of for below
"if he would land on the lower one",
e   palu di pa riba   ta   muri,
the tree of for above T-A die
"the higher tree would die",
esun   di pabou ta   biba.
the-one of below T-A live
"the lower one would live".

Ora e 0 lanta for di esun di pa bou,
when he T-A rise out of that-one of for below
"Whenever he would fly off of the lower one",
ku e 0 baha na esun di pa riba,
if he T-A lower in that-one of for above
"if he would land on the higher one",
esun di pa bou ta muri.
that-one of for below T-A die
"the lower one would die".
Esun di pa riba ta biba.
that-one of for above T-A live
"The higher one would live".

(Text 2, Folk Tale, 494-502)

The use of *ta* in the main clauses (and *0* in the subordinate clauses) is identical to the examples discussed so far where *ta* is used to depict general customary situations or events, whether present or past. The *ta* in this particular case is due to the need to show that the bird was flying up and down from one tree to another. This is an imperfective notion, filled by *ta*.

5. The Modal Auxiliaries *Ke, Mester,* and *Por*

Of the forms in group 2 of Table 3, I will only deal with the modal auxiliaries, since the other forms are of less relevance to the main thesis of this article. Goilo (1972:27, 58-59, 96-98) and Maurer (1986b) provide a detailed treatment of Papiamentu modal auxiliaries, and I will not attempt to duplicate their efforts here. My main purpose is to relate tense-aspect marking in modal constructions to my general thesis that the temporal morphemes *ta* and *a* mark aspect while *tabata* marks aspect and absolute-relative tense in basilectal Papiamentu. (For a discussion of "absolute-relative" as a type of relative tense, cf. Comrie 1985.)

Two of the three modal auxiliaries (*ke* and *mester*) have an independent existence as full verbs.[26] In addition, *mester* is also used, although in limited constructions, as a noun. In (22) mesté functions as a simple verb, while the same form is a noun in (23).

(22) *Pasó nan mesté hende pa vota.*
because they need people for vote
"Because they need people to vote".

(Text 1, Conversation, 864-65)

(23) *Ta   kuminda ku   kosnan   nan   tabatin   mesté numa.*
FOCUS food   with thing-PL they T-A-have need only
"The only things they really needed were **food** and stuff".
(Text 3a, Interview, 1062)

Similarly, *ke* is a simple verb in (24).[27]

(24) *Ta   ki   bo   ke   pa   nan   hasi?*
FOCUS what   you   want   for   them   do
"What do you want them to do"?
(Text 1, Conversation, 1437-38)

It may seem that *por* in (25) is also a full verb.[28] (25) is, however, simply an example of a truncated verb phrase, similar to the English equivalent.

(25) *No, den   eilandsraad   por.* [= *por tin*]
no   in   Island-Council can   [= can have]
"No, in the Island Council they can".
(Text 1, Conversation, 544)

Ke and *por* also occur frequently, especially in more formal usage, in the constructions *ker a* and *por a* with a frozen meaning of "would like" and "could", respectively. Examples of both can be seen in (26).

(26) *Mi ker   a   puntra señor   "G."*
I   want   T-A ask   mister G.
"I would like to ask Mr. G."
ku e   por   a   duna un punto mas   ariba . . .
if he   can   T-A give a   point more on
"if he could say a little more about (this) . . ."
(Text 4a, Public Forum, 347-48)

Another frozen expression is used for "I mean", as in (27). The construction mirrors Spanish *quiero decir* "I mean" (literally, "I want to say"), but the second verb is actually derived from the Dutch word for "mean".[29]

(27) *No. Akí shete aña mi ke   men.*
no   here seven year I   want mean
"No. Seven years from now, I mean".
(Text 1, Conversation, 250-51)

In the remainder of this section I will give examples of each of the three modal auxiliaries, first with present reference, then with past habitual reference, and finally with past punctual reference. With all three auxiliaries, the form of the present and the past habitual constructions is identical. Only when reference is made to a past perfective event (i.e. a singular, realized event) is the perfective marker *a* used. Examples (28), (29), and (30) show these differences with *mester*. In (29) the frequent use of the past imperfective clearly establishes the event as a past event, but the reference to "had to pass" is expressed by *mester pasa*, that is, with no explicit marking of past time, since this is a descriptive passage referring to habitual activities. Only in (30), where reference is made to a specific, singular event is *a* used. I take this as support for my claim that the main opposition in Papiamentu tense-aspect is between imperfective *ta* and perfective *a*. The past habitual (an imperfective) is explicitly marked only for imperfective aspect, not for past time.

(28) *Mené mesté konosé mi tawela.*
     sir   must know my grandfather
     "You must know my grandfather".
                             (Text 3a, Interview, 489)

(29) *Ma n' ta'atin   shon   Tams e   temp'ei.*
     but not T-A-have mister Tams the time there
     "But there was no Mr. Tams then".
     Shon Tams ta'ata   será.
     Mr.   Tams T-A-be closed
     "Mr. Tams's (place) was closed".
     Tur hende — ku nos tur ta'a bai skol —
     all people that we all T-A go school
     "Everybody — (all of us) who went to school —"
     mester pasa den "Witteweg".
     need pass in Witteweg
     "had to pass through 'Weiteweg'".
     No ta'atin   Santa Famia tampoko.
     not T-A-have holy family either
     "There was no Holy Family (Church) either".
                       (Text 3a, Interview, 329-34)

(30) *Nan a   ninga nan   morto na tera.*
     they T-A refuse their dead on land
     "They refused (to take) their dead on land".

Antó e barku mester a   bai tira   nan morto na awa.
then the ship   must   T-A go throw their dead   in water
"So the ship had to go and throw their dead into the sea".
(Text 3a, Interview, 1136-37)

We see the same distinctions in (31), (32), and (33) with *por. Por + V*
in (31) has present reference but in (32) the same construction has past reference. What they share is imperfective aspect, and explicit reference to
time is not encoded in the temporal marker. In (33), however, reference is
now made to a singular, realized event (hence not habitual and not imperfective), which thus requires *por + a + V.* My interpretation is that *a* is
required not because the event is in past time, but because it has perfective
aspect.

(31) *Nunka mi n' por kompronde*
     never   I   no can understand
     "I can never understand"
     kon un hende por ta bestia asina.
     how a person can be beast like-that
     "how a person can be such an animal".
                  (Text 3a, Interview, 1177-78)

(32) *Ma n'   tabatin   chèns   muchu*
     but not T-A-have chance   much
     "But there wasn't much chance"
     pa hend'e   koló bord'   e barku,
     for people-of color aboard of ship
     "for colored people on a ship",
     pasobra tur hende,
     because all people
     "because everybody",
     e   blankunan di tur nashon tabata nabegá.
     the white-PL of all nation T-A   sail
     "the whites from all nations were sailing".
     Un hend'e   koló no por haña un barku fasil.
     a   person-of color not can find a ship easy
     "A colored person couldn't find a ship easily".
     Ta   blo e barku di Red Dienst Line nan aki tabatin
     FOCUS only the ship of Red Dienst Line-PL here T-A-have
     "Only the Red Dienst Line ships here had"

yu'   i   korsow   bord' i   nan.
offspring of Curaçao board of them
"native Curaçaoans on them".
(Text 3a, Interview, 627-31)

(33) *Despues   a   bini   "Publikatie-Blad",*
afterwards T-A come Publication Sheet
"Afterwards came the 'Publication-Sheet'",
ku   a   bini   kuenta di buska   hende
that T-A come matter of look-for people
"and the business of looking for people"
pa bira   fast.
for become permanent
"to become permanent employees".
Ya   mi n' por a   bira . . .
already I   not can T-A become
"I couldn't become (permanent) by then . . ."
Ni   mi ni kola n' por a   bira,
neither I nor Cola not can T-A become
"Neither Cola nor I were able to become (permanent employees)",
pasó   nos edat ta'ata haltu kaba.
because our age was   high already
"because we were already too old".
(Text 3a, Interview, 755-60)

In the samples on which this article is based, I was unable to find an example of *ker a* with the perfective meaning of "wanted (to do something and did it)". All such uses were for the frozen meaning of "would like to" (see [36]). (34) and (35), however, provide the same type of evidence that a modal auxiliary with **no** tense-aspect marker encodes imperfectivity; the fact that (34) is present time reference and (35) is past indicates that it is imperfectivity that is being expressed rather than time reference.

(34) *"Swa   ke   baña"?*
brother-in-law want bathe
"'Do you want to take a bath?'"
(Text 2, Folk Tale, 124)

(35) *Nan a   bisa papa*
they T-A tell Papa
"they told Papa"

ku   mi n' ta   bai winkel di sapaté,
that I   not T-A go   shop   of shoemaker
"that I wasn't going to go (to work in) the shoemaker's shop",
pasó   mi n' ke   siña   sapaté.
because I , not want learn shoemaker
"because I didn't want to learn to be a shoemaker".

                              (Text 3a, Interview, 448-50)

(36) *E   pregunta ku   mi ker a   hasi . . .*
     the question that I   want T-A make
     "The question I would like to ask . . ."

                              (Text 4a, Public Forum, 294-95)

According to both Goilo (1972) and Maurer (1986b), both *ke* and *por* can be preceded by *tabata*.[30] In this data used for this article, the only example found of such forms was in the more formal register in Text 4a (Public Forum) — example (37). I suspect that both Goilo's and Maurer's frame of reference is that of the more formal register typical of public language (as in Text 4a). Nevertheless, the context is still appropriate for the use of *tabata*: its use places the time of reference of the "wanting" at some point prior to this point in the discourse.

(37) *Mi ta kontentu di tende*
     I   be happy   of hear
     "I'm happy to hear"
     ku   nos tin   diferente hende
     that we   have different people
     "that we have various people"
     ku   a   studia e   problema di petrólio,
     what T-A study the problem of oil
     "who have studied the oil problem",
     pero lokwal ku   mi ta'ata ke   repasá,
     but   which that I   T-A want review
     "but what I wanted to review",
     di for di tur e   kos,
     of out of all the thing
     "out of all the things",
     ta esaki.
     be this
     "is this".

                              (Text 4a, Public Forum, 475-79)

These examples of the three modal auxiliaries support, I believe, the interpretation of basilectal Papiamentu having basically an aspectual system.

6. Summary and Conclusion

This study of the temporal system of basilectal Papiamentu had at least three potential groups of "consumers" in mind: (1) creolists who have followed the literature on universal properties of creole languages, especially in the guise of Bickerton's (1981) bioprogram; (2) those, like myself, who see a need for a more empirically responsible comparison of the linguistic features of the Spanish and Portuguese creoles; and (3) applied linguists who have a need to make clear decisions regarding Papiamentu in areas of language planning and education.

For the first group, this analysis has considerable theoretical relevance. Bickerton (1981:85-88, 1984:177) has tried hard to account for the ways in which Papiamentu deviates from the prototypical TMA system. His only source for Papiamentu, however, is Goilo (1972), which is a good textbook but was not meant to be a sophisticated linguistic treatise.[31] In fact, Goilo is inadequate as a source on basilectal Papiamentu (and Bickerton's bioprogram only concerns the basilect); as one would expect of such a textbook, it more accurately reflects the formal usage of well-educated bilingual and multilingual speakers of Papiamentu. It is ironic that Bickerton, of all people, should overlook this fact, given his pioneering work on the creole continuum (Bickerton 1975, among other works). This article has shown that, when attention is primarily focused on basilectal Papiamentu, the Papiamentu tense-aspect system is much closer to Bickerton's bioprogram than he realizes. The primary opposition, if my interpretation and argumentation are correct, is that of a tense-neutral imperfective (*ta*) vs a tense-neutral perfective (*a*), which is what the bioprogram predicts, at least in terms of the semantics of the system, although not with respect to the expected zero marking of perfective aspect.

There still remain conflicts between bioprogram predictions and the way Papiamentu maps meaning onto form, as with the function of *ta'a* (and its variants) as a discourse- and pragmatically- governed marker of aspect and relative tense, the existence of two irrealis markers (*0* and *lo*), the lack of a clear anterior marker, the lack of a *0* marker for perfective aspect, and the "deviant" position of the irrealis marker *lo*. I will not address these issues here, other than noting that Bickerton's (1981:85-88) attempts to deal with the last three of these still deserve serious consideration. If he had had available the type of information this article provides, he might have been able to go farther than he did.

But are we dealing with a glass that is half full (i.e., Papiamentu is closer to the bioprogram than Bickerton realized) or one that is half empty (i.e., given that part of the Papiamentu temporal system is similar to that of other apparently unrelated creoles, what do we make of the features that are apparently specific to Papiamentu?)? If anything, this study reveals the inadequacy of comparisons that are based on pedagogical grammars, sentence-level studies that fail to capture the way tense-aspect and mood morphology actually functions, and sketchy inventories of forms that "seem" to be the same across creoles.[32]

This treatment of the temporal system of one particular Hispanic creole should have special value for the second audience, those who work on related Hispanic creoles and are interested in comparative research. We have had sentence-level grammars of these creoles for a long time and they have proven inadequate for an in-depth comparison of the Portuguese and Spanish creoles. I hope that I have provided a model for treating tense-aspect (and any other linguistic subsystem) within the total discourse context instead of the only other existing model, which is sentence-level semantics and syntax alone.[33] Without such a focus, it would have been impossible to carry out the present study. And without a similar approach for comparative research on the Portuguese and Spanish creoles (without neglecting the better studied English and French creoles, of course), we will never have an adequate basis for such comparisons.

The last audience, although very specialized and not the primary audience of this book, is very important for two reasons. First, over the past fifteen years I have benefited considerably from the native speaker intuitions of a large number of Papiamentu speakers, mainly in Curaçao, but also in Aruba and Bonaire.[34] These people opened their homes and their minds to me and without such assistance I could never have gotten this close to what I think is a more realistic picture of how Papiamentu tense and aspect really work. And, if I am wrong in some aspects (and I would not be surprised if I am), these are the people who can show where I am wrong and improve on this study. I hope this study helps pay them back in a small but significant way. Second, and equally important, Papiamentu has finally become a subject in the schools (where Dutch is still the language of instruction for all other subjects). There is a need for studies like this one to provide a sound empirical basis for decisions that affect the development of a complete curriculum in Papiamentu in the schools.

There is always a strong tendency in any society to take the speech (and writing) of the well-educated elite as the norm. In other work (Andersen 1983) I have argued for a multi-norm approach to such issues. This study, while focussing primarily on one norm, that of the basilect (and the least conscious norm), will hopefully make applied linguists in the Netherlands Antilles even more aware of the need to liberate themselves from a rigid European latinate tradition. The tense-aspect system of the multilingual educated elite is certainly a valid and real system, but it is only one of several. One assumption behind this article is that more basic to all speakers is the system described and exemplified in this study. Applied decisions regarding language cannot neglect this reality.

Notes

1. I am indebted to the following friends whose commentaries on an earlier draft of this paper have been very helpful. I did not always follow their wise advice and therefore apologize if the results do not match their high expectations: Derek Bickerton, Talmy Givón, Philippe Maurer, Jürgen Meisel, Salikoko Mufwene, Enrique Muller, Suzanne Romaine, Mario Saltarelli, Izione Silva, and Carmen Silva-Corvalán. I owe a very special debt to Enrique Muller for his detailed comments on this work, from his perspective as a native speaker of Papiamentu and a competent linguist, as well as his earlier patience with my endless questions. This study was supported in part by funding from the UCLA International Studies and Overseas Programs and the UCLA Committee on Research of the Academic Senate, for which I am very grateful.

2. I will use "temporal reference" and "tense-aspect" (or, occasionally, "tense-modality-aspect") interchangeably.

   Most morphological markers of tense, aspect, and mood in creoles are preverbal. At least one, however, is postverbal: the anterior marker -ba of Capeverdean Creole, Guinea-Bissau Creole, and Palenquero.

3. I have recently begun to collaborate with other creolists to develop a framework for carrying out more elaborate comparative linguistic research on the Portuguese- and Spanish-based creoles.

4. Until very recently Papiamentu, the native language of the students, has had no official role in the school, where Dutch is the official language of all instruction.

5. It is still not certain whether Papiamentu originated in the Netherlands Antilles (more specifically on the island of Curaçao), was transplanted from the African coast with subsequent relexification of original Portuguese lexicon in contact with Spanish, or, more probably, some combination of these. On this question, see Andersen (1974) and references cited there. See also Goodman (1987).

6.   Absolute tense is used "to refer to tenses which take the present moment as their deictic centre" (p. 36) and relative tense to tenses "where the reference point for location of a situation is some point in time given by the context, not necessarily the present moment" (Comrie 1985:56).

7.   See Andersen (1974, 1978, 1983) for details on this continuum.

8.   Comrie restricts telic to accomplishments and atelic to activities, a restriction I have not followed.

9.   *Sa* is more marginal and non-obligatory in comparison with the other tense-aspect morphemes, *ta*, *a*, and *tabata*. *0* represents the "zero" subjunctive morpheme in Table 3.

10. *Ta* has two other functions: (1) the copula, and (2) a focus marker. As a copula, the past form, when required, is *tabata*, identical to the past imperfective aspect marker:

    (i)   Copula *ta* and *tabata*:
        Piraña ta un "small fish"
        piranha be a   "small fish"
        "A piranha is a small fish"
        i   vietnam tabata un piraña pa merka.
        and Vietnam was a piranha for America
        "and Vietnam was a piranha for the United States".
                (Text 4a, Public Forum, 431-32)

    (ii)   Focus marker *ta*:
        Basta   n' ta   over di politik bo ta   papia ku mi, no?
        provided not FOCUS about of politics you T-A talk   with me, no
        "Provided you're not going to talk to me about **politics**, right"?

11. *Sa* will be dealt with separately from the three major tense-aspect markers.

12. I assume readers are aware of the distinction between basilectal (furthest from the lexifier language), acrolectal (closest to the lexifier language) and mesolectal (intermediate varieties) distinctions in creole studies, introduced by William Stewart and elaborated on by Derek Bickerton, John Rickford, and others. The term acrolect applies mainly to those creoles which co-exist in the same territory with the original lexifier language; e.g., standard Jamaican English is the acrolect to basilectal "deep" creole English. In the case of Papiamentu, however, although Spanish and Portuguese are the major lexifier languages, the government and school language is Dutch and thus it is not appropriate to speak of an acrolect for Papiamentu, in the same sense as with the English creoles.

13. The old man telling this story told it this way. As Enrique Muller has pointed out, however, he should have said, . . . *yena (un) makutu ku awa* ". . . fill (a) bucket with water".

14. It is interesting that Bickerton (1981:87), in trying to account for the various counterexamples Papiamentu presents for his bioprogram, speculated that Papiamentu originally had a form *taba* with anterior meaning. *Tabata* then arose, Bickerton hypothesized, as a combination of anterior *taba* and nonpunctual *ta* (i.e. durative or, in terms of grammatical aspect, imperfective).

15. As Philippe Maurer has pointed out (p.c.), *sa* is actually more like a modal auxiliary, since it can take *tabata*: *Tur día e tabata sa pasa den e kaya aki* "Every day he would pass through this street".

16. Actually one of them, *konosé* "know" can be used with *a*. However, it then loses its stative meaning, and means entry into a state. English conveys this meaning with "met". Given that Papiamentu is a Spanish- and Portuguese-based creole, it is worth noting that this same distinction occurs in Spanish and Portuguese. In Spanish, for example, the perfective form *conocí* means "I met", while the imperfective form *conocía* means "I knew". Neither Spanish nor Portuguese, however, has restrictions on whether a verb can occur in perfective or imperfective form similar to Papiamentu's restrictions. (Stative verbs do, however, occur much more frequently in imperfective form than perfective form in Spanish and Portuguese — see Andersen 1986a, 1986b, and Schmidt & Frota 1986.)

17. Goilo (1972:24) is the basic source here, although his information on restrictions on *a* is very limited and scattered. In addition, I include *sa* as a verb that does not allow *a* to precede it. On this Goilo says, "Although both forms of the past tense [*a* and *tabata*] are possible with this verb, we mostly hear the form '*tabata*'" (p. 61). I have not encountered the sequence *a sa* in any of my recordings. However, Enrique Muller (p.c. 12/4/87) states that, although when *sa* is used with perfective *a* it is most often preceded by *haña* "find" (*Mi a haña sa ken a hòrta e plaka* "I found out who stole the money"), it is possible to say *Mi a sa ken a hòrta e plaka*. As he points out, in this case *sa* is no longer a stative verb. In this sense *sa* can also be preceded by *ta*: *Mi ta sa ken a hòrta e plaka* (= *Mi ta haña sa* . . .) "I'm finding out . . ."

18. The three modal auxiliaries in this group (*ke*, *mester*, and *por*), however, have another means for past expression — actually the one more commonly used: the verb that follows the modal auxiliary can be preceded by *a* (unless, of course, that verb does not permit *a*). This is dealt with in greater detail later in this article.

19. Goilo is inadequate on this point and I have not determined myself which verbs are restricted in this use of *a*. Philippe Maurer (p.c.), however, states that he has examples of all verbs in this list with *a* in his data.

20. Izione Silva (p.c.) has suggested that this may be an indication that Papiamentu originally had zero marking for perfective, as most current Spanish and Portuguese creoles do.

21. Philippe Maurer (p.c.) has pointed out that in his most recent work he has begun to recognize that Papiamentu has relative tense (e.g. Maurer 1986a:137,140).

22. Both Enrique Muller (native speaker of Papimentu) and Philippe Maurer (based on his data) find this use of *ta'ata* in an embedded clause unusual. Both, independently, suggest that it would be more acceptable with a subordinator (e.g. *ku* "which"), but otherwise *ta* is more natural. Maurer cites Antoine Maduro's comment that such uses of embedded *ta'ata* are imitations of European languages. I have checked the example, however, and this is how it was uttered. Preference for *ta*, of course, is totally consistent with the main argument of this paper.

23. According to Philippe Maurer (p.c.), none of his informants accept sentences with *a* embedded as in example (17), clause 765. But he adds that he has heard that old people in the extreme ends of the island (Bandabou and Bandariba) do speak this way.

24. Curaçao really didn't have anything approaching the large plantations found in the South of the U.S. and in the larger English- and French-speaking islands of the Caribbean. In fact, *kunuku* literally means "countryside", or rural area, not "plantation" per se.

25. Enrique Muller informs me that *pa riba* "above" and *pa bou* "below" are not to be interpreted literally in this fashion, but rather as geographical direction: *pariba* "east side", *pabou* "west side". The two extreme ends of the island of Curaçao are called Bandariba "East End" and Bandabou "West End".

26. For *mester, mesté* is the usual form. *Mester* is used in formal registers and usually before *a*. *Mesté* also frequently gets treated like any other bisyllabic verb, acquiring the falling-rising tone and penultimate stress typical of bisyllabic verbs (see Andersen 1974 for more details), in both the form [mèsté] and [mèsé], where [..è..é..] marks falling-rising tone with approximately equal stress on both syllables.

27. *Ke* is the most typical phonological variant. *Ker* is used in formal registers (such as Text 4, the Public Forum) and in combination with *a*. Other alternate forms are *kyer* (formal) and *kye* (less formal).

28. The usual form is *por*. The *r*-less form, *po*, is markedly stigmatized as rural, uneducated, and substandard.

29. The source of the construction could also easily be Portuguese.

30. These three combinations are possible:
    a. *tabata + por/ke*
    b. *por/ke + a*
    c. *tabata + por/ke + a*   (Enrique Muller, p.c.)

31. This book continues to be, however, a rich resource of linguistic information about Papiamentu.

32. For example, the various inventories of features shared by creoles usually categorize a number of Papiamentu forms erroneously and fail to recognize similarities when they really do exist. To take one case from among several, Taylor (1971:294) lists Papiamentu as "-" for his feature (3): "The word for 'give' also functions as dative preposition 'to' or 'for'". All other similar inventories make the same mistake. "Give" in the formal register of Papiamentu is *duna*, while "to"/"for" is *na*. But basilectal "give" is *na*, which can be viewed as a variant of *duna*. (Probably, *na* is the basic form and *duna* a hypercorrect form based on Spanish/Portuguese *dar*.) His feature (3) should thus be marked "+" for Papiamentu, not "-". Comparative studies based on inadequate sources are not of much value.

33. We certainly cannot work without sentence-level semantics and syntax, which provide the basic essential tools for our work. The approach taken here, however, emphasizes and illustrates the need to work within a framework of total discourse. I owe my own interest in this model to Kenneth Pike and Ruth Brend, from my earliest linguistic training twenty years ago, and, more recently, to Wallace Chafe, Jack DuBois, Talmy Givón, Evelyn Hatch, and Sandra Thompson.

34. The list of names is too long to include here, but I would especially like to thank Enrique Muller for his patience in listening to me and answering my many questions, especially with regard to the topic of this paper, and his family for allowing me to take up so much of their time. I am especially grateful to Enrique for always using Papiamentu with me, even though he could pass as a native speaker of English. He is not responsible for any of my errors, however.

References

Andersen, Roger W. 1974. *Nativization and Hispanization in the Papiamentu of Curaçao, N.A.: A sociolinguistic study of variation.* Ph.D. dissertation, The University of Texas at Austin.

——. 1978. "Procesos fonológicos en el desarrollo del papiamentu". *Revista de Oriente* 2.135-44.

——. 1983. "One Norm or Several?: Linguistic variation in Papiamentu and its role in language planning". *Papiamentu, Problems and Possibilities* ed. by Enrique Muller, 65-84. Zuthphen, The Netherlands: De Walburg Pers.

——. 1986a. "El desarrollo de la morfología verbal en el español como segundo idioma". *Adquisición de lenguaje. Aquisição de linguagem*, ed. by Jürgen M. Meisel, 115-38. Frankfurt: M. Vervuert.

——. 1986b. "Interpreting Data: Second language acquisition of verbal aspect". Unpublished manuscript, UCLA.

——. 1988. "Mood and Modality in Papiamentu". Unpublished manuscript, UCLA.

Bickerton, Derek. 1974. "Creolization, Linguistic Universals, Natural Semantax and the Brain". *University of Hawaii Working Papers in Linguistics* 6(3).125-41. (Reprinted, *Issues in English Creoles: Papers from the 1975 Hawaii conference* ed. by Richard R. Day, 1-18. Heidelberg: Groos.)

——. 1975. *Dynamics of a Creole System.* Cambridge: University Press.

——. 1981. *Roots of Language.* Ann Arbor: Karoma.

——. 1984. "The Language Bioprogram Hypothesis". *The Behavioral and Brain Sciences* 7.173-221.

Bybee, Joan. 1985. *Morphology.* Amsterdam and Philadelphia: John Benjamins.

Comrie, Bernard. 1976. *Aspect: An introduction to the study of verbal aspect and related problems.* Cambridge: University Press.

——. 1985. *Tense.* Cambridge: University Press.

Goilo, E.R. 1972. *Papiamentu Textbook.* Aruba: de Wit Stores, N.V.

Goodman, Morris. 1987. "The Portuguese Element in the American Creoles". *Pidgin and Creole Languages* ed. by Glenn G. Gilbert, 361-405. Honolulu: University of Hawaii Press.

Juliana, Elis. 1970. *Echa Cuenta.* Amsterdam: Uitgeverij de Bezige Bij.

Maurer, Philippe. 1985. "Le système temporel du papiamentu et le système temporel proto-créole de Bickerton". *Amsterdam Creole Studies* 8.41-66.

————. 1986a. "El origin del papiamento desde el punto de vista de sus tiempos gramaticales". *Neure Romania* 4:129-149.

————. 1986b. "Los verbos modales POR, MESTER y KE del papiamentu: ¿un caso de transparencia semántica? *Akten des 2. Essener Kolloquiums zu Kreolsprachen und Sprachkontakten* ed. by Norbert Boretzky, Werner Enninger, & Thomas Stolz, 135-56. Bochum: Studienverlag Brockmeyer.

Meisel, Jürgen. 1985. "Les phases initiales du développement de notions temporelles, aspectualles et de modes d'action". *Lingua* 66.321-374.

Mourelatos, Alexander P. 1981. "Events, Processes, and States". *Syntax and Semantics, Vol. 14: Tense and Aspect* ed. by Philip J. Tedeschi and Annie Zaenen, 191-212. New York: Academic Press.

Naro, Anthony. 1978. "A Study on the Origins of Pidginization". *Lg* 54.314-347.

Schmidt, Richard W., and Sylvia Nagem Frota. 1986. "Developing Basic Conversational Ability in a Second Language: A Case Study of an Adult Learner of Portuguese". *Talking to Learn: Conversation in second language acquisition* ed. by Richard R. Day, 237-326. New York: Newbury House Publishers.

Taylor, Douglas. 1971. "Grammatical and Lexical Affinities of Creoles". *Pidginization and Creolization of Languages* ed. by Dell Hymes, 293-296. Cambridge: University Press.

Thompson, Roger W. 1961. "A Note on Some Possible Affinities Between the Creole Dialects of the Old World and Those of the New". *Creole Language Studies II* ed. by Robert B. LePage, 107-113. London: Mac-Millan.

Vendler, Zeno. 1967. "Verbs and Times". *Linguistics in Philosophy* ed. by Zeno Vendler, 97-121. Ithaca, NY.: Cornell University Press.

Whinnom, Keith. 1956. *Spanish Contact Vernaculars in the Philippine Islands*. London and Hong Kong: Oxford University Press.

————. 1965. "The Origin of the European-based Creoles and Pidgins". *Orbis* 14.509-527.

Time Reference in Kikongo-Kituba

Salikoko S. Mufwene
University of Georgia

1. Introduction

This chapter discusses especially what Fehderau (1966) identifies as the eastern dialect of (Kikongo-)Kituba, which is spoken in Zaire in roughly the part of the Bandundu region which lies south of the Kasai River. Aside from being one of the native languages of the writer, the variety was selected particularly because none of the dialects of ethnic Kikongo, its lexifier, are spoken in this area. It is in this region that the latter language must have undergone the greatest amount of restructuring during its pidginization and creolization (Mufwene 1988). Further, if decreolization is interpreted as a reverse systemic development toward the lexifier, it is this variety of post-formation Kituba that would have been subject to the least amount of decreolization. For the ultimate goal of determining some day which features are part of the formal universals of pidginization and creolization (be these absolute or typologically constrained — see Mufwene 1980), eastern Kituba (henceforth Kituba) is an apt language for study: it developed from the contact of non-European, primarily Bantu, languages (cf., however, Samarin 1982a, 1982b); and its lexifier is agglutinating.

The focus of this paper is the core morphosyntactic strategies of time reference in Kituba. In addition to the core strategies, there are a number of other, predominantly periphrastic, constructions that are often produced to convey some more precise temporal delimitations (e.g., terminative or ingressive constructions of recent past).[1] In this chapter these constructions are either ignored or discussed only very briefly, so that more detailed information may be provided about the basic delimitations. Although it is assumed here, as in Mufwene (1978, 1983a), that time adverbials contribute meaning to the temporal delimitation of sentences, only markers that delimit verbs as either inflections or "auxiliary verbs" are discussed fairly extensively.[2] Adverbials are dealt with only in connection with such markers.

Time reference is discussed below in generally the same framework as in Mufwene (1983a), especially where explicit comparisons with Atlantic pidgins and creoles (PC) are deemed helpful. For those who are not familiar with the work, its assumptions are reviewed in the course of the chapter, particularly in the light of recent theoretical developments in Mufwene (1984), Chung and Timberlake (1985), Comrie (1985), and Dahl (1985). An effort has been made to make explicit any changes from Mufwene (1983a) in assumptions and/or interpretation of facts.

Finally, although the tendency in the PC literature especially has been to mention tense and aspect in conjunction with mood (hence the common usage of the abbreviation TMA for tense-mood-aspect), generally the concomitant semantic analysis of mood has been scant. Indeed, mood has been considered mostly with regard to the position of its marker relative to those of tense and aspect. With the exception of future, the status of which remains problematic, no one has demonstrated in any way that mood is a sort of temporal delimitation.[3] Since Kituba provides no evidence for assuming that it is, and since this chapter is concerned especially with identifying semantic distinctions and the kind of marker (free or bound morpheme) used to express them, mood is mentioned only peripherally.

2. Tense and Aspect in Kituba

The bulk of Kituba's idiomatic time reference distinctions discussed below are the following:[4]

(1) a. *Béto ké(le) (kú+)dia.*   CONCOMITANT DURATIVE
         we   be   Infinitive+eat
         "We are eating".
     b. *Béto di+á(k)a.*   ANTERIOR PERFECTIVE
         "We ate".
     c. *Béto mé(ne) (kú+)dia.*   NEAR PERFECT (NPFCT)
         we   finish Inf+eat
         "We have eaten"./"We ate recently".

c'. *Béto mé(ne) di+á(k)a.*   REMOTE PERFECT (RPFCT)
   we   finish eat+ANTER
   "We ate a long time ago".

d. *Béto vand+á(k)a   (kú+)dia.* ANTERIOR DURATIVE
   we   be+ANTERIOR Inf+eat
   "We were eating".

e. *Béto (a)ta 'dia.*   SUBSEQUENT/FUTURE
   we   FUT eat
   "We will eat".

f. *Béto 'dia.*   SUBJUNCTIVE
   we   eat
   "Let us eat".

g. *Béto ké di+á(k)a.*   UNIVERSAL HABITUAL
   we   be eat+ANTER
   "We [usually] eat".

h. *Béto vand+á   di+á(k)a.*[5] ANTERIOR HABITUAL
   we   be+ANTER eat+ANTER
   "We used to eat".

i. *Béto ta   di+á(k)a.*   SUBSEQUENT/FUTURE
   we   FUT eat+ANTER   HABITUAL
   "We will [usually] eat".

j. *Béto 'dia.*   NARRATIVE
   "We ate".

One of the noteworthy features of Kituba is that it has a relative tense system. That is, the axis of reference (in Reichenbach's 1947 terms) or tense locus (according to Chung and Timberlake) keeps shifting in the discourse depending on the particular situation the speaker selects as the reference time (R).[6] While out of context the above constructions are interpreted relative to the speech event time (S), there are discourse contexts which require that they select either past or future events as R, as below.

(2) a. *Ntángu ya   María kwis+á(k)a,   múna béto méne*
       time   COMP Mary come+ANTER then we finish
       di+áka.
       eat+ANTER
       "When Mary came, we had already eaten [a long time/quite some time ago]".

b. *Ntángu ya María kwis+á(k)a, múna béto mé(ne) 'dia.*
   "When Mary came, we had eaten [not long ago]".[7]
c. *Ntángu ya María ata kwísa, múna béto méne di+á(k)a.*
   "When Mary comes, we will have eaten [a long time/quite a while ago]".
d. *Na   ki+ntéte   ngé   tub+áka   nde   María*
   LOC 9+Monday you-sg say+ANTER COMP Mary
   kwend+á(k)a na   ki+sálu mazóno.
   go+ANTER   LOC 9+work yesterday.[8]
   "On Monday you said that Mary had gone to work the day before (Sunday)".

Consequently, the traditional term PRESENT is rather misleading, if not downright inadequate, for characterizing situations whose time coincides with, or includes, R, especially when R is not the same as S. In relative tense systems, PRESENT is, strictly speaking, not asserted but contextually implicated. The metaterm CONCOMITANT (originally used in Mufwene 1978 and 1983a) seems to be more adequate.

In the same vein, the term PAST has acquired a deictic meaning in a great deal of the literature, even though it need not be interpreted this way. Based on how the precise interpretation of the delimitation *V+áka* changes from context to context (see, e.g., [1b] and [2d]), the metaterm ANTERIOR, which has been commonly used in the PC literature since Bickerton (1974, 1975) for situations which are anterior to R, seems not only to be less misleading for relative tense systems but also to facilitate the comparison of Kituba with other PC's. The main difference between this delimitation and the use of *ben/bin* in creoles such as Gullah and Jamaican and Guyanese lies in the fact that when R is S, or else once it has been clearly identified with some other time in the universe of discourse, the unmarked verb form is usually preferred in the latter languages (Mufwene 1983a).[9]

The delimitations with preverbal *mé(ne)*, identified in (1) as PERFECT, have sometimes been misidentified as COMPLETIVE or PERFECTIVE, owing in part to the fact that the term *perfect* also forms its adjective in *-ive* (see, e.g., the original version of Mufwene 1988 and the creole literature).[10] As Dahl emphasizes (see also Comrie, and Chung and Timberlake), PERFECT suggests some relation of a past event to R; Anderson's (1982) characterization of its prototypical meaning as CURRENT RELEVANCE seems quite adequate and this is adopted here. On the other hand,

COMPLETIVE/PERFECTIVE characterizes a situation as complete or as a whole (Comrie 1976) with no necessary relevance to R.

What Kituba's *mé(ne)* + *V* and *mé(ne)* + *V-á(ka)* delimitations denote is actually PERFECT; their meaning is based literally on the perception (hence presentation) of the event which is relevant to the current situation as completed, the literal meaning of *méne* (see also the discussion of states below). That the *méne* + *V* and *méne* + *V-á(ka)* constructions are not COMPLETIVE/PERFECTIVE is evidenced by the fact that they cannot combine with a time adverbial referring to an interval taken as a point, as below:

(3) a. **Béto mé(ne) dia búbu yáyi/mazóno.* NEAR PERFECT
         we   finish eat day this/yesterday
         **"We have eaten today/yesterday".[11]

    a'. *Béto di+á(k)a búbu yáyi/mazóno.* ANTERIOR
         "We ate today/yesterday".[12]

                                        REMOTE PERFECT
    b. **Béto mé(ne) bal+á(k)a*   *mvúla méne lúta.*
         we   finish marry+ANTER year finish pass
         **"We have (got) married last year".

    b'. *Béto bal+á(k)a mvúla méne lúta.* ANTERIOR
         "We married last year".

Kituba's closest counterpart to the Atlantic creole COMPLETIVE/PERFECTIVE is its *V+á(k)a* ANTERIOR delimitation. However, there is an interesting division of labor here between the ANTERIOR and the PERFECT constructions in expressing anteriority relations to situations which are not concomitant with S. The PERFECT delimitations are generally preferred when, aside from ANTERIORity, CURRENT RELEVANCE is also part of the meaning. Perhaps the best way to capture what is in effect here is an overriding principle (maybe language-specific) whereby the PERFECT must be used when there is conflict between ANTERIORity and CURRENT RELEVANCE.[13] Relating this paragraph to the preceding, Kituba's *V+á(k)a* construction corresponds to both COMPLETIVE and ANTERIOR in Atlantic PC's (as observed in note 9).

Kituba does not really have a morphological equivalent of the Atlantic English and French creoles' unmarked verb form, which is interpreted in some contexts as COMPLETIVE/PERFECTIVE with nonstative verbs, especially when context does not suggest otherwise.[14] The closest to this is what is identified in (1) as NARRATIVE, here, an inflectionally zero-tense delimitation of a verb which is also delimited with a null aspectual marker for PERFECTIVE (see below); it presents events as complete and "in the order they are supposed to have taken place" (Dahl 1985:112).[15] The NARRATIVE is used in Kituba primarily with nonstative verbs, especially when more than one verb is involved, which may sometimes result in a serial construction as below in (4b). This delimitation has the effect of making a macro-event out of the separate smaller events that are reported.

(4)   a. *Béto vand+áka   ku+sakána. Pételo kwísa ye   yándi*
         we   be+ANTER Inf+play   Peter   come and he
         banda ku+sokísa   Ida. Búna móno nganína yándi.
         start   Inf+provoke Ida. then   I   scold   him
         "We were playing. Peter came and started to provoke Ida.
         Then I scolded him".
      b. *Yándi sokis+áka   Ida; yó yína Ida 'wa   makási*
         he   provoke+ANTER Ida; it   that Ida perceive anger
         báka ńti   búla yándi.[16]
         take stick hit   him
         "He provoked Ida; this is why Ida got angry, took a stick,
         and hit him".

The NARRATIVE delimitation resembles the ANTERIOR PERFECTIVE in that they are both used for events perceived/presented as complete and are used in this function with no aspectual verb preceding them. Considering the semantic and functional kinship between the ANTERIOR tense (marked with the suffix *-á(k)a* on the verb) and the NARRATIVE tense (marked with zero), PERFECTIVE must thus be expressed by the absence of an aspectual verb before the verb. Cases of subjunctive and imperative modal delimitations set aside, the NARRATIVE is the only case where the verb is absolutely undelimited morphosyntactically; the normal trend otherwise is to have at least one marker, either a free morpheme before the verb or a suffix on the main verb.

Thus, Kituba often uses the ANTERIOR *V+áka* delimitation where Atlantic English and French creoles use the realis unmarked verb. In Kituba this is especially true at the beginning of a discourse, where the NARRATIVE is not permitted.[17] Kituba also uses the HABITUAL *ké(le) V+ á(k)a* construction where, for example, Gullah and Jamaican Creole still use the unmarked verb for habits (e.g., *Jaaj flai go a Miami ebri mont*

"George flies to Miami every month" in Jamaican Creole). The need for
overt delimitation of verbs extends to CONCOMITANT uses of statives,
which are delimited by the DURATIVE, as below:

(5) a. *Móno ké   'wa   nzala.*
         I   be/DUR perceive hunger
         "I am hungry".
     b. *Móno ké   'wa ngé mbóte.*
         I   be/DUR hear you well
         "I hear you well".
     c. *Yándi ké   kwikíla ngé vé.*
         He   be/DUR believe you not
         "He doesn't believe you".
     d. *Béto ké   fingíla ngé.*
         we   be/DUR wait   you
         "We are waiting for you".
     e. *Móno ké   zóla 'dia.*
         I   be/DUR want eat
         "I want/am about to eat".

The only exceptions to this rule are *zába* "know", the CONCOMIT-
ANT locative verb *ké(le)* "be", and *zóla* in the sense of "like, love", as in
the following constructions:

(6) a. *Yándi zóla Bea míngi.*
         he/she like Bea much
         "He likes Beatrice a lot".
     b. *Móno zába yándi vé.*
         I   know him/her not
         "I don't know him/her".
     c. *María ké(le) na zándu.*
         Mary be   at market
         "Mary is at [the] market".

Going back to the sentences in (5), it would be misguided here to
translate Kituba's DURATIVE state constructions with the progressive,
except where it is the only appropriate alternative in English, as is the case
of (5d). The English progressive would otherwise suggest marked interpretations which are not borne out by the originals.[18]
Used without (overt) morphosyntactic delimitations, the verbs in (5)
would be interpreted in the NARRATIVE tense (which, as noted above, is

also PERFECTIVE). They would concomitantly also be interpreted as
nonstative verbs, connoting change of state, rather than stative.[19] The
DURATIVE delimitation of stative verbs illustrated by the sentences in (5)
highlights TRANSIENT DURATION. This is proposed in Mufwene
(1984) as the basic meaning of the progressive (which is in turn defined as a
stativizing delimitation). The peculiarity of Kituba is that the delimitation
applies indiscriminately to virtually all verbs, regardless of whether they are
lexically stative or nonstative. Further, the DURATIVE delimitation
appears to be obligatory in the CONCOMITANT tense.

The DURATIVE occurs only in the CONCOMITANT and
ANTERIOR tenses and not in the SUBSEQUENT. However, CON-
COMITANT DURATIVE may have a future interpretation, suggesting a
plan, as below:

(7)   a. *Yándi ké   kwísa mbási.*
         He   be/DUR come tomorrow
         "He comes/is coming tomorrow".
      b. *Nki   yándi ké   lála   na   ńzo   na ngé?*
         COMP he   be/DUR sleep LOC house of you
         "Is he [planning on] sleeping at your house"?/"Have you
         planned for him to sleep at your house"?

No DURATIVE may, however, be used for imminent future; this is
expressed by the NEAR PERFECT construction used in combination with
no time adverb at all, as in (8). The event is thus described as already completed and being relevant to S:

(8)   a. *Móno mé kwénda.*
         "I am leaving".
      b. *Móno mé yantíka.*
         "I am about to start".

CONCOMITANT DURATIVE can occasionally also be used for
habits which are not quite fixed yet, as in (9), which is an extension of
TRANSIENT DURATION. This is the only case where the DURATIVE
may alternate with the HABITUAL, which is discussed below.

(9)   *Móno kéle   sála   áwa bilúmbu yáyi.*
      I   be/DUR work here days   DEM-PROXIMAL
      "I am working here these days".

There is an alternative to the DURATIVE delimitation of stative verbs, where the latter either is awkward or suggests a non-CONCOMIT-ANT interpretation as in (7b): the stative verb is delimited in the PER-FECT, as below:

(10) a. *Yándi mé   lála.*
          he   finish fall-asleep/lie-down
          "He is asleep".
      b. *Bó   mé   zóla   yándi.*
          they finish get-to-like him/her
          "They like him/her".
      c. *Bó mé kanga yándi.*
          "They have caught him [and he is still in their hands]"./"They
          have him".

As in the case of imminent future (discussed above and illustrated by [8]), the state is presented literally as an event that has just been completed. The stative meaning conveyed in this case is RESULTATIVE, convention-ally implicated rather than stated. This delimitation is preferred to the DURATIVE when the most obvious interpretation of the latter is that of a plan. The RESULTATIVE STATIVE is prototypically used with nonsta-tive verbs; when it is used with stative verbs, they are interpreted literally as change-of-state events with the stative meaning being only implicated. All this is consistent with the identification of the *mé(ne) V* and *méne V-á(k)a* constructions as PERFECT with the prototypical meaning of CURRENT RELEVANCE. The RESULTATIVE STATIVE meaning is thus one of the specialized interpretations of CURRENT RELEVANCE.

Kituba's HABITUAL also has its own peculiarities; its morphosyntac-tic expression is noteworthy, consisting of a combination of the locative-existential verbs *kéle* "be (at), exist" for universal habits or *vánda* (literally, "sit, be at, stay") for ANTERIOR habits; the main verb itself is delimited in the ANTERIOR. Insofar as the universal HABITUAL is concerned, this pattern is not consistent with other Bantu languages, where only the inflection on the main verb (in combination with no delimitative verb) is specialized for the HABITUAL delimitation. Even Lingala (another Bantu-based creole with which it has been in constant contact) follows the traditional Bantu pattern.

Unlike in some Atlantic PC's, these HABITUAL constructions have little competition, functionally, from the DURATIVE, the habitual interpretation of which is rather marked. Kituba is also unlike Atlantic PC's and more Bantu-like in another respect: its HABITUAL delimitation is fairly common with stative verbs; it is actually the most appropriate delimitation when a state transcends S and may be considered immanent. The specialization of its HABITUAL into UNIVERSAL, PAST, and SUBSEQUENT is also a common characteristic of Bantu languages, obvious counterevidence to a fairly widespread assumption that the HABITUAL is tenseless.[20]

Related to the above morphosyntactic considerations is the following question: what is the formal status of the free markers in the CONCOMITANT DURATIVE construction *kéle* + V and *méne* + V? Are they verbs or different kinds of markers?[21] The question arises particularly because they are most commonly heard in the contracted form.

At least one linguist, Ngalasso (1984) (also a native speaker), has hypothesized that they probably suggest a return to the Bantu agglutinating system, i.e., at least the shorter forms may be interpreted as prefixes. Even if Ngalasso's hypothesis is correct, the fact that the alternations of fuller and contracted forms are still current does not obviate the question raised here. Etymological considerations (such as suggested by the alternations) set aside, it is relevant to consider the marker *vand+á(k)a*, the substitute of *ké(le)* in the ANTERIOR. As *vand+áka* has the regular ANTERIOR suffix, like any other verb in the ANTERIOR delimitation, it is apparently justified to assume that *ké(le)* and perhaps *mé(ne)* must be used as regular verbs. Since the delimitative verb *ké(le)* is etymologically related to the locative-existential *ké(le)*, I assume that, like the latter, it is used in the CONCOMITANT non-DURATIVE and is one of the exceptions to the general rule which delimits concomitant states of affairs in the CONCOMITANT DURATIVE.[22] As for *mé(ne)*, which is etymologically related to the nonstative verb *mana* "finish", I assume, consistently with the hypothesis that nonstative verbs have no CONCOMITANT non-DURATIVE uses, that it is in the NARRATIVE. The fact that these verbs may not be assigned SUBJUNCTIVE and IMPERATIVE interpretations lends indirect support to these hypotheses.[23]

The formal status of the SUBSEQUENT marker *(a)ta* is less clear. It was originally a DURATIVE prefix in Kikongo-Kintandu (Fehderau 1966:104), and unlike the shorter DURATIVE and PERFECTIVE markers *ké* and *mé* it bears no high tone.[24] It would be easy to assume that it is a prefix if it did not have a fuller disyllabic form; prefixes are normally monosyllabic. I have no position on its status.

The general strategy of temporal delimitations in Kituba may not be completely assessed without taking into account the fact that the infinitival prefix *ku-* is often dropped after delimitative verbs. Although the resulting form is homophonous with the NARRATIVE verb form, I am reluctant to consider them as the same for the purposes of temporal delimitation. The fact that infinitival verb forms and verbal stems alternate after delimitative verbs (subject to the constraint stated above) but not in NARRATIVE environments (without a preceding delimitative verb) argues against equating them.

The above clarification taken into account, the following may further be stated about the morphosyntax of temporal delimitations in Kituba: the DURATIVE marker is the (delimitative) verb *ké(le)*, which assigns TRANSIENT DURATION to the main verb in the stem or infinitival form; the PERFECT marker is the delimitative verb *mé(ne)*, which assigns CURRENT RELEVANCE to the main verb. The REMOTE PERFECT is expressed by combining the verb *mé(ne)* with the main verb inflected with the ANTERIOR, which is independently marked by the suffix *á(k)a*. The absence of a free delimitative marker before a verb marks the PERFEC-TIVE; a main verb used alone with no inflection nor a delimitative verb (characteristics of the NARRATIVE-PERFECTIVE) must of necessity denote an anterior event (relative to R) perceived/presented as complete, except for the few stative verbs seen above.

HABITUAL delimitations are of peculiar interest: in the non-SUB-SEQUENT, the delimitative verbs *ké(le)* or *vand+á(k)a* assign CON-COMITANT DURATION or ANTERIOR DURATION, respectively, to a verb that is otherwise inflected with the ANTERIOR suffix *á(k)a*. Except for the fact that the ANTERIOR non-DURATIVE is PERFECTIVE and suggests at least one previous occurrence (as required by habits), I have no explanation for why this verbal form was selected over, for example, the NARRATIVE.[25] As for the form of SUBSEQUENT HABITUAL, which is expressed by combining the SUBSEQUENT preverbal free marker *(a)ta* with a *V+á(k)a*, this may have to be considered in connection with the lack of SUBSEQUENT DURATIVE in Kituba. A plausible explanation is the relative tense system, which makes it unnecessary to specify SUBSEQU-ENCE while expressing DURATION if this is already stated elsewhere. It is, however, possible that the system just has a gap here. In any case, anteriority to a R located in the future is expressed with a verb delimited either only with the ANTERIOR suffix *á(k)a* or, preferably, in the PER-

FECT (when CURRENT RELEVANCE is significant).

Except for the SUBSEQUENT delimitation, Kituba uses a combination of regular syntactic and morphological strategies for its tense-aspect system. The pattern seems to be inflections for realis tense and periphrasis or free markers for aspect.[26] Stating the aspectual delimitation pattern in terms of free marker may actually be more accurate, since it does not make an exception of PERFECTIVE: the free morpheme is, as indicated above, null in this case. This might suggest that the PERFECTIVE must be the unmarked aspect, on which other aspectual delimitations seem to operate; however, I see no strong evidence for defending this position here.

3. Summary and Conclusions

The tense/aspect system of Kituba may be summarized as follows:

1) There are three basic tenses: ANTERIOR, CONCOMITANT, and SUBSEQUENT. ANTERIOR situations may be delimited in either the DURATIVE aspect (which is IMPERFECTIVE) or the PERFECTIVE (or non-DURATIVE) aspect. CONCOMITANT situations are delimited only in the DURATIVE aspect (with the exception of the few stative verbs noted above), and SUBSEQUENT situations are delimited only in the PERFECTIVE (with no DURATIVE counterpart). The markers of ANTERIOR and CONCOMITANT are inflectional (counting the null suffix on the few stative and delimitative verbs used alone); that of SUBSEQUENT is a free morpheme.

The NARRATIVE tense deserves a special comment: it backgrounds the anteriority of the reported events relative to S; in fact, it brings them closer to S. It does not introduce a fourth time distinction, only a special style of reporting events which are otherwise as anterior as those expressed with a verb inflected with *á(k)a*.

2) Kituba has a relative tense system; in order to express anteriority or subsequence of a situation relative to R (where R is different from S), no re-orientation of tenses is required. This makes it difficult to hold a *de re/de dicto* distinction in reports of events.[27]

3) Kituba has four basic aspectual delimitations: PERFECT, DURATIVE, HABITUAL, and PERFECTIVE/COMPLETIVE. All are periphrastic delimitations. Stated differently, all aspects are expressed by a free morpheme, that of the PERFECTIVE being null. Something may now be added comfortably to the description in part 2: more specific aspectual

delimitations may be expressed in utilizing both the above basic delimitations and some general principles of complementation. For instance, witness how inchoation is expressed below:

(11) a. *María mé   yantíka *(kú+)dia.*
Mary finish start   Inf+eat
"Mary has started to eat".

b. *Ntángu ya   béto vánda,   múna Maria mé*
time   COMP we   sit-down-NARR then   Mary finish
*yantik+áka   *(kú+)dia.*
start+ANTER Inf+eat
"When we sat down, Mary had already started to eat/had started to eat [a long time ago]".

c. *Béto ké   yantíka *(ku+)longúka   mbási.*
we   be/DUR start   Inf+study   tomorrow
"We start/are starting to study tomorrow".

The obligatoriness of the infinitive prefix *ku-* on the last verb in the combination indicates that *yantíka* functions more like a regular verb with a nominal object (which the infinitive is in Bantu languages) than as an auxiliary aspectual verb. That it is itself aspectually delimited with *mé(ne)* is further evidence for the hypothesis.

4) The discrepancy between the number of aspectual distinctions and that of tense distinctions is not significant, unless SUBSEQUENT is treated as a mood.

For creolists a few other things must be noted here. First is the fact that Kituba's system is in part inflectional, which reduces relatively its dependence on context for the interpretation of some forms, e.g., the HABITUAL. This must be due in part to the fact that in the contact situation in which it developed all the languages present are agglutinating, hence inflectional (Mufwene 1988).

Secondly, Kituba has some distinctions not attested to in Atlantic PC's; for instance, it makes a distinction between REMOTE and NEAR PERFECT. It makes a clear morphosyntactic distinction between PERFECT and COMPLETIVE (or PERFECTIVE); in Atlantic PC's the distinction depends in part on the context, as Youssef (1986) shows regarding the interpretation of morphosyntactically undelimited verbs.[28] Kituba also makes a clear morphosyntactic distinction between especially the HABITUAL and both the NARRATIVE and the CONCOMITANT

DURATIVE. In some Atlantic PC's there is no formal distinction between the HABITUAL and the unmarked COMPLETIVE verb, and in others there is none between the HABITUAL and the DURATIVE; context specifies which semantic delimitation is being conveyed. There is apparently no Atlantic PC that has Kituba's three-way distinction of HABITUAL, DURATIVE, and unmarked verb form (NARRATIVE).

Thirdly, the role of the stative/nonstative distinction is not as significant in Kituba's tense/aspect system as it is in Atlantic creole systems. With the exception of the few verbs noted above in connection with the CONCOMITANT DURATIVE (and illustrated in the sentences in [6]), all verbs are delimited semantically and morphosyntactically in a uniform way. The only case where the stative/nonstative distinction seems significant is the NARRATIVE delimitation; it is more common with nonstative verbs, and the stative verbs which are so delimited are assigned a change-of-state interpretation.

Fourthly, Kituba's tense system is not articulated in terms of the same basic irrealis/realis or future/nonfuture distinction as the Atlantic PC systems. If anything, it is akin to the European past/nonpast system, since CONCOMITANT DURATIVE may be used for plans.

There are of course also some similarities. For instance, both Kituba and Atlantic creoles have relative tense systems; in both, the overt PERFECT delimitation (with *méne* or *done*) has the same effect on stative verbs, suggesting that the situation started a long time ago or has been in effect for quite some time.[29] Kituba's NARRATIVE is in some ways also reminiscent of (though not identical with) the Atlantic creoles' unmarked realis verb especially in that it may not refer to future.[30]

In a slightly different vein, the development of both Kituba and Atlantic PC's is characterized by some morphosyntactic restructuring, which has given periphrasis a great role to play in temporal delimitation. This cannot be denied for Kituba, since, as explained in Mufwene (1988), the system in ethnic Kikongo (the lexifier) is agglutinating and periphrastic constructions have generally been functionally marked, being used especially for emphasis.[31] If any question of significance arises here, it is why marked constructions have been selected. The notion of (perceptual) saliency suggested to me by Morris Goodman (p.c., Mufwene 1987) may hold a plausible answer to the question.[32]

Notes

*   I am grateful to John Singler both for inviting me to write this chapter and for a number of comments which have prompted me to clarify some of my positions. I assume alone full responsibility for all shortcomings.

1.   The term **delimitation** is used in this paper (after Bierwisch 1971) as a semantic cover term for the alternative morphosyntactic strategies (inflectional or periphrastic) whereby the language user specifies the tense, aspect, or mood of a sentence. Although delimitative markers are morphosyntactically most commonly associated with the verb (as affixes or auxiliary verbs), they may also occur as sentential adverbs, as with the perfective marker *le* in Chinese. Also, temporal inflections, auxiliaries, and adverbs are often used concomitantly in a sentence for a more precise delimitation, as in **Sometimes** *John* **comes** *to work at 8 A.M.* I refer to this below.

2.   Mufwene and Bokamba (1979) argue that in Lingala the verbs used in the periphrastic temporal delimitation of other verbs are strictly speaking not auxiliary verbs; normal syntax makes possible their delimitative uses. Although genetically the same position may be assumed about Kituba's delimitative verbs, the fact that at least two of the delimitative verbs, *kéle* "be" and *méne* "finish, end" have no infinitives (with the prefix *ku-*) suggests that they may indeed be auxiliaries in their delimitative functions. Corroborating this is also the fact that the main-verb form of "finish, end" is exclusively *(ku+)mana*, except in the idiomatic impersonal form *i+méne* "it [is] over/finished". However, the phonological alternations affecting these verbs in their delimitative function also affect the main verb *kéle* "be (at), exist". In both its main-verb and its delimitative verb uses *kéle* is replaced by *vánda* "sit, stay", both in the infinitive and in the ANTERIOR. I find the evidence rather inconclusive and I will use "delimitative verb" where others may prefer "auxiliary verb". (Additional evidence, presented in fn. 22, seems to support my decision.)

3.   For instance, Bailey (1966), Mufwene (1983b), and Chung and Timberlake (1985) assume that the future may be, or is, a modal delimitation, whereas Dahl (1985) thinks it is a tense.

4.   The word **idiomatic** is used here in reference to those fixed delimitations (syntactic or inflectional) that are routinely used for time reference. It excludes nonce constructions (involving regular complementation) whereby a speaker tries to convey temporal nuances which the basic system does not express, as in *Chantál yantíka ku+yímba* "Chantal started to sing". (*Ku-* is the infinitival marker.) The parentheses in all the examples below indicate possible contraction, except for the infinitive, where they indicate possible omission of the prefix. (The omission is actually not permitted when the delimitative verb has a full form.) Where only the shorter form is given, the full form sounds odd. I am not sure that the verb stem without the infinitival marker is also a contraction; the form seems to suggest development toward isolating morphosyntax (Mufwene 1988). Where no particular suffix is identified on the base of the main verb, the final vowel is identified in Bantu linguistics as a verb ending; the tense inflection is thus null.

5.   As noted in fn. 2, *ku+vánda*, which basically means "to sit, to stay", is also used as the ANTERIOR allomorph of *kéle* "to be" in all its uses as existential or locative verb or as DURATIVE marker.

6. Another term proposed in the literature is "deictic centre" (Comrie 1985). While it seems adequate when R is the speech event time (S), it applies only by brute force to any R other than S. Deictics are defined relative to the speech event; relative tenses are not so defined (see also Dahl 1985).

7. This translation should not be confused with the English *we had just eaten*. Kituba conveys the meaning of this English construction differently; in the case of sentence (2b), the second clause would be:

    (i)   *Múna béto méne katúka   kú+dia.*
          then   we   finish come-from Inf+eat

    A post-verbal adverbial corresponding to *just, káka sisépi yáyi* "only a while ago" (literally: "only short-temporal-distance this") is often used without the verb *katuka* "come-from" when R is S, as below:

    (ii) *Béto méne 'dia káka sisépi   yáyi.*
          we   finish eat only short-time this
          "We have just eaten"./"We just ate"./"We ate a short while ago".

8. LOC stands for "locative"; the digit before the gloss specifies the noun class. For more information see Mufwene (1988).

9. Note that in these languages the unmarked verb, which is also PERFECTIVE/COMPLE-TIVE, has an ANTERIOR meaning relative to S when nonstative verbs are involved (unless context, e.g. the presence of frequency adverbials in the same sentence, requires otherwise). *Ben/Bin* is used to express anteriority to R. Although the *ben/bin* delimitation is usually used at the beginning of narratives, the unmarked verb is often used at the beginning of conversations when nonstative verbs are involved. The main difference between this and Kituba's systems thus lies in the fact that Kituba uses one form for what is expressed by both the overt ANTERIOR with *ben/bin* and the covert one expressed with the unmarked verb.

10. Youssef (1986) makes the distinction for Trinidadian Creole, although she equivocates somewhat on the PERFECT meaning of *dɔn + V* constructions. She does a nice job, however, of highlighting the fact that some uses of the morphologically unmarked nonstative verb are PERFECT rather than COMPLETIVE. The question of whether this meaning is stated or implicated remains open.

11. There is an interpretation of sentence (3a) and its translation which is acceptable with the adverbial *búbu yáyi* "today", viz., "As for today we have eaten". (The adverbial would also have to be said with a different voice modulation.) However, this is irrelevant here, since the adverbial is interpreted to denote a period of time within which the perfect delimitation applies but not the time of occurrence of the event delimited in the perfect.

12. Periphrasis is not really what defines a construction as PERFECT rather than PERFEC-TIVE. For instance, although the French "passé composé" is periphrastic, it is in many cases a PERFECTIVE rather than a perfect. Its translation of sentence (3a) is well-formed:

    (i)   *Nous avons mangé hier/aujourd'hui.*
          *"We have eaten yesterday/today".

    (The English translation is all right if *today* is interpreted as period rather than as point in time.)

13.   The most unequivocal counterpart of Kituba's PERFECT in Atlantic creoles appears to
      be the *done + V* and *V + done* constructions (Mufwene 1983a) and those with *feni* in
      Liberian English, *finis* in Nigerian Pidgin English, and *fini* in "le français populaire
      d'Abidjan" (Singler 1983). One obvious difference between Kituba's PERFECT and that
      in these languages lies in the fact that the latter have no NEAR/REMOTE contrast. The
      match between the PERFECT constructions of all these languages goes up to the way the
      markers *mé(ne)*, *done*, and *feni* combine with stative verbs to indicate that the state of
      affairs either started a long time ago or has obtained for quite some time, the distance
      being determined rather subjectively. This interpretation is suggested in part by the fact
      that in Kituba the stative verb is normally delimited in the REMOTE PERFECT; at least
      to this writer the delimitation in the NEAR PERFECT denotes a recent inchoative event,
      instead. See:
      (i)   a. *Yándi mé(ne) zol+á(k)a Bea!*
                "He's loved Beatrice [for a long time]".
            a'. *Yándi méne zóla Bea.*
                "He has fallen in love with/loves Beatrice".
      (ii) *i dʌn lɔv beatrɪs.*   (Gullah)
      (iii) *Yu dɔn fat aredi.*   (Trinidadian English Creole, Youssef 1986)
      (iv) *Mi dɔn nuo se yu bɛn tɛl pan mi.*
            "I have known all along/for quite some time that you (had) told about me".
            (Jamaican Creole, Mufwene 1983a)
      (v)   *ši feni lezi.* (transcription phonetically adapted)
            "She is thoroughly lazy". (Liberian English, Singler 1983)

      The translation Singler assigns to sentence (v) may not be in conflict with the analysis
      proposed here. The construction may be interpreted as stating that the referent has been
      lazy for as long as the speaker can remember. My informants do not find the translation
      with "thoroughly" or "completely" quite adequate in similar Gullah constructions. How-
      ever, Singler (p.c.) has observed that there are some exceptions to my explanation. For
      instance, *feni ɔrenʃ* in the following sentence used by a nurse to describe the body of the
      late Liberian President Tolbert as it lay in the morgue must be interpreted as "com-
      pletely":

      (vi) *a se də mɛ ho su wə feni ɔrenʃ.*
            "I say the man['s] whole suit was completely orange (from blood)".

14.   Youssef indicates that some of these uses have a PERFECT interpretation, especially
      when reference is to a recent past and there is no time adverbial co-occurring with the
      nonstative verb. This is very similar to some uses of the French "passé composé".

15.   NARRATIVE is Dahl's metaterm. It seems to be more adequate for Kituba than the
      traditional term "historical present". Unlike in Western European languages where the
      historical present is actually a present tense form, Kituba's NARRATIVE is used exclu-
      sively with reference to past situations described with nonstative verbs. Except for a tiny
      subset of stative verbs (discussed below), there is no simple present form in Kituba.

16.   It is not clear to the writer that there should be any punctuation in the second part of sen-
      tence (4b); such sentences are normally spoken without pauses between the verbs.

17.   Inside the discourse the NARRATIVE is sometimes also obligatory, such as in the exam-
      ples (4), where the intent is to present the smaller event as parts of a macro-event. The
      constraints regarding this are related to limitations in the strategies of subordination,
      which cannot be discussed here.

18. As shown in Mufwene (1984), *wait* is among the state verbs that are normally used in the progressive in the present tense. The simple form conveys a habit instead.

19. In some contexts the verbs might also be interpreted as subjunctive or imperative (both of which are morphosyntactically unmarked), but this will not be dealt with here. What is presented here about Kituba seems to some extent to be the opposite of what Mufwene (1984) discusses about a number of English stative verbs such as *like* and *hate*, which may be assigned an inchoative interpretation when delimited in the progressive, although a transient durative interpretation is not excluded:

(i)   *Are you liking the world any better?*
(ii) *I think I am hating this protocol.*

However, in English, the problem is complicated by the fact that both the acceptability of a progressive construction and its interpretation as inchoative or in transient duration are determined by the position which a verb holds on the scale of stativity hypothesized in Mufwene (1984).

20. In Atlantic creoles the most obvious corroborative evidence for my position comes from those creoles such as Guyanese and Papiamentu which use CONCOMITANT DURA-TIVE also for universal habits, as in the following sentence from Papiamentu taken from Maurer (1985:50):

(i)   *E   ta   landa tur   dia.*
      he/she be   swim   every day
      "He/She swims every day".

21. My frequent reference to them as verbs in the earlier part of this chapter has so far been a matter of faith.

22. Since even the main verb *ké(le)* is subject to the phonological alternation and is substi-tuted by *vánda* in the ANTERIOR, we may assume that it is actually the same locative-existential verb which is used as main and delimitative verb. The following sentence from the western variety of Kituba actually weakens the auxiliary verb status of *ké(le)*:

(i)   *Yándi   kéle na kú+dia.*
      he/she be   at INF+eat
      "He/She is eating".

23. One paradigmatic detail weakens the above assumption for *mé(ne)*. Unlike *ké(le)*, it has neither a productive main-verb usage nor an ANTERIOR counterpart (which may be explained by the fact that Kituba has a relative tense system and does not need this dis-tinction). In the former respect it is somewhat similar to the SUBSEQUENT marker *(a)ta*. Unlike the latter, however, it is etymologically related to the verb *ku+mana* "finish, end".

24. As discussed in Mufwene (1988), the high tone is retained from the fuller forms *kéle* and *méne*, where, according to a dominant tone placement rule for polysyllabic words, a high tone is placed on the penultimate syllable (all the other syllables bear a low tone).

25. As conjectured in Mufwene (1988), it is possible that the HABITUAL suffix *ánga* in ethnic Kikongo (*-áka* in Kikongo-Kiladi) has merged in Kituba with the ANTERIOR suf-fix *-aka*. The addition of the DURATIVE delimitation to the original HABITUAL would thus prevent ambiguity. Note, however, that the SUBSEQUENT HABITUAL delimitation is not ambiguous.

26. This formulation excludes the SUBSEQUENT delimitation, which is considered by linguists such as Bailey (1966) and Chung and Timberlake (1985) to be a mood. This is actually the spirit of the realis/irrealis distinction proposed by Voorhoeve (1957). Morphosyntactic reasons for treating the SUBSEQUENT delimitation as a mood in Kituba would include the following: 1) the marker *(a)ta* corresponds to no verb in ethnic Kikongo (it was originally a PRESENT DURATIVE marker in Kikongo-Kintandu); 2) it is not a suffix (unlike the true tenses ANTERIOR, with *á(k)a*, and CONCOMITANT, with a null suffix); and 3) unlike the shorter forms of the aspectual verbs *kéle* and *méne*, it bears no high tone — it might well pass for a prefix. On the other hand, the fact that CONCOMITANT is not completely parallel with ANTERIOR (e.g., it does not have a simple form for most verbs) indirectly weakens the evidence for assuming that the SUBSEQUENT is a mood. I treat it by fiat here as a tense.

27. See Martin (1985) about this distinction. The following English examples illustrate the contrast:

(i)   *I learned that John is in Paris.*   [de re]
(ii) *I learned that John was in Paris.*   [de dicto]

28. For instance, *im gaan* has the PERFECT interpretation "he/she is gone" when used alone but the PERFECTIVE interpretation "he/she went" when used with a time adverbial specifying an interval considered as a point in time, e.g., *laas yia* "last year", or *yeside* "yesterday".

29. Kituba does not have adjectives, which makes it difficult to test the meaning "completely/thoroughly" assigned by Singler to constructions involving predicate adjectives, as in example (e), note 13.

30. Among the differences are, as noted above, the facts that NARRATIVE may not be used discourse-initially and is used almost exclusively with nonstative verbs.

31. This observation may not apply to all dialects of Kikongo, as I was reminded by Hazel Carter (p.c.).

32. Mufwene (1987) also addresses the question of why Kituba does not show as much restructuring as Atlantic PC's.

References

Anderson, Lloyd B. 1982. "The 'Perfect' as a Universal and as a Language-Specific Category". *Tense-Aspect: Between semantics and pragmatics* ed. by Paul J. Hopper, 227-64. Amsterdam and Philadelphia: John Benjamins.

Bailey, Beryl Loftman. 1966. *Jamaican Creole Syntax: A transformational approach*. Cambridge: University Press.

Bickerton, Derek. 1974. "Creolization, Linguistic Universals, Natural Semantax and the Brain". *Working Papers in Linguistics, University of Hawaii* 6(3).125-41. (Reprinted in *Issues in English Creoles* ed. by Richard R. Day 1980.1-18. Heidelberg: Groos.)

――――. 1975. *Dynamics of a Creole System*. Cambridge: University Press.
Bierwisch, Manfred. 1971. "On Classifying Semantic Features". *Semantics: An interdisciplinary reader in philosophy, linguistics, and psychology* ed. by D. Steinberg and L. A. Jakobovits, 410-35. Cambridge: University Press.
Chung, Sandra, and Alan Timberlake. 1985. "Tense, Aspect, and Mood". *Grammatical Categories and the Lexicon, Vol. 3: Language typology and syntactic description* ed. by Timothy Shopen, 202-58. Cambridge: University Press.
Comrie, Bernard. 1976. *Aspect: An introduction to the study of verbal aspect and related problems*. Cambridge: University Press.
――――. 1985. *Tense*. Cambridge: University Press.
Dahl, Östen. 1985. *Tense and Aspect Systems*. Oxford: Basil Blackwell.
Fehderau, Harold. 1966. *The Origin and Development of Kituba*. Ph.D. dissertation, Cornell University.
Martin, Robert. 1985. "Langage et temps *de dicto*". *Langue Française 67: La pragmatique des temps modaux*, ed. by C. Vet, 23-37. Paris: Larousse.
Maurer, Philippe. 1985. "Le système temporel du papiamento et le système temporel proto-créole de Bickerton". *Amsterdam Creole Studies* 8.41-66.
Mufwene, Salikoko S. 1978. "A Reconsideration of Lingala Temporal Inflections". *Studies in African Linguistics* 9.91-105.
――――. 1980. Review article of *The Ethnography of Variation: Selected writings on pidgins and creoles* by Hugo Schuchardt, edited and translated by T.L. Markey (Ann Arbor: Karoma, 1979). *Caribbean Journal of Education* 7.218-29.
――――. 1983a. "Observations on Time Reference in Jamaican and Guyanese Creoles". *Studies in Caribbean Language* ed. by Lawrence Carrington, 155-77. St. Augustine, Trinidad: Society for Caribbean Linguistics. (Revised version in *English World-Wide* 4.199-229. 1983.)
――――. 1983b. *Some Observations on the Verb in Black English Vernacular*. Austin: African and Afro-American Studies and Research Center, University of Texas.
――――. 1984. *Stativity and the Progressive*. Bloomington: Indiana University Linguistics Club.
――――. 1987. "Pidginization and Creolization: An evolutionary biology analogue". Lecture at Northwestern University.

————. 1988. "Formal Evidence of Pidginization/Creolization in Kituba". *Journal of African Languages and Linguistics* 10.33-51.

————. and Eyamba G. Bokamba. 1979. "Are There Modal-Auxiliaries in Lingala"? *Papers from the Fifteenth Regional Meeting of the Chicago Linguistic Society* ed. by Paul R. Clyne et al., 245-55. Chicago: Chicago Linguistic Society.

Ngalasso, Mwatha M. 1984. "Pidgins, créoles, ou koinés? A propos de quelques langues véhiculaires africaines". *Cahiers de l'Institut de Linguistique de Louvain* 9.135-61.

Reichenbach, Hans. 1947. *Elements of Symbolic Logic.* New York: Mac-Millan.

Samarin, William J. 1982a. "Colonization and Pidginization on the Ubangi River". *Journal of African languages and Linguistics* 4.1-42.

————. 1982b. "Goals, Roles, and Language Skills in Colonizing Central Equatorial Africa". *Anthropological Linguistics* 24.410-22.

Singler, John Victor. 1983. "Liberian English *feni*: AUX and ADV". Paper presented at the Annual Meeting of the Linguistic Society of America, Minneapolis.

Voorhoeve, Jan. 1957. "The Verbal System of Sranan". *Lingua* 6.374-96.

Youssef, Valerie. 1986. "The Emergence of the Aspectual Category of Perfect in Early Child Language in Trinidad". Paper presented at the Sixth Biennial Conference of the Society for Caribbean Linguistics, St. Augustine, Trinidad.

Tense, Mood, and Aspect in the Haitian Creole Preverbal Marker System[1]

Arthur K. Spears
The City College and The Graduate School
The City University of New York

During the past decade, a significant amount of work has appeared on French creoles generally and Haitian Creole (hereafter HC) particularly, and some of it has been concerned specifically with the verb system (Koopman and Lefebvre 1981, 1982; Magloire-Holly 1982; Piou 1982a, 1982b; Déchaine 1986; Déchaine and Lefebvre 1986). However, none of these recent works deal with the verbal system as a whole while focusing on tense, mood, and aspect.

In HC, tense, mood, and aspect (hereafter TMA) are expressed by means of two types of element in the verbal system. One kind, the principal concern of this article, is what is commonly referred to in the literature as a "preverbal marker". These are preverbal auxiliaries which meet the criteria typically advanced for auxiliaryhood, e.g. behavior as a unit with respect to syntactic and phonological rules; occurrence in second position in the sentence; inability to carry stress; and the expression of tense, mood, and/or aspect.

1. Semi-Auxiliaries

The other elements involved in the verbal expression of tense, mood, and aspect are what I will refer to, simply as a matter of convenience, as semi-auxiliaries. These function also as main verbs, so there is an important question as to whether they are always main verbs or whether there is a morphosyntactic basis for generating them in some cases as auxiliaries and in other cases as main verbs. In other words, whether all of the semi-auxiliaries are actually such from a morphosyntactic stándpoint remains to be determined.

In (1) are examples of some of the lexical items which might be included on a list of semi-auxiliaries:

(1) a. *Li **dwe**   te   pati.*
        3sg S-AUX ANT leave
        "She must have left".[2]
     b. ***Fòk**   li   pati.*
        S-AUX 3sg leave
        "She must leave".
     c. *Lòt   semenn nan pa **fouti**   peye l.*
        other week   DET NEG S-AUX pay 3sg
        "The other week, there's no way it can be paid".
     d. *Ou **mèt**   naje.*
        2sg S-AUX swim
        "You may (are permitted to) swim".
     e. *M **gen**   pou   m ale.*
        1sg S-AUX COMP 1sg go
        "I have to go".
     f. *M **gen dwa** ap   fè travay mwen . . .* (B.H105.1)
        1sg S-AUX   NPCT do work   1sg-POSS
        "I may be doing my work . . ."[3]
     g. *. . . w   ap   **plede** vin   anreta.*
           2sg NPCT S-AUX come late
        ". . . you're going to keep on coming late".

2. Preverbal Markers

2.1 *Introduction*

The auxiliary or preverbal marker system of Haitian has traditionally been described as tripartite, like that of other creoles, with the three TMA markers occurring in the order shown in Table 1:

Table 1

ANTERIOR	IRREALIS	NONPUNCTUAL
te	*ava*	*apr*
t	*av, va, a*	*ap, pr, ape*

The unreduced form of the marker is given on the first line of Table 1; the reduced form(s), on the second. With *apr*, one actually cannot consider *apr* or *ape* as a reduced form of the other; I have arbitrarily placed *apr* on the first line. *Te* may undergo vowel deletion when it precedes or follows a vowel. The full form *ava* is quite rare. Sylvain (1936) presents more tokens of it than any of the other grammars. In my data, it is almost non-existent.[4]

Allomorphs of the nonpunctual marker with /r/ occur only before the verb *ale* "go". The following examples show sentences with the full forms of the preverbal markers and some environments in which their phonological reduction may occur:

(2)   a. *Mwen te   pale avè l.*
          1sg   ANT talk with 3sg
          "I talked with him".

      b. *Mwen t   al avè l.*
          1sg   ANT go with 3sg
          "I went with her".

      c. *Mwen pa   t   pale avè l.*
          1sg   NEG ANT talk with 3sg
          "I didn't talk with her".

(3)   a. *L ava vin   doktè.*
      b. *Li va vin   doktè.*
      c. *L a   vin   doktè.*
          3sg IRR become doctor
          "She will become a doctor".

(4)   a. *M apr   al telefonen yon zami.*
      b. *M pr   al telefonen yon zami.*
          1sg NPCT go telephone ART friend
          "I'm going to telephone a friend".

      c. *M ap   pale ak   Mari.*
          1sg NPCT talk with Marie
          "I'm talking to Marie".

      d. *Ou p   ape fè   oun goud pa jou* . . . (CT203)
          2sg NEG NPCT make ART gourde per day
          "You're not going to make one gourde a day . . ."

2.2 *The Semantics of the Preverbal Markers*

In discussions of creole languages the semantic terms **anterior, irrealis**, and **nonpunctual** tend to be used in the sense established by Bickerton (1974, 1976, 1981). Bickerton has posited a "typical" or "classic" creole language preverbal marker system, one which he says that Haitian shares with several other creoles, among them Hawaiian Creole English, Guyanese Creole English, Sranan, and Saramaccan. For these languages, Bickerton says that the "ranges of meaning of the particles are identical" (1981:58). Since Bickerton's writings have had such an important impact on the field, it is necessary to cover in some detail the claims he has advanced concerning the preverbal markers, particularly since his claims concern the "typical" system, which Haitian supposedly has. His analysis, in other words, is a good starting point for the analysis of Haitian. Bickerton (1981) describes the meaning of the stem form of the verb as follows: the stem form of stative verbs expresses present tense, that of active (nonstative) verbs, past tense.

Bickerton (1981) describes the meaning of *te* as anterior, meaning that it marks past-before-past tense for active (nonstative) verbs and past for stative verbs (p. 58). In a footnote (fn. 5, p. 306), he acknowledges that the anterior-nonanterior distinction is "not an easy one for the naive speaker (i.e., anyone who does not speak a creole)" and refers readers to Bickerton (1975), Chapter 2. There he discusses anteriority in Guyanese Creole English. (As noted above, Bickerton claims elsewhere [1974] that Guyanese has the same preverbal marker semantics as Haitian.) He points out that difficulties arise in specifying the meaning of the anterior marker when it is used with active verbs (1975:35): while the anterior usually indicates past-before-past with such verbs, it sometimes signals remote past rather than past-before-past.

The crucial point to make in this connection, however, is that anterior tense markers mark a situation (event or state) as anterior to some reference time. Bickerton recognizes this in noting that an anterior "action does not have to be a 'past-before-past', since it could be regarded as both related and prior to a state of affairs at present in existence" (1981:46).

The meaning of the irrealis *va* is described by Bickerton (1981:58) as expressing the future and conditionals. He states more specifically (1976) that irrealis markers additionally express subjunctive mood, the gist of his remarks being that irrealis includes the three notions just mentioned (futurity, conditionality, and subjunctivity) and other related ones. Elsewhere (1975:42), he states that the irrealis system includes all situations (events and states) which have not actually occurred, whether these situations are expressed by the preverbal marker or by modals. This implies that those situations expressed by the irrealis preverbal marker lack reality, but not necessarily that the preverbal markers alone express all such situations; some are signaled by modals.

According to Bickerton, *ap*, the nonpunctual marker, expresses progressivity and habituality. Bickerton's specific comment is that this aspect marker expresses "progressive-durative plus habitual-iterative" (1981:58). These hyphenated terms muddle the issue since both progressives and habituals may be either durative (uninterrupted) or iterative (interrupted) (Comrie 1976). Observe the following English examples, which illustrate the distinctions:

(5)   a. *He is sitting motionless in the living room right now.* (progressive, durative)
      b. *He is hitting the nail with the hammer.* (progressive, iterative)
      c. *This statue used to stand in Central Park.* (habitual, durative)
      d. *He used to hit the bullseye.* (habitual, iterative)

It does appear, however, that Bickerton uses the pairs of terms as synonyms, i.e., progressive = durative, habitual = iterative. Thus, his claim can be interpreted rather straightforwardly as stating that the nonpunctual preverbal marker expresses progressive and habitual.

The preverbal system, including combinations of markers, is presented in Table 2. (It is adapted from Valdman 1977:177.) It should be pointed out that *pou*, claimed to be a preverbal marker in some works (Koopman and Lefebvre 1981, Sylvain 1936, Valdman 1978), is not considered in this discussion.

The semantics of the preverbal marker combinations, following Bickerton (1976, 1981), are mostly additive. So, for example, *t* + *ap* signals an anterior and nonpunctual, as the remarks above would indicate. The semantics of combinations involving *te* and *va* are not quite so transparent. These two in combination form not only the future-in-the-past, as in (6), as one might expect by "adding" the meanings of each marker, but also the conditional.

Table 2

	PUNCTUAL	NONPUNCTUAL	
	0	ap	NONANTERIOR
REALIS	te	t ap	ANTERIOR
	a	av ap	NONANTERIOR
IRREALIS	t a	t av ap	ANTERIOR

(6)   *M   te   di   m   t   a   pati.*
       1sg ANT say 1sg ANT IRR leave
       "I said that I would leave".

The semantics of the other combinations are straightforward, given what has been stated: *av ap* is basically a future progressive, and *t av ap* is a counterfactual conditional progressive. Concerning the counterfactual conditionals (progressive and nonprogressive), one should note that cross-linguistic patterns would lead one to expect — or at least not be surprised by — the formal identity of items marking the counterfactual and futurity-in-the-past.[5]

3. A Reanalysis of the Preverbal Marker System

In this section, I will present discussions indicating that the HC preverbal marker system differs from Bickerton's classic one. I will do so by discussing exceptions to his model.

3.1 *Ap,* *Va,* *T ap,* *and* *T a*

3.1.1 *Ap* *and* *Va* *as Futures*

It is quite clear that *ap* in HC is a future tense marker, in addition to its other semantic properties. It occurs in sentences such as the following:

(7) a. . . . *depi m jwenn oun ti   bagay, monchè,*
              after 1sg find   ART little thing my-friend
         m   ap   sove. (B.T45)
         1sg NPCT escape
         ". . . after I find another job, I'm going to quit".
     b. *Vant   a   ou ap   plen.* (C.H55.Ch)[6]
         stomach PREP 2sg NPCT full
         "Your stomach is going to be full".

All the major treatments of HC grammar agree on this. This use of *ap* is not, however, indicated by Bickerton's classic TMA system.

Va also serves as a future, and all treatments of HC grammar agree on this as well. They all agree also that in the negative, *va* never appears, but *ap* does instead. The sentences in (8) illustrate this.

(8) a. *N   a   rive.*
         1pl IRR arrive
         "We will arrive".
     b. *Nou p   ap   rive.* ([8a] negated)
         1pl   NEG NPCT arrive
         "We will not arrive".

Since both *va* and *ap* can be used as futures, a question arises as to whether there is any difference in meaning between them. Several grammarians have posited a difference, one that involves definiteness, with *ap* as a definite future and *va* indefinite. Further, native speakers, when asked what the difference is between the two, almost always say that *ap* expresses certainty, while *va* is less certain or is uncertain.

Valdman (1970:116) states that *ap* indicates the "near future," and expresses a situation "related to the present. To mark an action as clearly future we must use *a*". His remarks in Valdman (1978) are essentially the same. Hall (1943:31) states simply that *ap* marks the future in addition to its other uses. D'Ans characterizes *ap* as a near future generally and a general future after *pa*, where *va* is excluded.[7] Sylvain states that *ap* is used for

unfinished actions (1936:88) but provides several examples which she translates into French with *aller* ("going to") futures and simple futures, with the
future verbal suffix. She characterizes *va* simply as a future (p. 86).

I intend to expand and refine the claims about these two markers as
futures as well as *t a* and *t ap*, using as supporting evidence an analysis of a
conversational text. This analysis confirms that certainty and "near futurity" are among the notions distinguishing these two future markers but goes
further and asserts that in fact these two notions are minor characters in a
more complex drama. In the next section, I will describe the methodology
used in the analysis of all four markers, and in the section following that I
will present the results regarding their semantics.

3.1.2 *Methodology*

The pragmatic analysis of *ap* and *va* as futures along with *t a* and *t ap*
was based on a transcript of one and one-half hours of tape-recorded conversations. The conversational group consisted of two female and four male
HC speakers residing in the U.S. They range in age from early twenties to
mid-thirties. All left Haiti either in their late teens or as adults. They are all
originally from northern Haiti: Port de Paix, Cap Haïtien (both northern
coastal cities), and Ile de la Tortue, an island off the coast from Port de
Paix. The setting of the conversation is naturalistic in that the speakers
were doing something they normally do, having a communal dinner. In
many parts of the conversation, they are performing social work, e.g. urg-
ing people to go ahead and eat, to eat as much as they want, and the like.
One of the participants was responsible for making the recording and pulling the conversation out of lulls. The conversation transcript is
supplemented by elicited data provided by native speakers. (Elicited sentences are either not followed by a reference code in parentheses or have an
"E" as the second letter in the reference code.)

Since *ap* is used as a nonfuture also, tokens expressing the future had
to be separated from others. This presents some problems; in some cases, it
cannot be determined from context whether it is signaling future tense or
not. Such cases account for fewer than 5 percent of the total number of
tokens, however; and they were excluded from the analysis.[8]

A major problem with quantitative semantic studies is replicability.
This is true because so much hinges on how often different researchers will
be able to classify specific tokens in the same way, based on factors of
meaning and form. The occurrence of a form is determined by the meaning

a speaker wishes to convey and/or the formal (phonological, lexical, syntactic) context in which it appears. With formal factors, which are typically objective, there is little problem. But, when factors of meaning are involved, there is often disagreement. In this study, the problem was partially solved because formal factors allow one in some cases to predict which preverbal marker will occur. In some cases, the occurrence of the markers is lexically and syntactically predictable. These environments are also compatible with the meanings posited for the markers.

In other cases, there are no objective cues that can be used in replicating a particular study, more specifically, the assignment of a specific contextual meaning to a specific token. Replicability is also a function of how well terms have been defined and environments specified. However, the real point is that in doing a pragmatic analysis of a text, one can hope only to produce a coherent, explicit theory of the meaning of the forms under consideration. This theory should explain the actual uses of these forms, and explain when they are not used. In other words, this Jakobsonian approach should attempt to provide a *gesamtbedeutung*, or general meaning. In some cases, this may not be possible; all one can provide is a *hauptbedeutung*, or basic meaning, i.e. the primary meaning which accounts for many or most uses of a form. Of course, part of the problem in searching out a general meaning is avoiding simply providing a label that arbitrarily covers a wastebasket-full of specific notions. One's best guide is facts from a range of languages; semantic notions tend to travel together. Any findings for HC, then, should recall form/meaning relationships in other languages.

3.1.3 *Findings*

As implied above, the notion of definiteness, combining the subnotions of near futurity and certainty (which to some extent are mutually implicative), provides a very rough description of the semantics of *ap* and *va*. In this description, *ap* would be definite (marking near futurity and/or certainty), *va* indefinite.

The result of the pragmatic analysis was to provide a more adequate characterization of what distinguishes *ap* from *va* as futures and what distinguishes *t ap* from *t a*. (The last two both serve as futures-in-the-past and conditionals, but there are some meanings that they do not share, e.g. *t ap* is also an anterior nonpunctual.) The hypothesis in undertaking the study was that the semantic difference between *ap* and *va*, on the one hand, and *t ap* and *t a*, on the other, is parallel. This hypothesis was borne out: the *ap* forms (*ap* and *t ap*) are indicative mood, and the *va* forms (*va* and *t a*) are subjunctive.

In presenting a more adequate description, I will first define indicative mood for HC. Afterwards, I will present some reasons for having chosen this label instead of certain others. Finally, I will present supporting data.

Indicative mood in HC refers to the communication by a speaker of a situation as one which is normal or unremarkable — there is no need or desire to question its truth or to provide emotive information (such as surprise) regarding one's acceptance of its truth. In other words, the situation communicated by the speaker is accepted, or at least put forth to be considered as a fact, as true, without any expressed qualification that the situation has occurred, is occurring, or will occur. Furthermore, the situation is communicated in a direct, literal way and is not unexpected; in other words, the mind is prepared for it (Slobin and Aksu 1982). This, then, is what is communicated in the clause in which the indicative form occurs.[9]

If we can imagine a mood scale, the two indicative forms (*ap* and *t ap*) cover those modal subnotions which are subsumed under indicative mood in the sense elaborated above. The two subjunctive forms cover the rest of the scale. The meanings of the indicative forms, then, do not overlap with those of the subjunctive forms.

Another way of stating this is that the HC indicative is used in communicating situations which are **presupposed**, i.e. assumed to be facts, or **asserted**, i.e. merely communicated as facts (Hooper 1975). Table 3 shows approximately the range of modal subnotions expressed by each form:

Table 3

Ap — Indicative	*Va* — Subjunctive
Factive	Desiderative
Assertive	Purposive
	Hypothetical
	Counterfactive
	Resistant

Direct	Polite
Expected	Unexpected
Certain	Uncertain
	Dubitative
Literal	Figurative (e.g. joking)

For each of the moods, the subnotions under the line in Table 3 may more appropriately be thought of as pragmatic consequences of the core meanings, which are above the line. In any case, the characterization of the two moods will be considered as including all the notions in Table 3.

Bickerton's term **irrealis** is ostensibly as apt a term as **subjunctive**. However, in using the term, Bickerton did not realize that *ap* expresses futurity, not just *va*. The indicative/subjunctive distinction acknowledges the two futures and distinguishes between them. If *va* is to be labeled irrealis, it would seem straightforward to label *ap* realis. The problem, though, would be that *ap* as a future marker has patently irrealis properties. Thus, to label it realis would be unnecessarily misleading. Furthermore, Bickerton was apparently unaware that HC has two conditionals, not only *t a* but also *t ap*. The same problem exists for *t ap* and *t a* in using the terms realis and irrealis; conditionals containing *t ap* (as well as conditionals containing *t a*) refer to unreal, irrealis, situations. For these reasons, I have not used realis/irrealis. (Bickerton does use *subjunctive*, among other terms, to describe the meaning of *va*.)

While the indicative/subjunctive opposition exists in many languages, one reservation might arise about using it in HC. This reservation has to do with the fact that subjunctives in many languages are used for factives, whereas in HC they are not.[10] But on the other hand, there are languages which have both indicative and subjunctive forms and whose indicative mood subsumes factivity (e.g. English, with some exceptions). The indicative/subjunctive distinction I posit for HC, then, is not exactly equivalent to that found in certain other languages. However, this distinction in HC fits within the range of indicative/subjunctive distinctions found in other languages, matching some more closely than others (see Palmer 1986). Typological studies generally recognize explicitly that we find in many languages forms which are roughly equivalent semantically, enough so to warrant using one universal semantic term to label their meanings (e.g. Comrie 1976).

3.1.4 *Uses of the Subjunctive Forms,* **Va** *and* **T a**

In this section I present the specific usages found for *va* and *t a*. (Remember that *a* and *va* are allmorphs of the same morpheme, the full form of which is *ava*. What I refer to as *va* in this section is sometimes realized as *va*, sometimes as *a*, and sometimes as *av*.) There is considerable overlap in the contexts in which both forms occur. The facts are not yet fully clear.

One possibility is that *va* can occur wherever *t a* can occur and vice-versa, with *t a* expressing subjunctive notions more strongly. A second, perhaps more likely, possibility is that each form is exclusive in some environments, but both may occur in others. Whatever the exact relationship between *t a* and *va*, it may be complicated by a rule of *te* deletion that applies to *te ava* (*t a*) and leaves *va*.

After the discussion of the subjunctive forms, I will present and discuss data from *ap* and *t ap*, the indicative forms.

3.1.4.1 *Desiderative.* These occurrences of *t a* and *va* express a desired or hoped for situation in an attenuated or polite way. They can involve various types of predicates expressing a desire, e.g., *vle* "want", *renmen* "like", *espere* "hope", and *kontan* "happy".

(9) a. *M espere ke piti mwen an a vin doktè.*
 1sg hope COMP child 1sg DET IRR come doctor
 (CE11.93)
 "I hope that my child will become a doctor".[11]

The desiderative sense can also extend to verbs more generally in which case the predicate of liking or desiring is implicit, as in (10).

(10) *Ou konnen, m t av achte kay la.* (CT271.6L)
 2sg know 1sg ANT IRR buy house DET
 "I'd like to buy this house".

3.1.4.2 *Resistance.* The resistance under consideration refers to a resistance to accepting the reality or truth of what some clause expresses. *Va* expresses less resistance and *t a* more, the greater resistance in the latter case a consequence of the condition that is either implicitly or explicitly present. With both *va* and *t a* occurring in conditions, the distinction between them is roughly equivalent to that between *will/would* in English conditionals, a distinction illustrated in (11).

(11) a. *If you mow the lawn, I'll give you $5.*
 b. *If you mowed the lawn, I would give you $5.*

The types of resistance include the attentuation of belief or conviction; thus skepticism, doubt, or uncertainty is expressed, as in (12):

(12) *se sa fe m se oun moun, m t a panse,*
 it-COP that make 1sg it-COP ART person 1sg ANT IRR think

m   se   oun moun m ka   pran lajan . . . (CT216.4T)
1sg it-COP ART person 1sg be-able take money
"That's why I'm a person, I would think, I'm a person who could take money . . ."

The speaker certainly does not fully believe this. The parenthetical with *panse* "think" conveys the resistance.

Resistance may also involve surprise, amazement, or unexpectedness, as in (13).

(13) *Kounye-a m tande i   di m l   a   ban m . . .*
     now   1sg hear 3sg say 1sg 3sg IRR give 1sg
     venn   senk goud . . . (CT202.2.F)
     twenty five gourde
     "Now I hear him tell me he'll give me . . . (a raise to) $5 (per hour) . . ."

The speaker finds this raise almost too good to be true, and he notes that he would have been hard pressed to make a dollar a day in Haiti. Notice that the boss, if he spoke in HC, would surely have used *ap* to make it clear he was serious. Observe that the speaker has no reason to question or not believe his boss, so there appears to be a sound basis for distinguishing between surprise/amazement/unexpectedness and attenuated belief/commitment/conviction.

Possibility — the attenuated assertion of truth — can also be expressed. This is the case in (14).

(14) *Pou   nou met tèt   ansamn pou   nou wè si n   a   fè*
     COMP 1pl put head together COMP 1pl see if 1pl IRR do
     oun aktivite mache nan peyi   a,   monchè. (CT9.2,3T)
     ART activity work in   country DET my-dear
     "We should get ourselves together in order to see if we can make something work in Haiti, my friend".

The speaker is referring to the possibility of making something work; thus, the subjunctive is called for.

Va or *t a* sometimes attenuates a directive, the use of one of them signifying politeness (cf. Valdman 1970:116):

(15) *W a   rele m, w a   telefonen m . . .* (CT78.2)
     2sg IRR call 1sg 2sg IRR telephone 1sg
     "You call me, you telephone me . . ."

In contrast to (15) is the sentence in (16):

> (16) *M   pa   vle   Nani konn baay sa   yo menm.* (CT54.3C)
> 1sg NEG want Nani know thing DET PL same
> "I don't want Nani to know these things".

In (16) there is no *va* or *t a* before *vle*: the speaker certainly does not want Nani to know. Consequently, neither politeness nor softening is appropriate. A second type of attenuated directive conveys a type of exhortation: a pragmatic gloss for such sentences would be something such as "You should do this because it is necessary/urgent/important" or "It would make me happy if you did this". (17) illustrates this type of attenuated directive:

> (17) *I   nesese   pou   ou t   a   rive   demen.* (CE8.62)
> 3sg necessary COMP 2sg ANT IRR leave tomorrow
> "It would be/is necessary for you to leave tomorrow".

3.1.4.3 *Other Uses of* **Va** *and* **T a**.   The remaining ranges of use of *va* and *t a* are identified in each case with one of the two markers in particular (though the deletability of *te* in *t a* constructions muddies the distinction once more). The first of these involves figurative uses, and it is identified with *va*. An example of this is given in (18).

> (18) . . . *m   a   ba   ou oun disyonè.* (CT232.4.L)
> 1sg IRR give 2sg ART dictionary
> ". . . I'll give you a dictionary".

One of the men had asked where another found such sweet words to use in courting women. The speaker answers that the person in question got them from the dictionary and that he will give the questioner one so that he can find some good words for himself. The speaker clearly is not serious.

One usage which may be exclusive with *t a* involves purposive clauses introduced by the complementizer *pou*, e.g. (19). Similarly, a relative clause or complement clause on a nonspecific NP, e.g. (20), seems to take *t a* exclusively as well.

> (19) *Ou p   ape   fè oun goud   pa jou Ayiti, pou   ou t*
> 2sg NEG NPCT do ART gourde per day Haiti COMP 2sg ANT
> *a   mande pou   ou fè oun goud   pa jou . . .*
> IRR ask   COMP 2sg do ART gourde per day (CT203.5T)
> "You're not going to (i.e. can't) make one gourde a day in Haiti, for you to ask (i.e., to have asked, when you were in Haiti) to make one gourde a day . . ."

It is not entirely clear, but the *t a* in (19) is probably to be interpreted as a anterior tense subjunctive since, if this example is non-anterior, the *t a* would signal a weakness and/or politeness which seems quite unnecessary.

(20) *Men, m pa t   bay okazyon pou   i   t   a*
     but 1sg NEG ANT give occasion COMP 3sg ANT IRR
     di   sa . . . (CT187.7C)
     say that
     "But I didn't give her any reason to say that . . ."

Because *di* "say" refers to past time, this is another example of an anterior subjunctive (assuming that [19] is an anterior subjunctive).

Finally, *t a* (and *va* also) may occur in *si* clauses that refer to a future situation, as in (21). (In *si* clauses of conditional sentences, *te* by itself occurs in counterfactuals only.)

(21) *Menm si i   t   a   mouv, gwoup la   pa   t   ap   tonbe,*
     but   if 3sg ANT IRR move group DET NEG ANT IRR fall
     non, gwoup la   ap   toujou mache . . . (CT1955.5T)
     no   group DET NPCT always move
     "Even if he moves, the group won't dissolve; the group will always keep on going . . ."

(21) has to be interpreted as hypothetical rather than counterfactual since everyone known that the person referred to has said he will move and is undoubtedly able to.

3.1.5 *Uses of the Indicative Forms,* **Ap** *and* **T ap**

Subjunctives, as pointed out above, are used for a range of meanings clustering around desideration and resistance. Indicatives present a situation in a matter-of-fact way. The practical effect of the use of indicatives is in virtually all cases to convey certainty. Examples of this are given in (22)-(24).

(22) *Monchè, oun lè   m panse ke   tout bagay ap   fini.*
     my-dear ART hour 1sg think COMP all thing NPCT finish
     (CT15.3.T)
     "I think all that is going to end one day".

The conversation was recorded in 1981. The speaker is referring to the regime of Jean-Claude Duvalier, still in power at the time. In her mind, the demise of the Duvalier government is certain. She gives several reasons in the conversation why the regime cannot go on much longer.

> (23) . . . *an tou ka men sa k genyen, m ap lapriye.*
> in all case but that REL have 1sg NPCT pray
> (CT21.1T)
> ". . . regardless, I'm going to pray".

In (23) the introductory phrase itself, which translates as "regardless, in any case," is a marker of certainty.

> (24) *M t ap mande kòman li t ap . . . kòman*
> 1sg ANT NPCT ask how 3sg ANT NPCT how
> *l apr ale la a.* (CT195.2,3F)
> 3sg NPCT go there DET
> "I was asking him . . . how he was going to move".

(24) involves a future-in-the-past construction. The move in question is certain: the person under discussion has already been accepted to study in another city.

3.2 *Ap and T ap, Markers of Progressive and Habitual Aspect*

Bickerton's claims lead us to expect that *ap* is progressive in aspect. The issue of *ap*'s progressivity, however, requires some comment because the major, i.e. most useful, references for Haitian Creole, with the exception of d'Ans (1978) and Lefebvre et al. (1982), do not label it as such. The two studies labeling it thus do so without comment. One should also note, in fairness, that these references, not having a major concern with aspect, are not concerned with the details focused on in this writing. Among the major (general) references on HC, I am including, in addition to d'Ans, Valdman (1970, 1978), Sylvain (1936), and Hall (1953). My goal in the following discussion is to justify the use of the term **progressive** to label the semantic content of *ap* and to elaborate on some details related to *ap*'s occurrence with stative predicates.

I will follow Comrie in making a distinction between the following aspectual notions: **imperfective, habitual, continuous**, and **progressive**. **Imperfectivity** expresses a situation that is ongoing. It can be divided into habitual and continuous. **Habituality** classifies a situation as being

> . . . characteristic of an extended period of time, so extended in fact that the situation referred to is viewed not as an incidental property of the moment but, precisely, as a characteristic feature of a whole period" (Comrie 1976:27-8).

A clear sense of what habituality expresses can be gained best by considering sentences with forms that are semantically habitual, that is, which always express habituality. An example of such a form is the English *used to*:

(25) *Republicans used to have a large Black constituency.*

(26) #*Harry used to be eating the apple you see over there.*

(26) is crosshatched to mark its anomaly. A specific apple would not stay around long enough for the eating of it to characterize an entire period.

Continuous consists of ongoing situations other than habitual ones. These are of two types, either **progressive** or **stative**. As indicated by the examples in (5) above, habituals and progressives alike can be either durative or iterative. **Durative** means that the situation is uninterrupted; the situation is in effect at all times. **Iterative** means the opposite: the situation is interrupted. Thus, **situation** may actually refer to a series of situations that are considered as one situation-unit or event-unit. Thus, if one says *I'm coughing* in English, the situation actually referred to is one composed of several situations taken as subparts of one inclusive situation. The situation referred to in this case is necessarily iterative because the verb *to cough* is essentially **punctual**: it is conceived of as having no duration in time. Since this situation is iterative, it is therefore not durative, i.e. not uninterrupted.

As for **progressivity**, it differs from continuousness in that it is the combination of continuousness with nonstativity (Comrie 1976:35). Stated differently, progressivity does not co-occur with stativity; stative predicates in a language with progressive forms cannot occur in the progressive in the normal case. Thus, for example, the sentences with stative verbs in (27) are ungrammatical because these verbs are in the Progressive form. (Following Comrie, the names of verb forms in particular languages are capitalized, while semantic terms for various types of aspect are not):

(27) a. **John is knowing the answer.*
      b. **John is owning the house.*
      c. **John is being six feet tall.*

As Comrie, Bickerton (1975), and others have noted, the set of stative verbs varies from language to language. There is clearly a core meaning for the term; thus, the set of stative verbs in any one language will have something in common semantically with those in all other languages. It must also be noted that the stative/nonstative distinction is not a discrete one; rather, there is a continuum linking the two (Sag 1973).

Table 4 shows the relationships among the aspectual notions I have discussed:[12]

Table 4

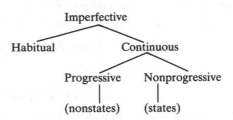

Ap must be classified as progressive; it does not (save one exceptional case) occur with statives except to impart an indicative future reading. Thus, a (present tense) sentence with a stative predicate such as *konnen* "know" is inadmissible in HC as its counterpart is in English:

(28) **m   ap   konnen ke   li   te   pati.*
      1sg PROG know   COMP 3sg ANT leave
      *"I am knowing that he left".

The special case is that involving predicates which would be expressed by COPULA + ADJ in English and French such as *be rich*. In this case, *ap* combines with the predicate and signals a processual state; it expresses a situation of becoming, as in (29):

(29) *m   t   ap   rich.*
      1sg ANT PROG rich
      "I was becoming/getting rich".

The contexts in which *ap* can occur in HC and the resulting meanings are parallel or at least very nearly so to those described by Corne (1981) for Ile-de-France Creole (IF). Roughly, his claim is that *pe*, the IF analog of *ap*, combines with predicates expressing processual states to signal becoming (as in [29]), while they do not combine with those expressing "pure" states. The two cases are illustrated in (30):[13]

(30) a. *i   pe   malad*. (PROCESS) (Corne 1981:105)
         3sg PROG sick
         "He is getting sick".

b. *i   pe   bet.   (STATE)
3sg PROG stupid
"He is (getting) stupid".

Previous studies of HC have not made explicit that, while *ap* is progressive (and therefore cannot co-occur with ordinarily stative predicates), it can occur with "processual statives". That is, there are exceptions to the general prohibition against stative predicates occurring with progressive aspect markers.[14] Magloire-Holly (1982:102-3) notes the non-co-occurrence of *ap* with statives generally but does not comment on the special status of processual statives. (There are times when *ap* does co-occur with statives other than processual ones, but it is my claim that in such cases they can only have a future meaning.)

Of the works considered, only in d'Ans is it made clear that *ap* may also express habituality. To this, one may add that *ap* is pragmatically durative or iterative. D'Ans provides the following example of *ap* being used habitually:

(31) *L-ap   vini.*
3sg-NPCT come
"He is always coming".

Unfortunately, no contextual justification for the habitual gloss is provided.

To reiterate, *ap* expresses both habitual and progressive aspect. One important question which I will not treat here is whether *ap* habituals are of a different type from zero verb form habituals, which, contrary to Bickerton's model, occur frequently in HC.

I have concentrated on *ap*, but what concerns *ap* in terms of aspect applies to *t ap* in its aspectual use, viz., anterior nonpunctual.

4. Conclusion

I have argued that the actual HC preverbal marker system differs significantly from that represented by Bickerton's "classic" system. I have not dealt at length with the zero verb or *t av ap*, but these two forms are discussed below in the summary of preverbal marker semantics. Specifically, I have put forward the following points:

1. *Ap* is used for nonpunctuals, i.e. habitual and progressive aspect, but also for indicative futures. Further, because *te* is subject optionally to deletion in most if not all environments where *t ap* occurs, this means that

ap also can express most if not all of the range of meanings expressed by *t ap* (see below). The following examples illustrate *te* deletion with conditionals:[15]

>   (32) a. Conditional with *te* present in both clauses
>   *Si m te etidye, m t ap konnen.*
>   if 1sg ANT study 1sg ANT NPCT know
>   "If I had studied, I would know".
>   b. Conditional with *te* deleted from both clauses
>   *Si m etidye, m ap konnen.*
>   if 1sg study 1sg NPCT know
>   "If I had studied, I would know".

In Bickerton's model, *ap* is not a future tense marker, nor does it occur in conditionals.

2. *Va* is used for subjunctive futures or simply as a subjunctive marker (e.g. in anterior subjunctives). Some occurrences of *va* may represent underlying *te va*'s that have undergone *te* deletion. The details of how *va* compares with *t a* semantically remain to be uncovered.

3. *T ap* is used for anterior nonpunctuals (i.e. anterior progressives and habituals), indicative futures-in-the-past, and indicative conditionals.

4. *T a* is used for subjunctive futures-in-the-past, anterior subjunctives, and subjunctive conditionals.

5. Zero verb forms are significantly different from what Bickerton claims. Specifically, their range of uses is considerably broader. In keeping with Bickerton's assertions, they are used to express present tense with stative verbs and past tense with active verbs. But they are also used to express present tense with active verbs, e.g. present habituality, and also present continuousness. (33) provides an example of the latter, particularly when it is uttered while the speaker is trying to convince the addressee of the truth of his or her claims.

>   (33) *M di ou se vre.*
>   1sg say 2sg it-COP true
>   "I tell/am telling you it's true".

It is particularly noteworthy that zero verb forms mark habitual aspect and future tense. That they mark habitual aspect is a point made by all the major grammars of HC, and zero habituals are not in any way rare in texts. These facts, taken together, indicate that the general meaning of zero verb forms is more like that of an aorist, in the sense the zero form signals reference to a situation pure and simple, with no further specification with respect to TMA.[16] In brief, the various meanings that the zero form may express are determined by context.

6. *Te* marks anterior tense and, optionally, occurs in the hypostasis of conditionals. Bickerton does not point out the second of these functions, although it is certainly compatible with his model.

7. *Av ap*'s semantics seem to be straightforwardly combinatorial in line with preceding discussions of *av* and *ap*. Specifically, *ap* adds the meaning of nonpunctuality to whatever meaning *va* is expressing in a particular context.

8. My data contain no occurrences of *t av ap*, although I have elicited it from a number of native speakers. (Verb forms with all three markers are generally considered to occur only in the most radical creoles, those which have least undergone decreolization.) In line with the foregoing discussions, this form should be used for nonpunctual futures-in-the-past and nonpunctual conditionals. My experience has been that it is difficult if not impossible to elicit it from speakers under thirty, regardless of how little time they have spent in the U.S. From native speakers, I have received the following claim: in some areas, e.g., Cap Haïtien, speakers use *t ap* for *t av ap*. Consequently, there is one form to do the work of both. In other areas, both forms are still used.

Notes

1.   The research presented here was supported in part by grants from the University of California, Santa Cruz, and the Professional Staff Congress of the City University of New York. I would like to give a special thanks to those who served as consultants.

2.   The IPN orthography for HC, the official orthography, is used throughout except where examples are taken from other works, in which case the author's notation will be used. Often, several straightforward English glosses are possible; ordinarily, I provide only one. Orthographic conventions with regard to the treatment of contracted forms such as preverbal markers and pronouns seem not to have stabilized. However, combinations of preverbal markers are usually written as one word. *Pa* "not" preceding one or more preverbal markers is written with those markers if *pa* is contracted or if the following marker is, e.g. *pat* "NEG ANT". For the convenience of the reader, I have left spaces between all morphemes.

3.   **Nonpunctual** (NPCT) is Bickerton's term for markers that signal habituality and progressivity.

4.   My recorded data, on which these comments are based, represent at least three easily distinguishable dialect areas (the cities of Port de Paix, Cap Haïtien, and Port au Prince).

One might well assume that patterns of phonological reduction are more predictable within one dialect area. In cases in which data presented in this study come from published works, the source will be indicated. Native speaker judgments come from students who have taken my courses at The City College, CUNY; taxi drivers (many of whom are Haitian in New York); colleagues; and acquaintances.

5.   For example, *would* in English serves to mark future-in-the-past, e.g., *Last week, I said I would leave yesterday*, and conditionals, e.g., *If I were you, I would leave now*.

6.   In some northern dialects of HC, possession is indicated by the sequence Possessed NP-*a*-Possessor NP, *a* being a preposition. In the Port-au-Prince dialect, the possessed NP is followed directly by the possessor NP. This speaker is from Ile de la Tortue.

7.   Curiously, d'Ans labels *va* as a certain future ("futur assuré"), one which cannot be denied (1978:125-6). This is a characterization of *va* that goes against what the others say about it.

8.   Also excluded from analysis were the following types of token:
     (1) instances in which *ap* appeared with the negative *pa*. (Because only *ap* co-occurs with the negative, the distinction between *ap* and *va* is neutralized in this environment.)
     (2) tokens of *va* before a word beginning with /p/. Since *va* is typically realized as *a*, one cannot always determine before a /p/-initial word which marker is involved.
     (3) tokens of *apr ale* ("go") + V, which were treated as instances of a third future form, *apr ay*; *ay* is a northern dialect form of *ale*. The investigation of this form remains for future research.
     (4) tokens occurring before a semi-auxiliary; it seems that semi-auxiliaries may alter the relationships among, and the functions of, the various markers.

9.   This definition might seem to exclude the presence of the indicative mood in questions, but questions too can be accounted for if they are thought of as consisting of a declarative sentence modified by a question about it. (i) shows this; (ii) presents the corresponding sentence with *va*. In both cases an elaborated English gloss is presented as a way of illustrating the differences between the two.
     (i)   *sa   n   ap   fè?*
           what 1pl AP do
           "(We will do something; what?) = What will we do?"
     (ii) *sa   n   a   fè?*
           what 1pl VA do
           "(We may/might/could do something; what?) = What might we do?"

10. For example, in Spanish:
     (i)   *Siento   que   no   lo   hayas   visto.*
           regret-1sg COMP NEG 3sg-masc PERFECT-SUBJ-2sg see-PST.PPL
           "I regret that you didn't see it".

11. I would predict that sentences with *t a* in main and embedded clauses also occur, e.g.
     (i)   *M t   a   espere ke   piti mwen an   t   a   vin   dokté*
           1sg ANT IRR hope COMP child 1sg   DET ANT IRR become doctor
           "I would hope that my child would become a doctor".

12. This table is an adaptation of Comrie's Table I (1976:25).

13. Corne is apparently referring to permanent states with his term "pure" states. His statement is certainly reasonable, but one wonders how permanence is determined in the grammar of that language: why could not "becoming stupid" be considered a process?

14. There are also exceptions to this general prohibition in English (Spears 1977, Smith 1983), e.g., *Our foreign exchange students are knowing more and more English upon arrival.*

15. Note again that *te* may also be present in only one of the clauses, either the hypostasis or the apodosis.

16. It might seem upon first consideration that zero verb forms should all be indicative mood. However, zero verb forms, both finite (with an overt subject) and nonfinite, occur in nonindicative contexts. Note the following:

    (i)   *M   t   a   byen kontan pou   ou fè sa   pou mwen.*

          1sg ANT IRR   well happy COMP 2sg do that for 1sg

          "I would be quite happy for you to do that for me".

References

d'Ans, André-Marcel. 1978. *Le Créole Français d'Haïti*. The Hague: Mouton.

Bickerton, Derek. 1974. "Creolization, Linguistic Universals, Natural Semantax and the Brain". *University of Hawaii Working Papers in Linguistics* 6(3).125-41. (Reprinted in *Issues in English Creoles: Papers from the 1975 Hawaii conference* ed. by Richard Day 1980.1-18. Heidelberg: Groos.)

————. 1975. *Dynamics of a Creole System*. Cambridge: University Press.

————. 1976. "Creole Tense-Aspect Systems and Universal Grammar". Paper presented at the Conference of the Society for Caribbean Linguistics: New Directions in Creole Studies, Georgetown, Guyana.

————. 1981. *Roots of Language*. Ann Arbor: Karoma.

————. 1984. "Creoles and Universal Grammar: The unmarked case?" Colloquium paper presented at the Annual Meeting of the Linguistic Society of America, Baltimore.

Comrie, Bernard. 1976. *Aspect: An introduction to the study of verbal aspect and related problems*. Cambridge: University Press.

Corne, Chris. 1981. "A Re-evaluation of the Predicate in Ile-de-France Creole". *Generative Studies on Creole Languages* ed. by Pieter Muysken, 103-24. Dordrecht: Foris.

Déchaine, Rose-Marie. 1986. "Opérations sur les Structures d'Arguments: Le cas des constructions sérielles en haïtien". Lefebvre et al. 1986.12-108.

Déchaine, Rose-Marie, and Claire Lefebvre. 1986. "The Grammar of Serial Constructions". Lefebvre et al. 1986.471-99.

Hall, Robert A., Jr. 1953. *Haitian Creole* (=*Memoirs of the American Folklore Society*, 43.) Philadelphia: American Folklore Society.

Hooper, Joan B. 1975. "On Assertive Predicates". *Syntax and Semantics 4* ed. by John Kimball, 92-125. New York: Academic Press.

Koopman, Hilda and Claire Lefebvre. 1981. "Haitian Creole Pu". *Generative Studies on Creole Languages* ed. by Pieter Muysken, 201-22. Dordrecht: Foris.

――――. 1982. "Pu: Marqueur de mode, préposition et complémenteur". Lefebvre et al. 1982.64-91.

Lefebvre, Claire, Hélène Magloire-Holly and Nanie Piou, eds. 1982. *Syntaxe de l'Haïtien*. Ann Arbor: Karoma.

Lefebvre, Claire, Jonathan Kaye, et al. 1986. *Projet Fon-Créole Haïtien: Etudes syntaxiques, morphologiques et phonologiques*. (Research report.) L'Université du Québec à Montréal.

Magloire-Holly, Hélène. 1982. "Les Modaux: Auxiliaires ou verbes?" Lefebvre et al. 1982.92-121.

Palmer, F.R. 1986. *Mood and Modality*. Cambridge: University Press.

Piou, Nanie. 1982a. "Le Clivage du Prédicat". Lefebvre et al. 1982.122-51.

――――. 1982b. "Le Redoublement Verbal". Lefebvre et al. 1982.152-66.

Sag, Ivan. 1973. "On the State of Progress on Progressives and Statives". *New Ways of Analyzing Variation in English* ed. by Charles-James N. Bailey and Roger W. Shuy, 83-95. Washington: Georgetown University Press.

Smith, Carlota S. 1983. "A Theory of Aspectual Choice". *Lg* 59.479-501.

Slobin, Dan I. and Ayhan A. Aksu. 1982. "Tense, Aspect and Modality in the Use of the Turkish Evidential". *Tense-Aspect: Between Semantics and Pragmatics* ed. by Paul Hopper, 185-99. Amsterdam and Philadelphià: John Benjamins.

Spears, Arthur K. 1977. "The Semantics of English Complementation", Ph.D. dissertation, University of California, San Diego.

Sylvain, Suzanne, 1936. *Le Créole Haïtien: Morphologie et syntaxe*. Wetteren, Belgium: Imprimerie de Meester.

Valdman, Albert. 1970. *Basic Course in Haitian Creole* (=Indiana University Publications, Language Science Monographs, 5.) Bloomington: Indiana University.

――――. 1977. "Creolization: Elaboration in the development of Creole French dialects". *Pidgin and Creole Linguistics* ed. by Albert Valdman, 155-89. Bloomington, IN: Indiana University Press.

――――. 1978. *Le Créole: Structure, statut et origine*. Paris: Klincksieck.

Tense and Aspect in Capeverdean Crioulo[1]

Izione S. Silva

The Republic of Cape Verde differs from many areas where a pidgin or a creole language is spoken. It did not have a native population when discovered by the Portuguese in 1460. But soon thereafter, Portuguese nobility and peasants along with African slaves began settlement of the largest of the nine presently inhabited islands. Thus started the first phase of Capeverdean society and its language, Capeverdean Crioulo.

Geographically and linguistically, this West African archipelago is divided into two major groups — Barlavento (windward) and Sotavento (leeward). Capeverdean Crioulo developed in the Sotavento region and subsequently spread to the Barlavento area. In this chapter I will analyze the Sotavento dialect; it is older and more basilectal than the Barlavento dialect.[2] I will use Derek Bickerton's paradigm to describe the Capeverdean tense-aspect system and then compare the Capeverdean system to Bickerton's "classic" one.

1. Tense and Aspect

Tense refers to the way temporal relations are expressed in language. Quirk and Greenbaum describe tense as the "correspondence between the form of the verb and our concept of time" (1975:40). Since the concept of time varies from one cultural group to another, the expression of tense may also vary between such groups. Aspect, on the other hand, is concerned with "the manner in which the verbal action is experienced or regarded" (Quirk and Greenbaum, p. 45). Thus, when considering time designation in a particular language, one must specify not only the time of occurrence of a situation but also whether it may be regarded as continuous, completive, habitual, iterative, or the like.

The linguistic literature does not always make clear the difference between tense and aspect, even in a language as well studied as English. As Comrie states, "the distinction between *he read, he was reading*, and *he used to read* in English is an aspectual distinction" (1976:1); but we rarely talk about aspectual distinctions in English. If this is so with English, then it is not surprising that much less is known about aspect in a little-studied language such as Capeverdean Crioulo.

The tense-aspect system of Capeverdean Crioulo has many similarities with that of other creole languages, both English-based (Voorhoeve 1957; Bickerton 1974, 1975; Herzfeld 1978) and Portuguese-based (Wilson 1962; Morais-Barbosa 1965; Valkhoff 1966; Scantamburlo 1981; Gomes and Mendonce 1981). But these similarities have not been clearly captured in previous studies of Capeverdean Crioulo (Coelho 1880; Costa and Duarte 1886; Brito 1887; Lopes da Silva 1957; Almada 1961; Meintel 1975; Santos 1979; Macedo 1979a; Veiga 1984), mainly because the paradigms used for analysis were inadequate to handle the data.[3]

Bickerton's "Creolization, Linguistic Universals, Natural Semantax and the Brain" (1974) and *Dynamics of a Creole System* (1975) offer the most comprehensive and direct background for the present study of Capeverdean Crioulo. I will begin by providing a taxonomy of the verbal forms, followed by an explanation of the range of functions available to particular forms. Data used for this analysis include my native speaker's intuitions of Sotavento Crioulo, sociolinguistic interviews with native speakers, and various written texts: a play (Macedo 1979b), a political speech (Duarte 1981), folktales (Parsons 1923), and a short story (reprinted in Macedo 1979a:201-11).

1.1 *The Verbal Forms and Their Combinations*

Capeverdean Crioulo has a particle *ta* and an auxiliary verb *sta* which occur preverbally; a postverbal suffix *-ba* and a clause-initial/clause-final particle *dja*. In addition, the unmarked form of the verb has many different functions.

Sta is an auxiliary verb as opposed to a particle, like *ta*, because:

(a) it occurs alone in a sentence like other verbs and modal auxiliaries.

(1)   *El sta na casa.*
       "She/He is at home".

(2)   *El mestê um casa.*
       "She/He **needs** a house".

(b) it contrasts with *e/ser* in designating temporary as opposed to permanent qualities.

(3)   *El sta bonito (hoji).*
       "He **is** handsome (today)".

(4)   *El e bonito.*
       "He **is** handsome".

(c) *ta*, on the other hand, cannot occur alone and must precede a verb.

(5)   **El ta na casa.*[4]
       "She/He (particle) at home"

(6)   *El ta sta na casa manhâ.*
       "She/He **will be** at home tomorrow".

(7)   *El ta cumprâ lete tudo dia.*
       "She/He **buys** milk every day".

(d) the anterior marker, *-ba*, attaches itself to *sta*, but not to *ta*.

(8)   *El staba na casa.*
       "She/He **was** at home".

(9)   **El taba na casa.*[4]
       "She/He (particle)+*ba* at home".

The preverbal particle and the auxiliary combine with each other:

$$\text{Subject} \quad \left\{ \begin{array}{c} \emptyset \\ ta \\ sta \\ sta\ ta \\ ta\ sta\ ta \end{array} \right\} \quad \text{Verb}$$

When the postverbal suffix *-ba* occurs, it is attached to the verb, unless the auxiliary *sta* followed by *ta* is present, in which case it attaches to *sta* to yield *staba ta V*.[5] The clause-initial/clause-final particle *dja* can co-occur both with *sta* and with *-ba*.

1.2 *Functions of the Various Forms*

The above sequences of forms can be analyzed by setting up a prospective tense system for Capeverdean Crioulo, where, following Ultan (1978:88), the present and the future are represented by the same markers. The forms containing *sta* and *ta* represent the nonpast (**both** present and future), whereas the presence of *-ba* indicates the anterior. Prior to discussing these forms, I will first examine the unmarked verbal form.

1.2.1 *The Unmarked Verbal Form (0 V)*

According to Bickerton, it is a general characteristic of creole languages that "the zero form marks simple past of action verbs and nonpast for state verbs" (1974:128). The situation in Capeverdean Crioulo is somewhat parallel.

Although the notion of stativity is a rather "fuzzy" semantic category (see Sag 1973) and Bickerton's definition is restricted to "stative propositions" as opposed to "specific lexical items" (1975:30), a stative verb will be defined, for the purpose of this discussion, as any verb which is [− imperative] and [−controllable]. The feature [imperative] by its very nature encompasses the feature [controllable]. The notion of controllability refers to the ability of the subject to exert control over the verb. It is closely associated with the imperative. Presumably, if one is ordered to do something, one must be in a position to exert control over the situation to be able to execute it. The reverse holds true as well: if one cannot carry out an order, one does not have control. To return to the issue of stativity: a stative verb is defined as one that cannot occur as an imperative and over which the subject of the verb cannot exert control.

Table 1 illustrates the criteria for dividing Capeverdean Crioulo verbs into statives and nonstatives. The stative/nonstative distinction is a crucial one for Bickerton's schema and for an understanding of Capeverdean Crioulo's tense-aspect system; thus, Table 1 will prove important in the discussion that follows. As noted, the statives are those which are [− imperative] and [− controllable]; they are the verbs that take a "−" in the first column. The combination of the auxiliary *sta* and the preposition *pa*, preceding a verb, signals a future intention or plan to do something; the inability of a verb to co-occur with *sta pa* signals the verb's inability to be controllable; thus, the results in the *sta pa* column re-inforce the notion of controllability. The sentences in (10) through (13) illustrate this.

(10) ·*El **sta pa tenê** *fome*.
"She/He **is planning on being** hungry" (literally, "**having** hunger").

(11) *El **sta pa parcê** *se pai*.
"He **is planning on resembling** his father".

(12) *El **sta pa creditâ** *na el*.
"She/He **is planning on believing** in her/him".

(13) El **sta pa tchigâ** *manhâ*.
"She/He **is planning on arriving** tomorrow".

The "past" column in Table 1 indicates whether the zero form of the verb takes a past reading or not. The final column of Table 1 indicates the ability or inability of a verb to co-occur with the auxiliary *sta*, the marker of continuous/progressive aspect. This last column is included only to demonstrate that the standard test for stativity (whether or not a particular verb is barred from entering into a progressive construction) is generally misleading and not operative in Capeverdean Crioulo.

Table 1

Stative and Nonstative Verbs in Capeverdean Crioulo

Verbs	Imperative/ Control	sta pa	Past	sta
GROUP I				
tem "have$_1$"	−	−*	−	−
tenê "have$_2$"	−	−	−	−
sta "be$_1$"	−	−	−	−
e/ser "be$_2$"	−*	−*	−	−
GROUP II				
sabê "know"	−	−	−	+
parcê "resemble"	−	−	−	+
crê "want"	−	−	−	+
crê X tcheu "love"	−	−	−	+
conchê "recognize"	−	−	−	+
debê "owe"	−	−	−	+
gostâ "like"	−	−	−	+

Verbs	Imperative/ Control	sta pa	Past	sta
GROUP III				
creditâ "believe"	−**	−	+	+
squicê "forget"	−**	−	+	+
sperâ "wait"	−**	−	+	+
ubí "hear"/"listen"	−**	−	+	+
odjâ "see"	−	−	+	+
tcherâ "smell"	−**	−	+	+
morrê "die"	−	−	+	+
vivê "live"	−	−	+	+
criâ "grow"	−	−	+	+
GROUP IV				
tchigâ "arrive"	+	+	+	+
mudâ "change"	+	+	+	+
abrí "open"	+	+	+	+
saltâ "jump"	+	+	+	+
trazê "bring"	+	+	+	+
bebê "drink"	+	+	+	+
entrâ "enter"	+	+	+	+

* Normally, *tem* is not preceded by *sta pa*, except in the fixed phrase *sta pa tem fidjo* "to be pregnant". *El/Ser* is an irregular verb and one can say *el sta pa ser professor* "He is planning on becoming a teacher".

** In negative sentences, these verbs can be [+imperative] and [+controllable.]

The verbs in Groups I, II, and IV of Table 1 confirm Bickerton's statement regarding the interpretation of stative and nonstative unmarked verbal forms. Groups I and II are [− imperative] and [−controllable] and are, according to the present definition, stative verbs. The zero forms of these verbs are also interpreted as nonpast. The verbs in Group I, however, are the only ones which behave according to the standard definition of stative verbs. That is, they do not enter into a construction with *sta*. The verbs in Group IV are nonstatives, being [+imperative] and [+controllable], and their zero form is interpreted as past.

The verbs in Group III are also stative verbs. They are [− imperative] and [−controllable]. But they are also [+past] and would not be considered as statives by Bickerton's definition. As a result two questions arise. First, can the basis for determining stativity in creole languages depend solely on the semantic interpretation of the verb as [−past]? Second, is there a semantic shift taking place specifically in Capeverdean Crioulo which may be neutralizing the clear-cut correspondence, found in other creole languages, between statives as [−past] and nonstatives as [+past]? For example,

    (14) *Pedro **gostâ** de Maria.*
        "Pedro **likes** Maria".

The verb, *gostâ*, belongs to Group II and is clearly a stative verb by both our and Bickerton's definition. It is [− imperative], [−controllable], and [−past]. But the verb in (15) is also grammatical and has the same interpretation as (14), yet it is preceded by the nonpast particle, *ta*.

    (15) *Pedra **ta gostâ** de Maria.*
        "Pedro **likes** Maria".

While the particle is optional for verbs like *gostâ*, it is required for the expression of nonpast interpretation of nonstative verbs. It is also required for Group III verbs. As a consequence, Group III verbs are stative verbs (since they are [−imperative] and [−controllable]) that behave like nonstatives. (Clearly, this issue needs to be explored further.)

    Still with regard to Group III verbs, the most plausible explanation for the existence of verbs like *creditâ*, *sperâ*, *morrê*, and *piorâ* with a past interpretation may be the basic semantic make-up of these verbs. Perhaps the normal state of affairs for these verbs may be a situation whose starting point reflects an event which results in the state. As pointed out by John Singler (p.c., November, 1988), "the initial endpoint of 'believe' is when the person 'started to believe' or 'came to believe'. That occurred in the past, and the result persists".

    The use of the unmarked verbal forms with past and nonpast interpretations is presented below.

Stative with nonpast interpretation
    (16) *Nha filho, bu necê hoji, bu **querê** ba toma lumi na cabo qui bu ca* **con'xê**! (Parsons 1923:14;31)
        "My child, you were born today, you **want** to go get fire in a place that you don't **know**"!

Stative with past interpretation
    (17) *Pert' di cas' di rei, êle **oubi** son' di pilon.* (Parsons 1923:16;35)
        "Near the king's house, he **heard** the sound of the *pilon* (mortar and pestle)".

Nonstative with past interpretation
(18) *Criad' **corrê**, ele **ba** f'ra rainha, ma rainha ca creditâ pamod esse homi era ses amigo.* (Parsons 1923:13;28)
"The servant **ran**, he **went** to tell the queen, but the queen didn't believe (it), because this man was their friend".

As in Guyanese Creole (Bickerton 1975:30-1), the unmarked verbal form is found following modals, in conditional and temporal clauses, and in imperatives. In these constructions, the time reference distinction between stative and nonstative verbs is neutralized, and nonstative verbs are interpreted as nonpast.

Following modals
(19) *Mi tambe 'n stâ quebrado, ma cumâ mala tchigâ hoje, algun cartinha de Merca **debê ben** certinho.* (Macedo 1979b:15)
"I'm broke, too, but since the mail arrived today, a little letter [with a few dollars] from America **should come** for sure".

In conditional clauses
(20) *. . . e raparigas de li **se bo papiâ** quese portugues es ta sinti brigonha . . .* (Macedo 1979b:7)
". . . and the girls here, **if you speak** with them in Portuguese, they'll get embarrassed . . ."

In temporal clauses
(21) ***Tó que nhós casâ** tudo cusa ta rumâ.* (Macedo 1979b:50)
"**When you get married**, everything will be okay".

Imperatives
(22) ***Tomâ** es bilhete . . .* (Macedo 1979b:28)
"**Take** this note . . ."

1.2.2 *The Preverbal Markers*

Ta is a nonpast marker and can be interpreted as present or future, depending on context.[6] In the present, *ta* indicates aspectual distinctions clustering around habituality and iterativity.

Present time:
Timeless truths such as proverbs (for equivalent examples in English, see Leech 1971:2)
(23) *Saco baziu **ca ta saquê**.* (Macedo 1979b:8)
"An empty bag **doesn't stand up**".

Simple present

(24) *Nhós* **ca ta dormi** *de note e dispós nhós* **ta quexâ**. (Macedo 1979b:17)

"You **don't sleep** at night and then you **complain**".

Habitual

(25) *Justiça é nós que* **ta fazê** *cumá no entendê*. (Macedo 1979b:55)

"Justice, we **(usually) dispense** it as we wish".

Iterative

(26) *Dja'n fraba bó cumá ses portugueses que* **ta ben** *nos terra, es ta ben djobê donde engostâ*. (Macedo 1979b:59)

"I had already told you that these Portuguese who **come** here (our country), they come looking for a way to live".

Future time:

(27) *'N ta* **mandâ** *Dani ca Iliza buscâ un bife de baca* . . . (Macedo 1979b:12)

"**I'll send** Dani to Iliza's house to get a steak . . ."

Sta is an auxiliary verb meaning "to be", marking the continuous/progressive aspect. In presenting *sta*, I will first present the meaning associated with certain groups of verbs when they co-occur with it and then describe its use more generally.

It has already been pointed out that, of the verbs listed in Table 1, *tem*, *tenê* "to have" and *sta*, *e/ser* "to be" are the only ones that cannot co-occur with the progressive auxiliary.

(28) a. *El* **tenê** *fome*.
"She/He **is** hungry" (literally "**has** hunger").

b. **El* **sta tenê** *fome*.
"She/He **is being** hungry".

(29) a. *Es lata* **tenê** *farinha*.
"This can **contains** flour".

b. **Es lata* **sta tenê** *farinha*.
"This can **is containing** flour".

(30) a. *El* **tem** *dos casa*.
"She/He **owns/has** two houses".

b. **El* **sta tem** *dos casa*.
"She/He **is owning/having** two houses".

(31) a. *El sta bonito.*
         "He is handsome (at this moment)".
      b. **El sta sta bonito.*
         "He is being handsome".

(32) a. *El e bonito.*
         "He is handsome (all the time)".
      b. **El sta ser bonito.*
         "He is being handsome".

The remainder of the verbs on Table 1 take *sta* with the following interpretations:

a) The verbs *sabê, parcê, crê, crê* [someone] *tcheu* seem to take *sta* to indicate that the state is not stable, or perhaps not yet completely achieved.

(33) *Cada dia el sta sabê mas tcheu.*
      "Each/every day she/he **knows/is knowing** more".

(34) *Cada dia cusas sta parcê midjor.*
      "Each/every day things **seem/are appearing** better".

(35) *Cada dia el sta crê um cusa diferente.*
      "Each/every day she/he **wants/is wanting** something different".

(36) *Cada dia el sta crêbu mas tcheu.*
      "Each/every day she/he **loves/is loving** you more".

b) The verbs *conchê, debê, parcê,* and *gostâ* seem to take *sta* to indicate limited duration of the state or of the process leading up to the state.

(37) *Bo ca sta conchê'n?*
      "Don't you recognize (**aren't you recognizing**) me"?

(38) *Tem um mes qu'n sta debê'l vinte dola.*
      "It is a month that I owe (**am owing**) him twenty dollars".

(39) *Gossi el sta parcê se pai.*
      "Right now he resembles (**is resembling**) his father".

(40) *Julio sta gostâ de Maria.*
      "Julio likes (**is liking**) Maria".

c) Verbs of "inert cognition" may take *sta* in situations where "mental activity" is implied.

(41) *'N sta 'ntendê tudo cusa que bo sta fra'm.*
      "I understand (**am understanding**) everything that you are telling me".

(42) *Gossi 'n sta imaginâ cuma mi e um princesa.*
      "Right now I **am imagining** that I am a princess".

d) Verbs of "inert perception" may also take *sta* in situations where there is active perception.

(43) *'N sta sinti friu.*
      "I am (**am feeling**) cold".

(44) *'N sta sinti um gosto margos na boca.*
      "I **am tasting** something bitter in my mouth".

e) "Transition" verbs may take *sta* to designate movement toward a state.

(45) *El sta morrê.*
      "She/He **is dying**".

f) Nonstative verbs routinely take *sta* to express the progressive/continuous aspect and also the future.

Progressive aspect

(46) *. . . e 'n ca crê odjâ Joana passâ cosé que 'n stá passâ.* (Macedo 1979b:41)
      ". . . and I don't want to see Joana go through what I **am going through**".

Future time

(47) *Sin — saudo 'n stâ fazê um badjinho.* (Macedo 1979b:34)
      "Yes — Saturday I'm **having** a party [literally, making a dance]".

Sta ta is the combination of the continuous aspect and the habitual/iterative aspect.[7] But it is very similar to *sta* in meaning; it is frequently used to describe or report events taking place at the moment of utterance. Even more so than with *sta* alone, there is a pronounced notion of continuity/progression. (*Sa ta* is a variant of *sta ta*; cf. fn. 4.)

(48) *Badjo dja cabâ, tudo dgente sa ta saí.* (Macedo 1979b:43)
      "The party (dance) is over, everyone **is leaving (going out)**".

In certain cases it also expresses iteration of a continuous event in existence over a period of time. But it appears that, as exemplified in (49) below, such a meaning is derived mainly from discourse factors rather than the form itself. The phrases *dja ten tempo* and *tudo ses dgentes* reinforce the notion of repetition over both time and space.

(49)   . . . *ma dja ten tempo que tudo ses dgentes* **sa ta dan** *recado pa'n dâ nha*. (Macedo 1979b:23)
". . . but it has been awhile that everybody **is giving** me messages for me to give to you".

While *sta ta* represents continuity/progression, *ta sta ta* represents a type of progressive iterative, progressive habitual, or future progressive, depending on the context.

(50)   *El* **ta sta ta comê** *tudo bez qu'm ba la.*
"She/He **is eating** every time I go there". (progressive iteration)

(51)   *El* **ta sta ta comê** *sempre qu'm ba la.*
"She/He **is (usually) eating** when I go there". (progressive habitual)

(52)   *O qui'm ba la manhâ, el* **ta sta ta comê**.
"When I go there tomorrow, she/he **will be eating**". (future progressive)

1.2.3 *The Postverbal Suffix,* **-Ba**

-Ba designates **anteriority** of states and actions. With stative verbs, it usually indicates simple past; and with nonstative verbs, past-before-past (see section 1.2.1, above).

-Ba with stative verbs of Groups I and II (Table 1)

(53)   *Lob'* **temba** *past'*. (Parsons 1923:10;17)
"The wolf **had** food".

(54)   *El olhâ cert' cuma esse homi é homi qui e's* **con'xeba**. (Parsons 1923:13;28)
"They checked to make sure that this man was a man that they **knew**".

-Ba with stative verbs of Group III (Table 1)

(55)   *Out'o dia Tobinh' sta passâ p'ra la, el olha func' que ele* **ca olhaba** *antes*. (Parsons 1923:24;49)
"The next day Tobinh' is passing by, he saw a hole that he **hadn't seen** before".

-Ba with nonstative verbs of Group IV (Table 1)

(56)   *Sim qu'ele chigâ ele começâ ta comê cusa que ele* **lebaba**. (Parsons 1923:16;36)
"As soon as he arrived he started to eat what he **had brought**".

The co-occurrence of -*ba* with various other markers signals a range of tense-aspect combinations. As previously stated, *ta* designates both present habitual and future (and does not, by itself, occur with verbs in the past). When it combines with a verb followed by the past marker -*ba*, the result is a past habitual or a past conditional (contrary-to-fact).

Past habitual

(57)   *Na tenpu di nu gubernador era gentis ki **ta rasebeba** tudo favor y privileziu di rizimi kolonial ki, ku tudo suberba **ta disprezaba** nos povu.* (Duarte 1981)

"In the era of His Excellency the Governor, they were the people who **used to receive** all the favors and privileges from the colonial regime, who with all arrogance **used to put down** our people".

Conditional (contrary-to-fact)

(58)   *'N **ta fritaba** nhose um obinho ma gossi na asagua tudo galinha stâ tchoca.* (Macedo 1979b:12)

"I **would have fried** some eggs for you, but now in the rainy season all the chickens are hatching".

Sta + *ba ta* (with -*ba* affixed to *sta* rather than the main verb) expresses the past continuous.

(59)   *'N pensaba nhós **ca staba ta ben**.* (Macedo 1979b:35)

"I thought that you **weren't coming**".

Finally, *ta staba ta* combines the habitual, continuous, and anterior markers to yield a type of past habitual progressive.

(60)   *Tudo dgente ta dixaba ele queto quanto ele **ta staba ta comê**.*

"Everyone used to leave her/him alone when she/he **used to be eating**".

1.2.4   *The Clause-Initial/Clause-Final Marker, **Dja***

Dja marks completion. When the subject is a pronoun, *dja* is found in a clause-initial position; but when the subject is a full noun phrase, it follows the subject and precedes the verb. It may, in addition, occur in clause-final position. As a completive marker, it combines with all of the preceding markers and their combinations, with the exception that it cannot co-occur with *ta* alone.[8]

When *dja* marks a stative whose zero form takes a nonpast interpretation, i.e. a Group I or II stative from Table 1, it signals that the state is in total existence in the present. There is sometimes no indication when the state commenced — only that at the moment of the utterance, the existence of the state is indisputable.

(61) *El ca sabê nadâ, ma el oubí Xobinho frâ, ele cu'dâ **ja ele sabê nadâ**, el buâ dent' di mar, el fogâ.* (Parsons 1923:25;54)
"He doesn't know how to swim, but he heard Xobinho say [that he did], and he believed that **he (already) knew how to swim**; he jumped into the sea and drowned".

In contrast, when *dja* marks a verb whose zero form takes a past interpretation, i.e. a Group III stative (62) or Group IV nonstative (63) from Table 1, it indicates situations from the past whose result is applicable in the present moment. (In this it is similar to a present perfect.)

(62) *. . . y e ku bastanti intusiasmu ki N sa ta bem li pamodi **ja N oja** na programa ki N dadu . . .* (Duarte 1981)
". . . and it is with much enthusiasm that I am coming here, because **I have seen** in the program that I was given . . ."

(63) *. . . ten otus **imigranti ki ja bira** inimigu di nos Partidu y Govérnu . . .* (Duarte 1981)
". . .there are other **immigrants who have become** enemies of our Party and our Government . . ."

In constructions with *dja + stative verb + ba*, the state is assumed to be complete and to have been in full existence during some period in the past.

(64) *Antes qu'el pô pé na cais de Furna, **dja'l sabeba** de nha Justa.* (Macedo 1979b:27)
"Before he set foot on the dock of Furna, **he already knew** of nha Justa".

In the sequence *dja + nonstative verb + ba*, the action is in the past-before-past and its result continues to hold in the past.

(65) ***Dja'n daba** nha palabra cumá badjo na casa de nha . . .* (Macedo 1979b:35)
"**I had already given** you my word that a party (dance) at your house . . ."

Notice, however, that stative verbs belonging to Group III continue to behave like nonstatives (Group IV).

(66) *Se pai **dja morreba**, quanto el bem Merca.*
      "His father **had already died**, when he came to America".

Consequently, the basilect of Capeverdean Crioulo may be said to exhibit the following correspondences:

1. −anterior +punctual −completive $\emptyset$
2. +anterior   −*ba*
3. −punctual +continuous   *sta*   .
4. −punctual −continuous   *ta*
5. +completive   *dja*

Depending on whether the verb is stative or nonstative, the preceding markers combine as follows:

1.   −compl +stat −ant $\emptyset$ *V*
2.   −compl +stat +ant   *V+ba*
3.   −compl −stat −ant +punct $\emptyset$ *V*
4.   −compl −stat +ant +punct   *V+ba*
5.   −compl −stat −ant −punct +cont   *sta (ta) V[9]*
6.   −compl −stat +ant −punct +cont   *sta+ba ta V*
7.   −compl −stat −ant −punct −cont   *ta V*
8.   −compl −stat +ant −punct −cont   *ta V+ba*
9.   +compl −ant   *dja...$\emptyset$ V*
10. +compl +ant   *dja...V+ba*

2. Comparison of the Capeverdean Crioulo System with Bickerton's Analysis of Creole Tense and Aspect

The description of the Capeverdean tense-aspect system provided above deviates in a number of ways from the "classic TMA pattern" (Bickerton 1981:73). Others have also noticed divergence from Bickerton's classic system. According to Bickerton,

> . . . an earlier work of mine (Bickerton 1974) that was limited to a discussion of TMA systems has been the subject of a number of criticisms, several to the effect that there were a number of exceptions to the generalizations made therein (1981:73).

Bickerton lists five "deviations from the regular creole TMA system" (p. 77). Two of these relate to the Capeverdean system.

1. In Bickerton's system, the anterior marker precedes the verb. But in Guinea-Bissau Crioulo, the anterior marker -*ba* follows the verb.

2. In Bickerton's system, the nonpunctual incorporates both the progressive/durative and the habitual/iterative. But in some creole languages the iteratives/habituals appear to have merged with either punctuals or irrealis, leaving the nonpunctual category to consist only of progressive/durative.

These two "deviations" are both characteristic of Capeverdean Crioulo. In Capeverdean Crioulo, the anterior marker -ba is identical to that of Guinean Crioulo; the iterative/habitual and the irrealis are expressed by the same marker, *ta*, while the nonpunctual *sta* expresses only the progressive/durative. In addition the completive marker, *dja*, plays a central role in the tense-aspect system.

2.1 *The Anterior Marker, -Ba*

Bickerton's response to the data from Guinea-Bissau Crioulo is based on the assumption that the syntactic position of Guinean Crioulo -ba is due to the persistence of pidgin-like features. He states:

> Most creoles have an "earlier" form which is derived from a verb with the meaning "finish"; in addition to [Hawaiian Creole] *pau*, we find Indian Ocean Creole *(fi)n* from Fr. *fini* "finished (p. part.)", English creole *don* from another past participle, Eng. *done*, and Portuguese creole *(ka)ba* from Pg. *acabar* "finish" (*kaba* is found in Sranan also) (p. 80).

Bickerton also states (p. 80) that, depending on the creole language, the syntactic position of these markers falls into one of "three distinct distributions":

1. "they remain as marginal particles, occurring optionally in clause-final position", e.g. *kaba* in Sranan and in Papiamentu;
2. they become part of the AUX without combining with other AUX constituents; or
3. they become part of the AUX and combine freely with other AUX constituents.

In Guinean Crioulo, -ba "retained clause-external position," according to Bickerton (p. 81).

An account that attributes the postverbal position of -ba to the persistence of pidgin-like features seems improbable to me. First, the basic assumption regarding the retention of this pidgin feature must be questioned. Although Bickerton states that in Hawaiian Pidgin English the marker to express "earlier" is *pau*, and the marker for "later" is *baimbai*, it is also a fact that

> [w]hen HCE [Hawaiian Creole English] developed out of HPE [Hawaiian Pidgin English] neither *pau* nor *baimbai* underwent any change of meaning, nor were they incorporated into Aux. Two quite different forms, *bin* and *go*, were selected to express anterior and irrealis, respectively (p. 79).

Since the "earlier" and "later" markers in HPE drop out of the verb system in HCE, the reverse argument to Bickerton's can also be true: when a pidgin develops into a creole, new lexical items are incorporated to express the anterior and the irrealis markers.

A second argument pertaining to the persistence of pidgin features in Guinea-Bissau Crioulo relates to whether it is a pidgin or a creole language. Bickerton states that the available evidence is inconsistent: Alleyne (1979:91) states that it has no native speakers, while Wilson (1962:vii) states that it ". . . is the first language of many who are born and bred in the main towns". Bickerton takes the mediating position that Guinean Crioulo probably creolized slowly and that a small number of native speakers existed within "a wide lingua-franca penumbra" (p. 82); this would allow for the persistence of pidgin-like features in Guinea-Bissau Crioulo. But all of the sociohistoric evidence points to the development of Guinean Crioulo (and possibly other West African creole languages) in the Cape Verde Islands, not on the West African mainland.[10] According to Carreira (1983:17), the African coastal area known as Guinea (extending from present-day Senegal to Sierra Leone) was discovered in 1446, fourteen years before the discovery of Cape Verde Islands; but it was not until the latter half of the seventeenth century that,

> . . . os portugueses tentaram com maior êxito, a criação e consolidação de centros de comércio com reduzido número de habitantes europeus à mistura com *lançados* ou *tangomaos* oriundos de Cabo Verde; e mesmo assim enfrentando séria oposição das populações (p. 22).
>
> ". . . the Portuguese attempted with greater success, the establishment and consolidation of trade centers with a small number of Europeans and *lançados* or *tangomaos*, natives of Cape Verde; and even so facing serious opposition from the native populations".

Carreira continues:

> A nosso ver o *Crioulo* começou a ser usado, timidamente, nos "rios" pelos *Lançados* ou *Tangomaos* oriundos das ilhas de Cabo Verde no período da formação das Praças e Presídios, isto em consequência intensa

penetração comercial operada pelos homens brancos de Santiago [Cabo Verde]. E mesmo assim o seu uso ficou limitado aos habitantes permanentes nas concentrações, ex[c]luindo portanto a gente do mato (p. 35).

"It is our view that *Crioulo* began to be used, timidly, in the "rivers" by the *lançados* or *tangomaos* originally from the Cape Verde Islands during the time of the formation of the *Praças* and *Presídios*, this being due to the intense commercial penetration operated by the whites of Santiago [Cape Verde]. And even so its [Crioulo's] use remained limited to the permanent residents in the concentrations, therefore excluding the people from interior".

It is precisely this restriction to urban centers of Crioulo's use and its absence from the interior of Guinea-Bissau that has led some to claim that it is a pidgin and not a creole. But, as Carreira states, it was not until the war for independence, which started in 1961, that Crioulo spread more widely and began to function as the lingua franca.

. . . mais de 80% da população rural, até a mais relutante, aceitou o crioulo como língua de contacto com as etnias diferentes. Adquiriu assim o estatuto de *língua-franca*, sobretudo no comércio.
Mas . . . repare-se que isto se deu na transição do século XX pra o XXI (p. 36).
". . . more than 80% of the rural population, even the most resistant, accepted Crioulo as the language of contact between the different ethnic groups. As a consequence it acquired the status of *lingua franca*, especially in trade.
"But . . . notice must be taken of the fact that this took place during the transition period of the twentieth to the twenty-first centuries".

The linguistic connection between Guinean and Capeverdean Crioulos is further reinforced by the fact that in Capeverdean Crioulo the anterior marker is also *-ba* (see section 1.2.3). Therefore, any explanation based on the persistence of pidgin-like features in Guinean or Capeverdean Crioulos can be readily rejected on sociohistoric grounds alone.

A third argument against Bickerton's explanation concerns his etymological derivation of the Crioulo anterior marker, *-ba*, from the Portuguese verb, *acabar* "to finish". Bickerton seems to have confused the anterior marker with the completive marker. The so-called anterior forms, which he designates as the "earlier" markers in pidgins, are actually associated with the "completive" category, not the "anterior" category. For example, *don* in Guyanese is the completive marker, and *bin* is the anterior marker (Bickerton 1975); *(fi)n* in Seychelles Creole is the completive marker, and *ti* is the anterior marker (Bickerton 1981:85). Therefore we must question whether the anterior marker, *-ba*, of Guinean (and Capeverdean) Crioulo could be linked to Portuguese *acabar* "to finish", realized in Papiamentu and Sranan as the completive marker, *kaba* (*ibid.*, p. 80).[11] In the examples from creole languages other than Crioulo that Bickerton provides, the "earlier" markers are not "anterior" markers but "completive" markers.

A more plausible explanation for the derivation of *-ba*, found in Guinean and Capeverdean creoles, is the ending *-va*, found in the first and third persons singular of the "past imperfect tense" of all Portuguese verbs terminating in *-ar*.

2.2 The Irrealis and Nonpunctual

Unlike English-based and French-based creole languages with a separate irrealis marker, in Capeverdean Crioulo the irrealis is expressed by modal auxiliaries and by the marker *ta*, which is also used for habitual/iterative aspect. In this, Capeverdean Crioulo parallels Guinean Crioulo and São Tomense.

Bickerton (1981:256) attempts to explain this feature of Guinea-Bissau and São Tomé Crioulos, by pointing out that, according to the work of Bronckart and Sinclair (1973), "there is more than one way of looking at iteratives". First, Bickerton says, they may be regarded as nonpunctual if habitual/iterative sentences like *John walks to work* are not viewed as single events, but as "ill-defined series" of instances which have already taken place in the past and will probably continue into the future. Second, iteratives may be regarded as punctual, if each isolated event within the series of *John walks to work* is viewed as a single event. The third way of looking at iteratives is to examine the conditions necessary "to establish the truth value of an iterative predication" (p. 256). Bickerton concludes, "Since the realis category embraces real events in real time, it could be concluded that the iterative 'really' belongs in the irrealis category" (p. 257).

Although these views explain how, semantically, iteratives are capable of covering the irrealis meaning, they do not explain why, in some creole languages (English- and French-based), irrealis and iterative/habitual have distinct markers while in others (Portuguese-based) they do not.

2.3 *The Completive Marker,* **Dja**

Two of the three possible syntactic positions (refer to 2.1 above) that Bickerton postulates for the "earlier" marker are found in Portuguese-based creoles. But the marker is the completive, *dja*, rather than the anterior, *-ba*. Examples can be found in São Tomense, Guinean, and Capeverdean creoles. In both Guinean and São Tomense, *dja*, *za*, or *ja* occurs clause-finally.

Guinean Crioulo

(67) /i **bay ja**/. (Wilson 1962:23; Morais-Barbosa 1965, reprinted 1975:139)
"He **has gone (recently, and is still away)**".

(68) *N **cume dja**.* (Scantamburlo 1981:53)
"I **have just eaten**".

São Tomense

(69) /*kasó **detá-za**/.* (Morais-Barbosa 1965; reprinted 1975:141)
"The dog **has (already) lain down**".

(70) *n-**fla za**.* (Valkhoff 1966:111)
"I **have said all I have to say, and now I have fallen silent**"./"I've spoken already".

In Capeverdean Crioulo, on the other hand, one encounters *dja* repeated in both clause-initial and clause-final positions; in clause-initial position only; and within the Aux, if the subject NP is not a pronoun.

(71) **Dja'l comê dja**.
"She/He **has eaten already**".

(72) **Dja'l comê**.
"She/He **has eaten**".

(73) **El **dja comê** (dja).*
"She/He **has eaten (already)**".

(74) **Dja** Maria **comê** (dja).
"Maria **has eaten (already)**".

(75) Maria **dja comê** (dja).
"Maria **has eaten (already)**".

(76)   *Maria dja comeba (dja) quanto no tchigâ.*
       "Maria **had (already) eaten** when we arrived".

In order to interpret the variation in the syntactic position of the completive marker in the three Portuguese-based creoles, we must follow Bickerton's lead in finding explanation in the dynamic model. These three creoles, which are still in association with their superstrate, represent different stages in the decreolization process. In all three creoles, adjusting for phonological differences, the form of the marker is the same. In São Tomé and Guinea-Bissau, the position is still "marginal". But in Cape Verde, there is evidence that the form has started to grammaticalize, perhaps influenced by the use of the Portuguese form *já* as a model. Sranan and Papiamentu *kaba* (refer to 2.1 above) may represent the earliest form for this function; it has not been replaced by *dja* and, since these two creoles are no longer in contact with Portuguese, probably will not be.[12]

3.   Conclusion

I have described the tense and aspect system of Capeverdean Crioulo and I have shown that it differs in a number of ways from Bickerton's "classic" tense-aspect system. Thus, while Bickerton predicts that tense-aspect markers will be independent preverbal markers, the Capeverdean Crioulo marker of anteriority is postverbal, a suffix. Bickerton's attempts to explain this fact away in Guinean Crioulo fail there as well as in Capeverdean Crioulo. A further difference between Capeverdean Crioulo and the classic system involves a division of nonpunctual into progressive/durative and habitual/iterative, with the habitual/iterative marker also indicating futurity. Finally, the classic system contains no place for a completive marker, yet such a marker is an integral part of Capeverdean Crioulo's tense-aspect system.

While I have pointed out these departures from Bickerton's system, I have not offered alternative explanations for them. Rather, I have simply added to the list of differences already in the literature, and have shown that the explanation provided in Bickerton (1981) does not adequately deal with the data. Perhaps as more is known about Portuguese-based creole languages in general, these differences will be better understood.

Notes

1. This chapter is based on my 1985 Georgetown University dissertation. I would like to thank Ralph Fasold, Susumu Kuno, Cléa Rameh, John Singler, and Jyoti Tuladhar for helpful discussion and comments.

   The specific orthography which I use to write the word /kriolu/ and other Capeverdean /kriolu/ sentences throughout this chapter should not be taken as either an endorsement or a rejection of any type of standardized orthographical proposals presently being debated. Examples from written texts are faithfully reproduced, and my own examples and those from the tape-recorded interviews have been written in the manner that was most expeditious to me.

2. For further details see Silva (1985).

3. See Silva (1985) for detailed review of these works.

4. Under certain conditions, a phonological rule changes *sta* to either *sa* or *ta*. I suspect that the two resulting forms reflect dialectal (Sotavento vs. Barlavento) variants. Under these circumstances and on the basis of form and function, sentences (5) and (9) would appear to be grammatical. But on semantic grounds, they are definitely different. Nonetheless, further examination of the phonological constraints is needed.

5. The syntactic position of the anterior marker appears to be in variation when both an auxiliary and a main verb are present. In my "idiolect", *-ba* definitely follows the auxiliary *sta*. That is also the case for many of my informants. But Veiga (1984:119) shows *-ba* attaching itself to the main verb. On the other hand, I have observed variation with other auxiliaries like *mestê* "need" and *podê* "can":

   (i) *El **mestê cumpraba** quel libro.* vs. *El **mesteba cumprâ** quel libro.*
        "She/He **needed to buy** that book".
   (ii) *El **podê cumpraba** quel libro.* vs. *El **podeba cumprâ** quel libro.*
        "She/He **could have bought** that book".

   John Hutchison (p.c.) first called this type of variation to my attention. Its examination is beyond the scope of this article.

6. *Ta* also occurs in what may be called nonfinite verbal constructions:

   (i) . . . *Djeje **ficâ ta razâ ta pedi** Nhór Dés pa djudâ'l co sé plano* (Macedo 1979b:29)
        ". . . Djeje **kept on praying and asking** God to help him with his plan".

   Ta is also used in agentless passive constructions.

   (ii) ***Ta credo** Maria tcheu.*
        "Maria **is loved/liked**".

7. *Ta sta*, on the other hand, occurs simply as the auxiliary verb *sta* preceded by the particle *ta*.

   (i) *El **ta sta** na casa tudo dia.*
        "She/He **is** at home every day". (iterative)
   (ii) *El **ta sta** na casa manhâ.*
        "She/He **will be** at home tomorrow". (future)

(iii) *El* **ta sta** *na casa sempre.*
"She/He **is** usually at home". (habitual)

8. *Dja* does not occur with *ta* alone. But it combines with *sta ta V* and *sta + ba ta V* to designate ingressive meaning:

(i) ***Dja nhos sa ta 'ntendê*** *cumpanhero midjor?*
"**Are you beginning to understand** one another better?"

(ii) ***Dja no staba ta 'ntendê*** *cumpanhero midjor qanto el 'mbarcâ pa strangero.*
"**We were already beginning to understand** each other better when he went abroad".

9. As previously stated, *ta* has several interpretations. It marks the habitual, the iterative, and the future. Apart from this, in the list of feature specifications, *ta* shows up both as [+continuous] and [−continuous]. This is to be explained by the fact that, while *sta* is [+continuous] and *ta* is [-continuous], they can co-occur, in which case the resultant form is [+continuous]. (See the discussion of *sta ta* in 1.2.2 above.)

10. See Silva (1985).

11. I use the designation "completive marker" for *kaba* in Papiamentu. It should be noted that Andersen (this volume) calls it a "completive adverbial".

12. Cléa Rameh (p.c., September, 1984) states that in Brazilian Portuguese the present perfect tense is not used very often. The tendency is to use *já* accompanied by the simple form of the verb, as in (i) and (ii).

Brazilian Portuguese:
(i) ***Já li*** *o livro.*
"I **(already have) read** the book".
(ii) ***Tenho lido*** *o livro.*
"I **have read** the book".

In addition, *já* co-occurs regularly with either the present or past perfect tenses in Portuguese.

Continental Portuguese
(iii) ***Já tenho lido*** *o livro.*
"I **have already read** the book".
(iv) *Eu* ***já tinha lido*** *o livro quando el chegou.*
"I **had already read** the book when he arrived".

There are also regular phonological correspondences between Portuguese /ʒ/ and Capeverdean Crioulo /j/. In fact, in the Barlavento region, /ʒ/ is used more often than /j/. In addition, unlike English, which has no way to express the completive, Portuguese does use *já*. Therefore, whereas in Capeverdean Crioulo the completive *dja* plays a central role in the grammar, when the perfective category begins to appear as decreolization sets in, the completive does not disappear. What probably happens is that the semantic range of the completive is restricted, to allow for the perfective to be expressed. This issue is discussed in Chapter Five of Silva (1985).

References

Alleyne, Mervyn C. 1979. "On the Genesis of Languages". *The Genesis of Language* ed. by Kenneth C. Hill, 89-107. Ann Arbor: Karoma.

Almada, Dulce. 1961. *Cabo Verde: Contribuição para o estudo do Dialecto Falado no seu Arquipélago*. Lisbon: Junta de Investigação do Ultramar.

Andersen, Roger W. this volume. "Papiamentu Tense-Aspect, with Special Attention to Discourse".

Bickerton, Derek. 1974. "Creolization, Linguistic Universals, Natural Semantax and the Brain". *University of Hawaii Working Papers in Linguistics* 6(3).125-41. (Reprinted in *Issues in English Creoles: Papers from the 1975 Hawaii conference* ed. by Richard Day 1980.1-18. Heidelberg: Groos.)

————. 1975. *Dynamics of a Creole Continuum*. Cambridge: University Press.

————. 1981. *Roots of Language*. Ann Arbor: Karoma.

Brito, Antonio de Paula. 1887. "Dialectos Crioulos-Portuguezes. Apontamentos para a Gramática do Crioulo que se Fala na Ilha de Santiago de Cabo Verde". *Boletim da Sociedade de Geografia de Lisboa* 7.611-69. (Reprinted in Morais-Barbosa 1967.329-404.)

Bronckart, J.P., and H. Sinclair. 1973. "Time, Tense and Aspect". *Cognition* 2.107-30.

Carreira, Antonio. 1983 [cover date 1984]. *O Crioulo de Cabo Verde: Surto e expansão*. Lisbon: Gráfica Europam.

Coelho, Francisco Adolfo. 1880-1886. "Os Dialectos Românicos ou Neo-Latinos na Africa, Asia e América". *Boletim da Sociedade de Geografia de Lisboa* 1880.129-96, 1882.451-78, 1886.705-55. (Reprinted in Morais-Barbosa 1967.1-234.)

Comrie, Bernard. 1976. *Aspect: An introduction to the study of verbal aspect and related problems*. Cambridge: University Press.

Costa, Joaquim Vieira Botelho, and Custodio José Duarte. 1886. "O Crioulo de Cabo Verde. Breves Estudos Sobre o Crioulo das Ilhas de Cabo Verde Oferecidos ao Dr. Hugo Schuchardt". *Boletim da Sociedade de Geografia de Lisboa* 6.325-88. (Reprinted in Morais-Barbosa 1967.235-328.)

Duarte, Abílio. 1981. Speech in *Voz di Povo*, November 26. Praia: Republic of Cape Verde.

Gomes, Adriano, and João Gomes Mendonce. 1981. *Essai de Grammaire Créole de Guinée-Bissau*. République de Guinée-Bissau: Ministère de l'Education Nationale, Départment de l'Education des Adultes.

Herzfeld, Anita. 1978. "Tense and Aspect in Limon Creole: A sociolinguistic view towards a creole continuum", Ph.D. dissertation, University of Kansas.

Leech, Geoffrey. 1971. *Meaning and the English Verb*. London: Longman.

Lopes da Silva, Baltasar. 1957. *O Dialecto Crioulo de Cabo Verde*. Lisbon: Agência Geral do Ultramar.

Macedo, Donaldo P. 1979a. "A Linguistic Approach to Capeverdean Language", D.Ed. dissertation, Boston University.

——. 1979b. *Descarado*. Boston: Atlantis Publishers.

Meintel, Deirdre. 1975. "The Creole Dialect of the Island of Brava". Valkhoff 1975.205-56.

Morais-Barbosa, J. 1965-1966. "Cabo Verde, Guiné e São Tomé e Principe: A Situação Linguística". *Cabo Verde, Guiné, S. Tomé e Principe, Macau e Timor: Curso de Extensão Universitária Ano Lectivo de 1965-1966*, 149-64.. Lisbon: Instituto Superior de Ciências Sociais e Política Ultramarina. (Reprinted in Valkhoff 1975.)

——. 1967. *Crioulos*. (*Reedição de Artigos Publicados no Boletim da Sociedade de Geografia de Lisboa*). Lisbon: Academia Internacional da Cultura Portuguesa.

Parsons, Elsie Clews. 1923. *Folk-Lore from the Cape Verdean Islands*. 2 volumes. Cambridge, MA, and New York: American Folklore Society.

Quirk, Randolph, and Sidney Greenbaum. 1975. *A Concise Grammar of Contemporary English*. New York: Harcourt Brace Jovanovich.

Sag, Ivan. 1973. "On the State of Progress on Progressives and Statives". *New Ways of Analyzing Variation in English* ed. by Charles-James N. Bailey and Roger W. Shuy, 83-95. Washington: Georgetown University Press.

Santos, Rosine. 1979. "Comparaison entre le Créole du Cap-Vert et les Langues Africaines". Paper presented at the *Primeiro Colóquio Linguístico sobre o Crioulo de Cabo Verde*. São Vicente, Cape Verde: Ministry of Education and Culture.

Scantamburlo, Luigi. 1981. *Gramática e Dicionário da Lingua Criol da Guiné-Bissau (GCr)*. Bologna: Editrice Missionaria Italiana.

Silva, Izione S. 1985. "Variation and Change in the Verbal System of Capeverdean Crioulo", Ph.D. dissertation, Georgetown University.

Ultan, Russell. 1978. "The Nature of Future Tenses". *Universals of Human Languages* ed. by Joseph Greenberg, 83-123. Stanford: University Press.

Valkhoff, Marius F. 1966. *Studies in Portuguese and Creole*. Johannesburg: Witwatersrand University Press.

————, ed. 1975. *Miscelânea Luso-Africana*. Lisbon: Junta de Investigações Científicas do Ultramar.

Veiga, Manuel. 1984. *Diskrison Strutural di Lingua Kabuverdianu*. Praia, Cape Verde: Institutu Kabuverdianu di Livru.

Voorhoeve, Jan. 1957. "The Verbal System of Sranan". *Lingua* 6.374-96.

Wilson, W.E. 1962. *The Crioulo of Guiné*. Johannesburg: Witwatersrand University Press.

The Tense-Mood-Aspect System
of Berbice Dutch

Ian E. Robertson
The University of the West Indies Saint Augustine

There are two vital and related characteristics of the creole languages of the Caribbean area which are often ignored but which ought to be taken into account in any description of the tense-aspect system. The first is that the temporal zero-point relative to which all temporal deixis is to be measured is, as a general rule, determined by the speaker and may have little to do with the actual time of discourse.

The second feature is that time values are not obligatorily marked within the verb system but may be signalled by temporals or, more importantly, may be clarified by features of the discourse context shared by the participants in the conversation. One obvious consequence of this is that once time values have been set further overt marking is optional.

Another consequence of this second point is that attempts to isolate the tense-aspect markers of Berbice Dutch and indeed of all creole languages ought to be based on the examination of the entire predicate system rather than be restricted to the verbal and adjectival subcategories of predication. Such analyses should also be sensitive to any additional information which may be provided by the discourse context.

Berbice Dutch (BD) is one of two Dutch-lexicon creoles which developed in the former Dutch colonies of Berbice and Essequibo, now part of Guyana. BD was originally spoken on plantations on the Berbice River and its two major tributaries, the Canje and Wiruni Creeks. The language spread to those Amerindian groups which were in close contact with the plantations. BD is dying: its speakers are all older than sixty years. (For further discussion of BD, particularly with reference to substratal influence from the Niger-Congo language Ịjọ, see Smith, Robertson, and Williamson 1987).

The data used for this analysis are derived in the main from field work that I carried out between 1975 and 1980. In addition I have benefited from access to the more recent data collected by Silvia Kouwenberg. The earlier data were amassed primarily in discursive, expository settings rather than by elicitation and interview.

The defining characteristic of a predicator in Berbice Dutch (BD) is the ability to combine with the particle *wa* as in the following examples:

(1)   *ori wa kori.*
      he (wa) work
      "He worked".

(2)   *ori   wa jɛndɛ.*
      it/he (wa) exist
      "He existed".

(3)   *ori wa ʃiki.*
      he (wa) ill
      "He was ill".

(4)   *ori wa jɛndɛ daŋga.*
      he (wa) LOC   there
      "He was there".

(5)   *ɛkɛ wa nimi dida ka.*
      I   (wa) know that not
      "I did not know that".

(6). *ori wa di domni.*
      he (wa) the priest
      "He was the priest".

Berbice Dutch is unique among basilectal creoles of the Caribbean in its use of a mixture of preverbal particles and suffixes in its tense-aspect system. The actual isolation of those markers that are to be considered genuinely BD is complicated; as BD moves towards extinction, it seems to have incorporated items from Guyanese Creole English (GCE), from which it is under constant pressure. This is particularly true of the modals.

Verbal predicators may be subclassified according to which tense-aspect markers and which combinations of tense-aspect markers they permit. In this regard stativity is crucial. However, there are some predicators that are normally, i.e. cross-linguistically, considered statives yet which occur in BD with markers that are usually limited to nonstatives. These include *fiki* "sick", *suku* "know", and *nimi* "want". The number of such predicators is not great enough to justify abandoning the division; in fact, it seems more appropriate to retain the division but adjust the parameters for membership in the stative and nonstative classes. Such an adjustment would not be confined to BD. The predicators in question in BD, the traditional statives that can occur with "nonstative marking" such as the ones listed above, are the same that occur with marking unlikely for statives (Lyons 1977:707) in the English-lexicon creoles of the Caribbean.

1. BD Tense Aspect Markers

Predicators in BD may appear with the following markers:

(a)	Base form only	*brɪŋgi*
		"bring"
		habu
		"have"
		jɛndɛ
		locative copula
		fiki
		"ill"
		enfi frɪndi
		we friend
		"our friend"
(b)	Base form + *-a*	*brɪŋgia*
(c)	Base form + *-tɛ*	*brɪŋtɛ*
(d)	*wa* + Base form	*wa brɪŋgi*
		wa fiki
		wa habu
		wa jɛndɛ
(e)	*wa* + Base form + *-a*	*wa brɪŋgia*
(f)	*wa* + Base form + *-tɛ*	*wa brɪŋtɛ*
(g)	*ma/sa* + Base	*ma brɪŋgi*
		ma ha
		ma jɛndɛ
		ma fiki

(h) *wa* + (*sa/ma*) + Base *wa sa/ma brıŋgi*
           wa sa/ma ha
           wa sa/ma jɛndɛ
           wa sa/ma fiki
(i) *fama* + Base   *fama brıŋgi*
(j) Base + *-tɛ* + *fama*   *brıŋtɛ fama*

Base

The use of the base form in Berbice Dutch best illustrates the earlier point on the signalling of temporal values outside of the verb system. The tense-aspect interpretation given is usually determined by factors outside the predicator itself, including the discourse context as in sentences (7)-(13):

(7) *krıkıt   kap di gʋtʋap   dʋŋgru.*
  cricket   cut the thing-PL night
  "Crickets usually cut the things at night".

(8) *ɛkɛ jef skelpata kanɛ.*
  I   eat turtle   not
  "I do not eat turtle".

(9) *ɛk onli kop di bita   an   kop di gari.*
  I   only   buy the cloth and buy the thread
  "I only used to buy the cloth and buy the thread".

(10) *aftə   ju   kom fan daŋ . . .*
  after you come from there
  "After you came from there . . ."

(11) *a   nʌ kom   wari   ka.*
  He not come home not
  "He hasn't come home".

(12) *an   ba di kɛnap dʒakasap.*
  and kill the people donkey-PL
  "And killed the people's donkeys".

(13) *bebia mira ba ju.*
  red   ants kill you
  "Red ants will kill you".

In each of these cases it is the discourse context which provides a tense-aspect interpretation. The base form must therefore be considered neutral for tense and aspect.

-A (-Arε)

The suffix -a is derived from the Eastern Ịọ imperfective form arε. The full form is very seldom used in my data, it being more evident in the data elicited by Kouwenberg (cf. Kouwenberg and Robertson 1988). Even here, however, its use is not widespread. This suffix is added to the base to signal both durative and iterative aspect, e.g.

(14) εkε st∧di-a   da wat   en   d∧z mia   ju.
     I   studying is   what they do   make you
     "I'm wondering what they do to you".

(15) εkε mu-a   kınki.
     I   going church
     "I am going to church"./"I usually go to church".

As the examples in (16) through (19) indicate, this suffix is not subject to any time restrictions:

(16) di   fruku   di   εkε bifi-a . . . .
     the morning this I   saying
     "This morning I was saying . . ."

(17) εkε jefi-a   nɔu.
     I   eating now
     "I'm eating now".

(18) so rumalo   pantε εkε bi   dat ju   kom-a di   fruku
     so Romalho told   me say that you coming the morning
     di   hiri.
     this here
     "So Romalho told me that you would be coming here this morning".

(19) ivri   daka εkε luru-a   moto.
     every day I   looking motor
     "Every day I look at motor boats".

In (16) the time is already marked by the temporal phrase di fruku di, while in (17) the time nɔu clearly shows the action to be nonpast. In (18), the time value of the verb in the subordinate clause is derived from the fact that the time value of the verb in the main clause, *pantɛ*, is past. Finally, in (19), *ivri daka* marks iteration; once again it is the hearer's knowledge that the speaker still looks at motor boats that causes this time interpretation to be given. If the entire story from which the particular utterance is taken were cast in the past, the past interpretation would be the acceptable one.

The suffix -*a* is not used with stative predicators as a general rule. The only exception to this rule in the data is *suku* + -*a* "want".

In addition there are a few examples in the data in which the suffix is replaced by a preposed particle. The process of change is exemplified in (20) and (21); IMP signals an imperfective marker, whether suffix or preposed particle.

(20) *ju   kiki dat di   jɛrma a   sɛt-a   di tron   enfi fa.*
      you see that the lady   IMP sit-IMP the throne us   of
      "You see that the lady is reigning over us".

(21) *ɛnɛ   a   kɔrɔ.*
      rain IMP fall
      "It is raining".

The presence of the preposed particle is probably the direct result of pressure from the GCE imperfective marker *a*, a preposed particle. The double marking of the continuous imperfective in (20) suggests a feature in transition, the double marking representing an intermittent stage en route to the resolution of the change. In BD *a*, whether as suffix or preposed particle, expresses a wide range of imperfective meanings: iterative, durative, continuous, and habitual. In the terminology, then, of the prototypical TMA system proposed by Bickerton (1974), *a* is the BD marker of nonpunctual aspect.

-Tɛ

The suffix -*tɛ* is one of two markers in BD which are used with past time reference, the other being *wa*. However, while *wa* expresses past, -*tɛ* signals the perfect. Some examples of the use of -*tɛ* are given in (22a) through (25).

(22) a. *a   mo-tɛ   mɛt eni.*
          he go-PERF with them
          "He has gone with them".

(23) a. *a kɔrə-tɛ.*
          it fall-PERF
          "It has fallen".

(24) a. *ɛkɛ paʃ-tɛ   eni   fa   sms   eni   kal   kal   tʌkapu.*
          I   care-PERF them from since they small small child-PL
          "I took/have taken care of them since they were little children".

(25) *ori grui-tɛ   wɪruni.*
       she grow-PERF wiruni
       "She grew/has grown up at Wiruni".

The foundation for analyzing *-tɛ* as perfect lies in part in the relative recency implied by the marker's use; as a result, there is frequently the implication that the state induced by an action marked by *-tɛ* may continue to obtain at the reference time (the temporal zero-point). This is most clearly illustrated by the verb *mu* "go" in (22); the use of *mo* + *-tɛ* signals that the subject of the sentence has gone but has not returned. In other cases, the implication with reference to current state is not so strong but remains probable. Thus, it is likely that in (23) the thing that fell is still down. Finally, in the final two examples, no assumption in either direction can be made about whether the "caring" has ceased or continues in (24) or likewise with the residence at Wiruni in (25).[1]

As a general rule *-tɛ* is not used with any but dynamic (Lyons 1977:707) predicators. There are, however, some exceptions: *ʃikitɛ* "ill", *blɛntətɛ* "blind", *nintɛ* "know" all appear in the data. In the specific case of *nintɛ* it is instructive that the *-tɛ* form never occurs with the negative particle. This seems to suggest that *-tɛ* is only used if the state has already been realized. Both *ʃikitɛ* and *blɛntətɛ* are used where the states are continuing into the present or where there is no clear indication that it has passed. These uses support the assertion that recency — and also currency — are the crucial dimensions. That is, *-tɛ* expresses "current relevance" in BD; this is precisely the definition of perfect put forth by Anderson (1982).

This analysis is further confirmed by utterances such as:

(26) *sʌtɪti   andɛ gʋtʋ jɛndɛ ʃi ben wati   wonɔu-tɛ.*
       sometimes some thing LOC it   in   what worn-out-PERF
       "Perhaps there is something in it which has worn out".

(27) *ɛkɛ jɛ kop-tɛ   kosn   sakap   ka, ɛk mia   ɛkɛ egɲjɛ.*
     I   buy-PERF pillow sack-PL not I   make my   own
     "I have not bought pillow cases, I make my own".

In the former example the part that is worn is still in the recorder referred
to, and in the latter the practice of making pillow cases, rather than buying
them, is still current.

Wa

By contrast with *-tɛ*, *wa* combines freely with all predicators.

(28) *ə wa   jɛndɛ hiri.*
     it PAST LOC   here
     "It was here".

(29) *ori wa   ʃiki.*
     he   PAST ill
     "He was ill".

(30) *tit   ɛk wa   jʊŋgʊ jɛrma . . .*
     when I   PAST young woman
     "When I was a young woman . . ."

(31) *en   wa   bifi   mɛtɛ ju   daŋʃi.*
     they PAST speak with you there
     "They spoke with you there".

In each case cited here, the predication is seen as something that is not current. The difference between *wa* (expressing past) and *-tɛ* (expressing perfect) in this regard can be seen by comparing (22a)-(24a), presented earlier,
with (22b)-(24b).

(22) b. *a wa   mu mɛt eni.*
        he PAST go with them
        "He went with them".

(23) b. *a wa   kɔrɛ.*
        it PAST fall
        "It fell (but is now up again)".

(24) b. *ɛkɛ wa   paʃ eni fa   sɪns   eni kal   kal   tʌkapu.*
        I   PAST care them from since they small small child-PL
        "I took/had taken care of them from since they were small".

Particularly, then, in its contrast to -*te*, *wa* can be characterized by its relative remoteness and completion.

A further point with regard to tense marking in BD is the status of the bare verb form. In other Caribbean creoles, this form ordinarily expresses the simple past for nonstative verbs. In BD, as was noted earlier, the base form expresses a wide range of tense and aspect; it is by no means confined to simple past. The fact that the base form did not develop into a marker of simple past may be explained in part by the fact that BD already had an overt marker of past tense, *wa*.

Fama

In addition to *wa* and -*te* as potential past time markers, *fama* may also be used. Derived from the verb that means "to finish", the form signals completion though not necessarily pastness. In its ability to occur in non-past environments, as in (32) below, *fama* contrasts with *wa*. A further point about the completive marker *fama* is that its distribution parallels that of *don* in GCE (Bickerton 1975) and *caba* in Sranan (Taylor 1956).

(32) ɛk   ma   plandi ə fama.
     I   FUT   plant   it COMP
     "I will plant it all out".

(33) enfi mo-tɛ   mu plandi ə fama.
     we   go-PERF go plant   it COMP
     "We went to plant it all out".

(34) enfi na   fama   plandi ka.
     we   not   COMP   plant   not
     "We haven't finished planting".

(35) ɛk fama jefi.
     I   COMP eat
     "I have finished eating".

Fama is unique among BD markers in that it can occur both preverbally and clause-finally. In this, it is like Liberian English *feni* (Singler 1983) and GCE *don*.

Ma/Sa

Futurity in BD is marked by *ma* or *sa*.

(36) *dɛn ɛk ma pama di kɛnap en mə wakti fi ju.*
　　 then I FUT tell the people they must wait for you
　　 "Then I will tell the people that they should wait for you".

(37) *a bi a ma kap ə.*
　　 he say he FUT cut it
　　 "He says (that) he will cut it".

(38) *ju ma tɪmi kori ka.*
　　 you FUT able work not
　　 "You will not be able to work".

(39) *ɛkɛ ma tɪmi fragi ka en sa ha fi du.*
　　 I FUT able ask not they will have to do
　　 "I will not be willing to ask; they will have to be enough".

(40) *wanɛrɛ ju draɪ wɛrɛ enʃ sa biʃi.*
　　 when you return again we FUT talk
　　 "When you return we will talk".

(41) *a sa help enʃi kop riʃ.*
　　 it FUT help us buy rice
　　 "It will help us to buy rice".

(42) *a sa luru lɔmbə fi bi a ma bɔrə.*
　　 it FUT look bad to say he FUT pass
　　 "It will seem terrible to say that he will pass".

The two particles *ma* and *sa* may be derived from Eastern Ịjọ and Dutch respectively. In the case of *ma*, I have argued elsewhere (1979) that it may well have been further influenced by the Yoruba future particle *maa*. If, on the other hand, the form is purely Eastern Ịjọ in origin, then it represents another instance of the use of the verb meaning "go" (*mu* + -*a*) to signal futurity. This is a frequent occurrence in the world's languages and, in particular, in the creoles of this region, cf. Bickerton (1975) on *sa* and *go* in GCE.

There is considerable overlap in the function of *ma* and *sa*. The only possible difference is that the use of *ma* implies a greater commitment to the realization of the future action; however, the evidence at hand is not adequate to establish this. Certainly a sentence like (43), where *ma* and *sa* are present in tandem, does not support the claim of a difference in force between the two.

(43) *ɛk sa   pi   ju   andə tablɪt an   ɛk ma pi   ju   mɛsrɛ*
     I   FUT give you   some tablet and I   FUT give you medicine
gʊtʊ fi   bu.
thing to   drink
"I will give you some tablets and I will give you medicine to drink".

There seems to be a transition in progress, from *ma* to *sa*. If this is so, it may be argued that this process was initiated but not completed before BD began to decay. On the other hand, such a transition is somehow at odds with a contemporaneous transition in GCE. Bickerton (1975:42) gives evidence that *sa* was the principal irrealis marker in late-nineteenth-century GCE; in contrast, *go* now dominates GCE. Thus, if *sa* was supplanting *ma* in BD, the change was occurring at the same time that it was itself being supplanted in GCE.

Though the examples presented above all illustrate the use of *ma* and *sa* to mark futures, both of them mark conditionals as well. The combination of future and conditional yields the category **irrealis**. Strictly speaking, then, *ma* and *sa* are irrealis markers (rather than simply future).

2.   Combinations of Tense-Mood-Aspect Markers

The markers presented thus far form the basic tense-mood-aspect system of Berbice Dutch. The following combinations manifest themselves in the data:

wa + *ma/sa*
wa + *-a*
wa + *-tɛ*

The distributional restrictions noted earlier for individual markers still apply when those markers co-occur with other markers.

Wa + *Ma/Sa*

Unrealized conditions are signalled in Berbice Dutch by a combination of the *wa* "past" and *ma* or *sa* "irrealis".

(44) *aʃ ɛk wa   nintɛ,   ɛk wa   sa   mu.*
     if I   PAST know-PERF I   PAST FUT go
"If I had known I would have gone".

(45) *ɛk wa   sa   pi   ju   en   giof.*
     I   PAST FUT give you one blow
     "I would have given you a severe blow".

(46) *a wa   ma   mu mɔi.*
     it PAST FUT go well
     "It would have gone well".

Wa + -A

The imperfective marker *-a* may combine with the past marker *wa* to signal that an event or action took place repeatedly or was stretched over a period of time. Since *-a* is rarely used with statives there are, as expected, no examples in the data of this combination occurring with statives.

(47) *a   wa   kap-a   tun.*
     he PAST cut-IMP field
     "He was cutting a field".

(48) *ɛkɛ wa   kriki-a kos   dʋŋgru.*
     I   PAST get-IMP fever night
     "I was getting fever at night".

(49) *mɛt ori sʌ   ɛk wa   stop-a.*
     with him there I PAST stay-IMP
     "I used to stay there with him".

It is vital to note that *-a* and *-tɛ* never combine. The most likely reason for this is that such a combination would produce two suffixes in a language which has already shown a marked reduction in the use of suffixes (particularly when compared to its two parent languages, Dutch and Ịjọ).

Wa + -Tɛ

The combination of the past particle *wa* and the perfect suffix *-tɛ* is illustrated in (50)-(52) below:

(50) *a wa   grui-tɛ   hɔgə.*
     it PAST grow-PERF tall
     "It had grown tall".

(51) *ʃi   tʌkʌ wa   draɪ-tɛ   gu.*
     his child PAST become-PERF big
     "His children have become big".

(52) *ɛk wa   mo-tɛ   oɪti.*
I PAST go-PERF out
"I had gone out".

3. Modals

The modals discussed here are those which may be considered genuinely BD, rather than being more recent borrowings from GCE.

Muti

Obligation or certainty is signalled by *muti*.

(53) *ju   muti ful   moɪ ka.*
you must feel well not
"You must feel ill".

(54) *ju   muti kiki ə bika   da nali   ka.*
you must see it because is needle not
"You must see it because it is not a needle".

(55) *ju   muti kriki kali help fɔrə   ju   draɪ ju   landi wɛrɛ.*
you must get   little help before you return your land back
"You must get some help before you return".

(56) *a   kiba, dɪs kol   a muti bi∧ntə   alma dɪ gʊtʊap.*
he short this make he must remember all the thing-PL
"He's short. That's why he must remember everything".

Mə

Desirability is expressed by *mə*.

(57) *ɛk t∧k∧ bi ju   mə   bi∧ntə dida ka.*
my child say you should believe this not
"My child said, 'You should not believe that'".

(58) *ju   mə   treɪ kom fruku*
you should try come early
"You should try to come early".

(59) *ju   mə   kom tɪti   ɛk mɛtɛ marian.*
you should come when I   and Marian
"You should come when Marian and I do".

Tɪni and Ka

Willingness and ability are expressed by *tɪni* and *ka*. (This *ka* is to be distinguished from the negative particle.)

(60) ɛk tɪni kori ka.
     I   can work not
     "I cannot work".

(61) ɛk tɪni fi mia di tun kori ka.
     I   able to make the field work not
     "I cannot work in the field".

(62) ɛk ɪni tal   mɛrɛ ka.
     I able count more not
     "I cannot count any more".

(63) ɛk ka mu.
     "I can go".

The modal system in Berbice Dutch is the grammatical area in which the influence of English is most strongly felt. For example, *k∧da* and *ʃ∧da* have come to express unrealized possibility and unrealized desirability respectively. These forms are obvious intrusions from Guyanese Creole English. The original marker of unrealized possibility is *aka* (< *wa* + *ka*) but it is used only once in the entire corpus.

(64) ɛk aka   mu.
     I   was-can go
     "I could have gone".

Because Berbice Dutch does not permit the co-occurrence of suffixes, the question of the order of occurrence of tense, mood, and aspect markers arises only for preverbal markers. In fact, when more than one marker appears preverbally, the tense marker precedes the modal, as (65) and (66) illustrate.

(65) ɛk wa tɪni fi mu en plɛkɛ ka lahan eni ka.
     I   PAST able to go one place not leave them not
     "I was not willing to go anywhere (and) leave them".

(66) ɛk wa ka mu luru fi ori b∧ tɪti ɛk mo-tɛ . . .
     I   PAST can go look for him but when I   go-PERF
     "I could go to look for him but when I did go . . ."

4. Summary

The mixing of preverbal particles with suffixes makes the system of predication in BD unique among basilectal creoles of the Caribbean. As Smith, Robertson, and Williamson (1987) demonstrate, the suffixes are derivable from the parent language(s). While undergoing alteration in their meaning, these suffixes survived the creolization process.

In contemporary BD, there is clear evidence of features in transition. The transition, however, is part of the process of language death. The set of modal auxiliaries that BD now uses as well as the competition between suffixal and preverbal *a* illustrates the growing inroads of Guyanese Creole English into the Berbice Dutch tense-mood-aspect system.

Note

1. Another use of *-tɛ* is in the antecedent clause of conditionals:
    (i) *aʃ ju   meʃ-tɛ   en hɔlə ju   ha   fi loʃ   di hɛlə.*
       if you miss-PERF one hole you have to loose the whole
       "If you miss one hole, you have to unravel everything".

    (ii) *dʒ ʌs   kɛkɛ   a ju   dek-tɛ   nali . . .*
        just   as   if you take-PERF needle
        "Just as if you took a needle . . ."

References

Alleyne, Mervyn C. 1980. *Comparative Afro-American*. Ann Arbor: Karoma.

———. 1987. "Predicate Structures in Saramaccan". *Studies in Saramaccan Language Structure* (= *Caribbean Culture Studies*, 2) ed. by Mervyn C. Alleyne, 71-86. Amsterdam: Instituut voor Algemene Taalwetenschap, University of Amsterdam, and Folklore Studies Project, University of the West Indies.

Anderson, Lloyd B. 1982. "The 'Perfect' as a Universal and as a Language-Specific Category". *Tense-Aspect: Between semantics and pragmatics* ed. by Paul J. Hopper, 227-64. Amsterdam and Philadelphia: John Benjamins.

Bickerton, Derek. 1974. "Creolization, Linguistic Universals, Natural Semantax and the Brain". *University of Hawaii Working Papers in Linguistics* 6(3).125-41. (Reprinted in *Issues in English Creoles: Papers from the 1975 Hawaii conference* ed. by Richard Day 1980.1-18. Heidelberg: Groos.)

————. 1975. *Dynamics of a Creole System*. Cambridge: University Press.

————. 1981. *Roots of Language*. Ann Arbor: Karoma.

————. 1984. "The Language Bioprogram Hypothesis". *Behavioral and Brain Sciences* 7.173-221.

Comrie, Bernard. 1976. *Aspect: An introduction to the study of verbal aspect and related problems*. Cambridge: University Press.

Gibson, Kean. 1986. "The Ordering of Auxiliary Notions in Guyanese Creole". *Lg* 62.571-86.

Kouwenberg, Silvia, and Ian E. Robertson. 1988. "The Marking of Tense, Mood and Aspect in the Berbice Dutch Creole Language". *Beiträge zum 4. Essener Kolloquium über "Sprachkontakt, Sprachwandel, Sprachwechsel, Sprachtod"*, ed. by Norbert Boretzky, Werner Enninger, and Thomas Stolz, 151-74. Bochum: Dr. N. Brockmeyer.

Lyons, John. 1977. *Semantics 2*. Cambridge: University Press.

Mufwene, Salikoko S. 1983. "Observations on Time Reference in Jamaican and Guyanese Creoles". *Studies in Caribbean Language*, ed. by Lawrence Carrington, 155-77. St. Augustine, Trinidad: Society for Caribbean Linguistics. (Revised version in *English World-Wide* 4.199-229. 1983.)

Robertson, Ian E. 1979. "Berbice Dutch — A Description", Ph.D. dissertation, University of the West Indies.

Singler, John Victor. 1983. "Liberian English *feni*: AUX and ADV". Paper presented at the Annual Meeting of the Linguistic Society of America.

Smith, Norval, Ian E. Robertson, and Kay Williamson. 1987. "The Ịjọ Element in Berbice Dutch". *Language in Society* 16.49-89.

Taylor, Douglas R. 1956. "Use and Disuse of Languages in the West Indies". *Caribbean Quarterly* 5(2).67-77.

Nigerian Pidgin English in Old Calabar in the Eighteenth and Nineteenth Centuries

Joan M. Fayer
University of Puerto Rico

In the eighteenth century Old Calabar was a well known trading center. The Efiks who settled in the Cross River estuary, in what is now southeastern Nigeria, probably came there in the middle of the seventeenth century. Their trade, first in slaves and later in palm oil, was almost exclusively with the British, and an English-based pidgin was the language used. One of these traders, Antera Duke, kept a diary for his own personal use in a large folio in which he recorded his daily trading, community, and family activities. In the nineteenth century the diary was taken to Edinburgh by a missionary and was eventually placed in the library of the United Church of Scotland. Just how the missionary acquired the diary is not known. A copy of portions of the diary was made, and it is only this copy that survived the bombing of the library in World War II. This copy of portions of the diary from the years 1785-1788 is published in Forde (1968). The *Diary of Antera Duke* (*DAD*) provides evidence that the pidgin English used in Old Calabar was not just a spoken language but also had written functions (Fayer 1986). It also provides some of the earliest evidence of the pidgin that continues — as Nigerian Pidgin English (NPE) — to be spoken in the area today.

Antera Duke was not the only Efik trader who kept records. In his diary there are references to the *coomy* book, "customs" book, of another Efik trader, Duke Ephraim, and to a letter written by the Efik traders to the captain of a ship. Unfortunately these have not been preserved. There are, however, other texts, six letters written by Efik traders to Liverpool merchants from 1763 to 1777 (Williams 1897).

In the early nineteenth century there are brief letters written by some of the prominent Efiks to British captains whose ships were anchored in Old Calabar (Holman 1834) as well as letters they wrote about stopping the slave trade (McFarlan 1946; Waddell 1970). After the middle of the nineteenth century there are more texts. In 1846 the first mission was established by the United Presbyterian Church. The diaries kept by the missionaries (Goldie 1890; Marwick 1897; Waddell 1970) and articles they wrote about their work for the *Missionary Record of the United Presybterian Church* contain letters written by the Efiks in NPE. After the arrival of the missionaries, the functions of the language expanded, with English now being used as one of the languages of education and religion.

All the data used in the following analysis have been taken from texts written by the Efiks. While there are differences between written and spoken language, in Old Calabar these differences may not have been as great as they are in communities in which printed material is available. Some of the Efik traders could write and read their own writing and the handwritten letters and records of others, but there are several references to the fact that they could not read printed material. Holman (1834:399) says, "There is not one of them who ever read English, or any other language in print. . ." He adds that one prominent Efik trader regretted not being able to read a newspaper. Waddell (1970:280) finds that when the missionaries arrived this still was true. He says, "It was a curious fact that while not one could peruse a printed book, a certain number had learned to use the pen in the way of trade". For the Efiks, writing in NPE was a way of keeping records and communicating with the captains of the ships and merchants who supplied them with the goods they wanted from Britain. While they may have used their best NPE when writing, their writing probably was closer to their speech than would be the case in a community that has access to printed material.

The exact date of the development of an English-based pidgin in West Africa cannot be determined. Mafeni (1971:97) states that it probably began with the first contacts with the British in the sixteenth century. There are no written data from the period. Tonkin (1971) discusses the replacement of a Portuguese-based pidgin and sets the date for English-based pidgin in Nigeria about 1750. This seems to be late since there are authentic texts in the pidgin from 1763, and it seems only likely that spoken varieties of the pidgin were in existence before the written ones. Mafeni's estimate may be too early, but Tonkin's seems to be too late.

Over the years, varieties of this pidgin continued to be used in the area, and the pidgin changed in function and form. In Nigeria today NPE has widespread use (Mafeni 1971; Agheyisi 1971, 1984; Tonkin 1971; Adekunle 1972; Nwoye 1978; Shnukal and Marchese 1983). Agheyisi (1984) finds that there are two varieties of NPE. One variety, which "approximates the purest form of the English-based Pidgin" (p. 214), is used in daily transactions and is a first language for many people. It is a "stable linguistic system, manifesting more consistently typical pidgin features". The second is a type of interlanguage used by those who do not have full competency in NPE.

The linguistic features of NPE as it is used today have been analyzed by Mafeni (1971), Barbag-Stoll (1983) and in more detail by Agheyisi (1971). A complete description of how this pidgin developed will probably never be possible. Sufficient data have not been found to document the long history of this language. The earliest authentic data that have been found, that of the letters written by the Efik traders and the *DAD*, do enable analysis of the eighteenth century varieties of the language. In the early nineteenth century the letters of the Efik traders to the British captains and later the letters to the missionaries make it possible to continue the diachronic description. A linguistic summary of a late nineteenth century variety of the pidgin used in West Africa is found in Grade (1892). Thus, beginning in the eighteenth century, there are data that can be used in the synchronic and diachronic analysis of NPE. It should be noted that the use of written texts presents some limitations. The absence of any given form in the data does not mean that the writer did not know the form and use it in other forms or discourse or even in other written discourse that did not survive.

In the discussion that follows, I use the distinctions between tense and aspect made by Comrie:

> Tense relates the time of the situation referred to to some other time, usually the moment of speaking (1976:1-2).
> Aspect is not concerned with relating the time of the situation to any other time point, but rather with the internal temporal constituency of the one situation (1976:3).

Thus, tense is "situation external time" and aspect "situation internal time" (1976:5).

1. The Diary of Antera Duke (DAD)

The most extensive early text in NPE is the *DAD* which consists of 188 entries of approximately 13,000 words. Since this is the longest eighteenth century text, it will serve as the basis for the analysis of the eighteenth century verbal system that follows.[1] Written data from the other Efik traders are also used as a way of analyzing the variation of the period.

In the *DAD* punctuation and capitalization were not often used to mark the beginnings and ends of sentences. Subjects occur immediately before verbs. This invariant word order is one of the ways to determine the subject and verb of each sentence. A typical entry is:

(1)   *about 6 am   in aqua Landing with small fog morning*
       about 6 a.m. in Aqua Landing with small fog morning
       and I walk up to see Egbo Sherry play wee wer   new
       and I walk up to see Egbo Sherry play we   wear new
       cloth   and at 12 clock   night Captin   Fairwether
       clothes and at 12 o'clock night Captain Fairweather's
       tender go way   with 280 slaves (p. 102)
       tender go away with 280 slaves
       "About 6 a.m. in Aqua Landing with small morning fog. I walked up to see an Egbosherry play. We wore new clothes, and at 12 o'clock at night Captain Fairweather's tender went away with 280 slaves".[2]

The verbs in the *DAD* are usually unmarked for tense or aspect. Verbs are also not marked for person or number.

All the sentences in the entries do not have verbs or copulas. Of the missing elements, it is most often a form of *be*. In the cases where the zero verb is not *be*, the immediate and general contexts most often suggest meanings such as "see", "hear", and "have".

(2)   *wee news about new ship* (p. 101)
       we news about new ship
       "We heard the news about the new ship".

Thus, in the *DAD* it is possible not only for *be* to be missing, but other statives as well.

In the *DAD* 93 percent (729/783) of the verbs that refer to past actions or states are unmarked. Of these 20 percent (147/729) are stative verbs. Like unmarked action verbs, unmarked statives can refer to the past. In the diary, Antera Duke recorded past events and future ones. There are no examples of verbs there with present time reference; still, it seems probable that unmarked verbs could also have present time reference, which would be indicated by context or temporal marking.

The most frequent way in which the time reference of unmarked verbs is determined is by adverbial words and phrases, most often occurring at the beginning of sentences. Individual entries in the diary usually begin with these markers, as in (1) above. The time refers either to the time the day's activities began or to the time that the events described began. With the exception of examples such as (21) below, most other events follow from this initial temporal reference point. Events in the diary are described in chronological order: what happened first is recounted first. (And results follow causes.)

Sentences in the *DAD* begin not only with temporal markers but also with conjunctions. The most frequently used is *so* with the meaning of "as a result" or "then". When *so* is used like this to indicate temporal sequence, it can be used in successive sentences.

(3)   *so I have all Captin   com   ashor so I Little sick*
      so I have all captains come ashore so I little sick
      so I not drink no mimbo all Day (pp. 82-3)
      so I not drink no mimbo all day
      "So I had all the captains come ashore. I was a little sick, so I did not drink any mimbo (palm wine) all day".

The conjunction with the next highest frequency is *and*. An example is in (1) above. *And* also can be used in successive sentences. Conjunctions and adverbial temporal markers can also be used together to set the time reference of the verb, as in (4):

(4)   &   *my first Boy com   from Curcock with slave*
      and my first boy come from Curcock with slaves
      and 12 clock   night wee go to Savage (p. 82)
      and 12 o'clock night we   go to Savage
      "And my first boy came from Curcock with slaves. And at twelve o'clock at night we went to Savage's ship".

With the possible exception of *sam time*, all the conjunctions and adverbials signal the sequence of events in the entries and relate the events to the external situation; as such, they are tense markers. *Sam time*, which occurs with very low frequency, seems to be different. It can indicate progressive aspect.

(5)   *so I firs one great gun for Crek   sam   time I*
      so I fire one great gun in Creek same time I
      find Coffe   Duk   Heer (p. 95)
      find Coffee Duke here
      "So as I was firing a great gun in the creek, I found Coffee
      Duke here".

There are three occurrences of *sam time* where it moves closer to the verb;
however, in these instances, *sam time* occurs immediately after the verb
rather than before it, as in (6). In addition, there are several other examples
of temporal markers after verbs, as (7) illustrates.

(6)   *so my canow get som   time* (p. 84)
      so my canoe get same time
      "So my canoe got (there at the) same time".

(7)   *so wee com   back in 5 clock time* (p. 100)
      so we   come back in 5 clock time
      "So we came back at five o'clock".

In those sentences with no adverbs or conjunctions the invariant word
order of the sentences indicates the beginning of each new sentence. Events
can be sequenced without any overt indication of their order, as in (8).

(8)   *so I &   Esin go bord   Cooper for brek   Book for*
      so I and Esin go board Cooper to   break book for
      4   slave arshbong Duk   son com   hom for
      four slaves Archibong Duke's son comes home from
      Orroup with slav (p. 92)
      Orroup with slave(s)
      "So Esin and I went on board Cooper's ship to break book (to
      begin trading) for four slaves. Archibong Duke's son came
      home from Orroup with (a) slave(s)".

Not all the verbs in the *DAD* appear in unmarked forms. There are
twenty occurrences of verbs which at first seem to be past tense forms:
killd, *don(e)*, *arrived*, and *drishst* "dressed". Closer analysis reveals that
these are the base (monomorphemic) forms of the verbs and occur in the
same constructions in which the base form of other verbs is used. Thus, just
as the zero form *tak* is used in (9), so the form *drishst* is used in (10).

(9)   *and I Did tak   one goat for mak   Doctor at my*
      and I did take one goat to   make doctor at my

god Bason (p. 94)
god's basin
"And I did take one goat to make doctor (a sacrifice) at my
god's basin".

(10) *so wee 3   Did Drishst whit   men* . . . (p.84)
so we three did dress   white men
"So we three did dress as white men . . ."

In these eighteenth century data verbs may have alternate spellings,
but with few exceptions verbs have a basic form, one that is usually derived
from the uninflected present tense SE verb.

However, not all of the verbs in the *DAD* occur in invariant forms with
no modification; some occur with auxiliaries. These constructions all have
low frequencies. The most common auxiliary is *did*, which occurs 55 times.
Although *did* is taken from a SE past form, I will argue that its primary
function is to indicate emphasis or contrast. In his analysis of the grammatical role of SE *do*, Twaddell (1960:15) finds that it is "the semantically
empty auxiliary" which in one function "bears the stress of truth-value insis-
tence". This seems to be the function of *did* in the *DAD*.[3]

An alternative analysis of the function of *did* is that it simply signals
past time. However, the data contain several examples of compound verbs
in the past; only the second verb and never the first is marked with *did*, as
in (11):

(11) *soon after we walk up to see wee town &   Did tak*
     soon after we walk up to see our town and did take
     one great guns to putt for   canow for two   Egbo
     one great gun to put in   canoe for two of Egbo
     Young   men   Bring hom   in aqua Landing (p. 79)
     Young's men   to bring home to Aqua Landing
     "Soon after that we walked up to see our town and did take one
     great gun to put in the canoe for two of Egbo Young's men to
     bring home to Aqua Landing".

If *did* were a past time auxiliary, it surely would have preceded the first
verb.

As noted above, tense in the *DAD* is ordinarily signalled by sentence-
initial conjunctions and temporal adverbs. There is only one example of *did*
in a sentence without these markers. Given that a diary entry would already

have past time indicated by sentence-initial temporal markers, it does not seem likely that in the *DAD* this is the function of *did* as well.

John Singler (p.c.) argues for still another analysis, one in which *did* functions to re-inforce temporal sequencing. That is, where the purpose of an anterior marker in many Atlantic pidgins and creoles is to signal the disruption of temporal sequencing, *did* in the *DAD* performs a converse function, signalling instead the preservation of the time sequence. That is, when *did* occurs, it is when the sequence in which events are reported matches the sequence in which they occurred. There are examples of such markers in Liberian varieties of pidgin, *waz* in Kru Pidgin English (see Singler, this volume) and *feni* in basilectal Liberian English more generally (see Singler, forthcoming). While this analysis takes care of those instances of the use of *did* where its emphatic or constrastive character seems hard to see, it still must be questioned. Given that the structure of the diary is overwhelmingly linear, with events reported again and again in the sequence in which they occur, it seems odd that Antera Duke would ever feel the need to signal the sequencing that occurs virtually all of the time. Moreover, there are six examples in the diary where a *did*-marked sentence is followed by a *did*-marked sentence (and, in at least one instance, that sentence is followed by a *did*-marked sentence). The strings of *did*-marked sentence are, I would argue, better accounted for by an analysis that is independent of questions of temporal sequentiality.

With regard to other auxiliaries: while there are no examples of *do* in the diary, there is one occurrence of *don('t)*.

(12)   *so wee say wee Don   know before wee settle   about*
        so   we   say we   don't know before we   settle about
        King of Callabar first (p. 105)
        King of Calabar first
        "So we said we didn't know before we first settled about the King of Calabar".

This example is unusual because negation (*no/not/never*) in all other cases is found before the verb without *do*. (Throughout the diary there are other examples of SE constructions, such as passives, within sentences that are otherwise in pidgin.)

In the *DAD* the construction *was + V* occurs 28 times. In five of these, its presence indicates simple past, as in (13); in the rest, it signals past before past, as in (14). (Thus, in the framework of Bickerton 1974, it can be argued that *was* marks anteriority.) *Was* is invariant, occurring with both singular and plural subjects.

(13) *and wee putt head   together to carry him on bord*
    and we   put heads together to carry him on board
    ship for putt his for iron and two his slav   I
    ship for put him in   irons and two his slaves I
    was carry his on bord my self (p. 102)
    carried   him on board myself
    "And we put our heads together to carry him on board ship to put him in irons and two of his slaves. I carried him on board myself".

(14) *and after 7 clock   night wee have all us   town*
    and after 7 o'clock night we   have all our town
    genllmen   meet for Coffee   Cobin to settle everry
    gentlemen meet at   Coffee's cabin   to settle every
    Bad bob   we was mak   sinc wee father Dead (p. 105)
    bad quarrel we had   made since our   father died
    "And after 7 o'clock at night we had all our town gentlemen meet at Coffee's cabin to settle every bad quarrel we had had since our father died".

There are only two examples of the auxiliary *been*. These, too, signal anteriority:

(15) *and so Callabar beagain ask him what make*
    and so Calabar began   ask him what make
    Been Run way   on Bord (p. 111)
    run   away on board
    "And so the Calabar people began to ask him what made him run away on board".

(16) *so wee say never Been hear that for   weer grandy*
    so we   say never heard   that since our   grand
    grandy father (p. 105)
    grand   father
    "So we said that we had never heard of that since our great-grandfather's time".

Future tense verb forms are not frequent in a diary such as this which records daily activities. In the few examples that are in the diary, future time is indicated by the auxiliary *will*.

> (17) *so his will pay 1000 copper for every Callabar* (p. 110)
>   so he will pay 1000 coppers for every Calabar
>   "So he will pay 1000 coppers for every Calabar person".

There are just two auxiliaries in the *DAD* that indicate aspect. One of these is *have*, which is used with both singular and plural subjects. It occurs preverbally 58 times. Though in some instances it seems to indicate necessity or obligation (cf. English *have to*), most often it seems to indicate the perfect, as in (18).[4]

> (18) *and I hear one my Ephrim abashey Egbo Sherry*
>   and I hear one my Ephrim Abashey Egbo Sherry
>   *women have Brun two son one Day* (p. 112)
>   women have born two sons one day
>   "And I heard one of my Ephrim Abashey Egbo Sherry women
>   bore (has/had borne) two sons in one day".

Support for an extensive use of *have* to mark the perfect in the *DAD* may also come from the substrate. In the Efik verbal system there is a present/completive construction (Welmers 1968:31). Thus, what is seen in English as a present tense is expressed in Efik by a completive. The Efik equivalent of "I see" is better translated into English by "I have sighted" or "I have caught sight of". This is a likely source for such examples in the *DAD* as (19):

> (19) *after 3 clock   noon   I have see us   Boostam*
>   after 3 o'clock afternoon I have seen our Boostam
>   *canow com Down with 5 slave   and yams* (pp. 90-1)
>   canoe come down with 5 slaves and yams
>   "After 3 o'clock in the afternoon I saw our Boostam canoe come
>   down with five slaves and yams".

(At other times, however, the use of *have* just seems to mark a past action in a series of events that are not otherwise overtly marked for tense.)

There are three occurrences of *done*, an auxiliary which also seems to express perfect aspect.

> (20) *so I Done pay Captin OSatam for all I owe* (p. 86)
>   so I have   paid Captain Tatam   for all I owe
>   "So I have paid Captain Tatam for all that I owed".

With so few examples, it is hard to determine much about *done*, e.g. whether or not it is linked in any way in the *DAD* to *did*, and what its relationship is to the aspect marker *don* in twentieth century NPE.

Sam time as a marker of progressive aspect was discussed above. *Goin(g)* in some of its occurrences also seems to have progressive meaning.

(21) *about 4 clock   wee goin   in   Town plaver   house* (p. 101)
     about 4 o'clock we   going into town palaver house
     "About 4 o'clock we were going into the town palaver house".

However, there are other examples in which *goin(g)* seems simply to be a variant of *go*.

(22) *I come up to my work plase and goin   to Egbo plaver*
     I come up to my work place and going to Egbo palaver
     house (p. 108)
     house
     "I went up to my work place and went into the Egbo palaver house".

There are also two examples of *to goin*, further evidence that at least in some cases *goin* is an alternate form of *go*.

With regard to modality, one way of expressing necessity is by the use of *mush* "must". There are three tokens of it; they do not co-occur with any of the preverbal tense or aspect markers.

(23) *Dick must Loos one his hand by   that guns* (p. 99)
     Dick must lose   one his hands because of that gun
     "Dick must lose one of his hands because of that gun".

As can be seen, tense and aspect auxiliaries are few in number. Those that do exist occur with very low frequencies. There are no examples of aspect and modal auxiliaries co-occurring with tense auxiliaries. This may mean that they did not co-occur, or it may mean that there are simply no examples in the data. The first explanation seems more likely.

2.   Other Eighteenth Century Efiks

There are fewer data from other eighteenth century Efiks. But the letters written by Grandy King George, Robin John Otto Ephraim, Otto Ephraim and Egboyoung Coffiong to Liverpool merchants (Williams 1897) provide, in particular, examples of the present tense forms. They also illustrate the variation that existed in NPE in Old Calabar at that time. It should be noted that the letters of Grandy King George contain approximately 1500 words and are longer than those of the others. Like Antera Duke, these writers did not often use punctuation. Subjects usually occur immediately before verbs, but there are several examples of a prepositional phrase coming between the simple subject and the verb. There is no other variation in word order.

As in the *DAD*, verbs can be deleted. This includes *be* and the stative *have*. Verbs with present tense meaning occurring with third person singular subjects can occur with and without inflection. This inflection can also be extended to both first and second person forms, as in the example from Grandy King George given in (24).

(24) *I dar say you knows that place* (Williams, p. 547)
      "I dare say you know that place".

The verb *be* is sometimes inflected for person, number, and tense, but there are also examples of singular forms used with plural subjects.

The three Efik traders who write about past events use both inflected and uninflected forms but with different frequencies. Grandy King George uses inflected forms most often (86%). Otto Ephraim uses them less often (65%), and Robin John Otto Ephraim uses very few (31%). If the frequency of marked past tense forms is used as a measure of the variation that existed in eighteenth century NPE in Old Calabar, Grandy King George is nearest the acrolectal variety and Robin John Otto Ephraim nearest the basilectal. This ranking is supported by the analysis of the other verbal constructions these Efiks use. While all three writers use the present perfect, i.e. *have*, Grandy King George is the only one to use the past perfect and passive forms. Only Robin John Otto Ephraim uses the auxiliary *been*, in the sentence given in (25).

(25) *I been send you one Boy by Captain Fairweather* (Williams, p. 547)
      "I sent you a boy by Captain Fairweather".

The auxiliary *will* is used for the future tense. There are in the data two occurrences of Standard English progressive constructions and only two occurrences of the preverbal modal *can*.

In the letters there is only one example of *did* with positive emphatic meaning. Antera Duke's use of this construction may just be idiosyncratic. He may have been a person who used more emphatic language. His writing is also different from the writing of the others in that it was for his own personal use and not meant to be seen by others. Whatever the explanation for his use of this form, it is not one that was used by the others and did not become a part of NPE as it developed.

If the analysis of the data from these Efik traders is compared with that from the *DAD*, a more complete description of the verbal system is possible. A great deal of variation exists in this early form of written NPE. The verbal system of Grandy King George includes many SE verbal forms. The others not only use fewer SE forms, but those that they do use occur with lower frequencies. Egboyoung Coffiong and Antera Duke use a basilectal variety in which verbs were invariant in form.

3. Data from the Nineteenth Century

In the first half of the nineteenth century before the arrival of the English-speaking missionaries, there are several brief letters written by Efiks to British captains of ships in Old Calabar (Holman 1834) and letters from the ruling Efiks, King Eyo Honesty and King Eymaba V, to a British commander about abandoning the slave trade (McFarlan 1946; Waddell 1970). In these texts *be* can occur in forms inflected for person, number, and tense; it can also be deleted. There is no inflection of other present tense forms. Of the 25 verbs used to express past action, only one has the past inflection *-ed*. The time of the action can be determined by context or by adverbial temporal marking, as in (26):

(26)   *I am very glad you come and settle treaty proper and thank you for doing everything right for me yesterday.* (Waddell, p. 664)

There is one occurrence of the auxiliary *have*, none of *done*, and two of *been*, one of which is presented in (27).

(27)   *if you please send me that Rum I been beg you* (Holman, p. 398)

Past progressive action in the letters of King Eyo Honesty and King Eymaba V is indicated by sentence-initial *long time*.

(28)   *Long time I look for some Man-of-war, and when French man come I think he want war, . . .* (Waddell, p. 664)

In these data future actions are marked by *will*. The preverbal modals are *can*, which expresses ability, and *must*, which indicates necessity.

When the missionaries arrived in 1846, a major change began in Old

Calabar. The ship captains and their crews lived on their ships and remained in Old Calabar for limited periods of time. The missionaries brought their wives and children and established residences. Now English-speaking people lived in the community. There was also another change. English became one of the languages for religion and education.

There are much more data from this period. From the thirty-one years following the arrival of the missionaries, forty-nine letters have been found. In this set of data, verbs other than *be* can still be deleted. *Be* occurs in both inflected and uninflected forms. Other than the verb *be*, 29 percent of the third person singular present tense verbs are inflected (35/121). There are just nine examples of third person singular inflection added to verbs that do not have third person singular subjects.

Of all the verbs with past time meaning in positive constructions, 55 percent (231/420) are zero forms. In these instances past time can be indicated by context or by adverbial temporal modifiers in sentence-initial or sentence-final position. In a compound predicate, the first verb can be inflected and the other not:

(29)   *I was very vex when I tied up this girl and flog her* . . . (*Missionary Record* [*MR*] 1870:213)

Of the non-zero forms, two strategies emerge for marking the past. The more frequently occurring is the inflection of the verb (140/189). The other is the use of preverbal *been*, occurring either with the bare verb or with the past participle of an irregular verb, as in (30) and (31) respectively:

(30)   *and only two men been see him.* (*MR* 1849:7)

(31)   *Also, my dear friend, please to remember me for what thing I been told you to bring for me.* (*MR*, 1853:7)

Been occurs 49 times in these data. The increased frequency of *been*'s occurrences signals its move from the periphery to the core of the system of tense.

Future action is almost always indicated (98 percent of the time) by the auxiliaries *shall* and *will*, with *go* marking the future in only 2 percent of all cases. The use of emphatic *do* is very limited; there are only three examples.

In these post-missionary data there are several aspect constructions. Some SE progressive constructions occur, i.e. marked both by a form of *be* and an *-ing* suffix on the verb. There are other instances where either *be* or the suffix is absent. *Have* is used to mark the perfect and occurs both with the bare verb form and with the past participle. Some Efiks use one or the other, and some use both. Further, the SE construction *used to + V* is used for past habitual action. Finally, the preverbal AUX *done* occurs but infrequently, only twice in these data. One instance is given in (32):

(32) *and when they done clean the place they put fire to the dry bush* (Waddell, p. 329)

Modals in the post-missionary data have the same forms and meanings as they have in SE. Necessity is most commonly expressed by *must + V* but *have + V* also occurs. *Can* is the auxiliary for ability. Both *may* and *might* are used for possibility.

The data analyzed in this period again demonstrate the variation in NPE in Old Calabar. Big Adam Duke (*MR* 1869:275) is representative of the basilectal speakers who use invariant *be*, deleted verbs, many unmarked past forms as well as the auxiliary *been* to mark past actions and the auxiliary *go* to indicate future action. There are also those whose writing includes more SE features such as Ekpenyung Eshen, who lived with one of the missionaries (Waddell 1970:646). He deletes verbs and uses the auxiliary *done* but also inflects half of the verbs in the present and past tenses and uses both *go* and *will* for the future.

4. Summary

The verbal system of eighteenth century NPE written data as analyzed above is basically one in which verbs are unmarked. Past tense is ordinarily indicated by context or by temporal marking, marking that occurs most often at the beginning of the sentence. In the nineteenth century data, most past tense verbs are still unmarked but there is more evidence of inflected past forms in the second half of the century, probably reflecting greater influence from SE. At the same time, the use of the past tense auxiliary *been* gradually increases. Also, in all the texts analyzed, unmarked stative verbs can refer to past states. Indeed, unlike Atlantic pidgins and creoles generally, the written NPE of the eighteenth and nineteenth centuries makes no distinction between stative and nonstative verbs. Finally, future tense is marked by the auxiliary *will/shall* until the second half of the nineteenth century when *go* begins to occur.

The verbal system in the eighteenth century is basically a tense system. There are few occurrences of perfects and few of progressives. Along these lines, there are no attestations of the twentieth century nonpunctual aspect markers *de* and *wan*. The absence of these forms is not proof that they did not exist. All that can be said is that they did not exist in these texts. Similarly, twentieth century NPE has a wide range of modals, including *sabi*, *fit*, and *fo*. The limited nature of the data may account for their absence from the eighteenth and nineteenth century texts, but it may equally be the case that these forms developed later.

The early data do not support the claim that aspect develops before tense since there are very few verbs in the written texts that are marked for aspect. The only modal constructions that are found in the early data are those expressing necessity and capability. Given the infrequency of marking for mood and aspect, it is not possible to determine if there was any ordering of tense, mood, and aspect markers. There are no co-occurrences of these forms in the data.

While some of the forms found in the early written data have dropped out over time, still others have persisted, their domain expanding. Used infrequently in the *DAD*, *been* and *done* have over time established themselves as the mainstays of the NPE tense system.

Clearly, there have been many changes in NPE — in its verb system and throughout the language — in the two centuries since Antera Duke kept his diary. It is through the study of such documents that the nature of the evolution and change in NPE and, indeed, of pidgins in general can be better understood.

Notes

1. The analysis of the verbal system of eighteenth century NPE and the verb systems of the other periods is a revision of a section of my 1982 dissertation.

2. The morpheme by morpheme and free glosses of the *DAD* are mine. The modern English version of the *DAD* found in *Efik Traders of Old Calabar* (Forde 1968) was used only to clarify names of people and places. For excerpts cited from the *DAD*, the page numbers refer to Forde (1968).

3. There may also be another source not for the form but for the meaning of this verbal construction: the Efik verb system. According to Welmers (1968), Efik has a neutral past that is "commonly used just to state what happened without any particular emphasis on any word or phrase in the sentence" (p. 17). Contrastive past constructions "serve somewhat the same function as contrastive stress and intonation do in English" (p. 39). The contrasted item can be before or after the verb. In the present tense, there is no difference between contrastive and noncontrastive forms (p. 44). The Efik past constructions are illustrated in (i)-(iii).

(i) *(ḿmá) ńdép ḿboró.*
I bought bananas (neutral past)
"I bought bananas".
(ii) *(ḿḿa) ŋkedèp* **ḿboró**
I bought bananas (contrasted item follows verb)
"I bought **bananas**".
(iii) **àmi** *ŋkedép ḿboró.*
I bought bananas (contrasted item precedes verb)
"**I** bought bananas". (taken from Welmers 1968:41,72)

Thus, the DAD use of *did* to signal emphatic/contrastive meaning may have just English as its source or it may have both English and Efik sources.

4. In addition, there are 69 tokens of *have* in the construction *have + NP + V*; here *have* expresses causation:

(i) *so wee have all Captin com to chop to Esim new house*
so we have all captains come to chop to Esim's new house
about new year (p. 93)
about New Year
"So we have all captains come to eat at Esim's new house for the New Year".

References

Adekunle, Mobolaji A. 1972. "Multilingualism and Language Function in Nigeria". *African Studies Review* 15.185-207.

Agheyisi, Rebecca Nogieru. 1971. "West African Pidgin English: Simplification and simplicity", Ph.D. dissertation, Stanford University.

———. 1984. "Linguistic Implications for the Changing Role of Nigerian Pidgin English". *English World-Wide* 5.211-33.

Barbag-Stoll, Anna. 1983. *Social and Linguistic History of Nigerian Pidgin English: As spoken by the Yoruba with special reference to the English derived lexicon.* Tubingen: Stauffenberg Verlag.

Bickerton, Derek. 1974. "Creolization, Linguistic Universals, Natural Semantax and the Brain". *University of Hawaii Working Papers in Linguistics* 6(3).125-41. (reprinted in *Issues in English Creoles: Papers from the 1975 Hawaii conference* ed. by Richard R. Day 1980.1-18. Heidelberg: Groos.)

Comrie, Bernard. 1976. *Aspect: An introduction to the study of verbal aspect and related problems.* Cambridge: University Press.

Fayer, Joan M. 1982. "Written Pidgin English in Old Calabar in the 18th and 19th Centuries", Ph.D. dissertation, University of Pennsylvania.

————. 1986. "Pidgins as Written Languages: Evidence from 18th century Old Calabar". *Anthropological Linguistics* 28.313-19.

Forde, Daryll, ed. 1968. *Efik Traders of Old Calabar*. London: International African Institute.

Goldie, (Reverend) Hugh. 1890. *Calabar and Its Missions*. Edinburgh: Oliphant, Anderson and Ferrier.

Grade, P. 1892. "Das Neger-Englisch an der Westküste von Afrika". *Anglia* 14.362-93.

Holman, James. 1834. *Voyage Round the World Including Travels in Africa, Asia, Australia, America*. London: Oxford University Press.

Mafeni, Bernard. 1971. "Nigerian Pidgin". *The English Language in West Africa* ed. by John Spencer, 95-112. London: Longman.

Marwick, William. 1897. *William and Louise Anderson*. Edinburgh: Andrew Elliott.

McFarlan, Donald M. 1946. *Calabar: The Church of Scotland Mission 1846-1946*. London: Thomas Nelson and Sons Ltd.

Missionary Record of the United Presbyterian Church. Edinburgh.

Nwoye, Onuigbo Gregory. 1978. "Language Planning in Nigeria", Ph.D. dissertation, Georgetown University.

Shnukal, Anna, and Lynell Marchese. 1983. "Creolization of Nigerian Pidgin English: A progress report". *English World-Wide* 4.17-26.

Singler, John Victor. this volume. "The Impact of Decreolization upon TMA: Tenselessness, mood, and aspect in Kru Pidgin English".

————. forthcoming. "On the marking of temporal sequencing in Liberian English". To appear in *Proceedings from the Thirteenth NWAVE Meeting* ed. by Sharon Ash.

Tonkin, Elizabeth. 1971. "Some Coastal Pidgins of West Africa". *Social Anthopology and Language* ed. by Edwin Ardener, 129-55. London: Tavistock.

Twaddell, W. F. 1960. *The English Verb Auxiliaries*. Providence, RI: Brown University Press.

Waddell, Hope Masterton. 1970. *Twenty-Nine Years in the West Indies and Central Africa: A review of missionary work and adventure 1829-1858*. London: Frank Cass & Co., Ltd. (Original work published 1863.)

Welmers, William E. 1968. *Efik*. Ibadan: University of Ibadan, Institute of African Studies.

Williams, Gomer. 1897. *History of the Liverpool Privateers*. London: William Heinemann.

The Impact of Decreolization upon T-M-A: Tenselessness, Mood, and Aspect in Kru Pidgin English[1]

John Victor Singler
New York University

1. Introduction

The importance to creole studies of David DeCamp's (1971) proposal of the creole-continuum model and Derek Bickerton's (1974) delineation of the prototypical creole tense-mood-aspect (TMA) system is well-established. The validity of extending DeCamp's and Bickerton's work to pidgins, particularly to those pidgins that are stable and long-established, depends upon the typological relationship of these pidgins to creoles. In the case of West Africa, both Tonkin (1971a) and Todd (1974) have commented upon the linguistic equivalence of the English-lexifier pidgins and creoles found there, with Todd (1974:5) using the term **extended** to describe the pidgins of the region.[2]

In the spirit of Tonkin and Todd, I argue in Singler (1984) for the applicability of creole models, beginning with the creole continuum, to pidginized Liberian English. Indeed, not only are the creole models applicable to pidgin varieties, the evidence from pidgin varieties can serve to inform and refine these models. In terms of the continuum, the Liberian case is unusual only in that there are two pidgin basilects (rather than one); they converge on a single mesolect. One of the two is an older coastal pidgin with a largely Kru substrate (Kru Pidgin English), and the other is a twentieth-century interior pidgin with a largely Mande substrate (Liberian Interior English).[3] The second is a repidginized descendant of the first.

The present article concentrates on TMA in the first pidgin, Kru Pidgin English (KPE). It draws upon Bickerton's model as a point of reference and focusses on the current state of TMA in the pidgin, as illustrated by data from six hours of recorded interviews with KPE speakers.

1.1 *Kru Pidgin English (KPE)*

Linguistically, KPE is of interest in part because of the unusual degree of homogeneity that characterizes its substrata. Its speakers have as their first language a Kru language, most often Klao or Grebo. (Singler 1988a explores this homogeneity and also discusses the social and historical factors surrounding KPE's use.)

KPE is the modern variety of the speech of the "Krumen", the mariners and migrant workers who went up and down the West African coast for nearly two centuries. Their own importance in the spread of pidginized English along the West African coast has long been acknowledged. As Tonkin states with regard to the Krumen:

> They must have been important diffusers and standardizers of Pidgin English, for their employers included slavers, traders, explorers, and the English Navy, and they worked for them even as far as South Africa. . .
> (1971b:143)

In the 1790's, if not earlier, a pattern had developed whereby an individual Kruman would grow up in a monolingual village on the southeastern Liberian coast, and then at the age of fifteen or so join a work gang. These gangs would work on board ships or in neighboring British colonies. Their world was overwhelmingly Kru. That is, if they were on board ship, it was usually as part of a Kru crew. If they worked on land, they lived in Kru enclaves. After a year or two or more, the gangs would return home, and individuals would remain home for a while before joining a new gang. The pattern would recur for an individual, often until he was forty-five or so. While the language of the home village would remain a Kru language, the language of the work gang was Kru Pidgin English (KPE). This was so on board ship and in the Kru enclaves of Sierra Leone, Nigeria, and the Gold Coast, i.e. modern Ghana.[4]

At the beginning of the Kruman tradition, Sierra Leone was the principal destination for Kru migrant workers. In the course of the nineteenth century, Sierra Leone was largely supplanted by Nigeria and, to a lesser

extent, the Gold Coast. Then, from World War I to the demise of the Kruman tradition in the second half of this century, the Gold Coast (Ghana,
after 1957) was the principal site of Kruman labor. However, Krumen also
continued to go to Nigeria and Sierra Leone and, when possible, to work on
ships.[5]

1.2 The Speakers

In order to study Kru Pidgin English in more detail, I carried out field
work in the Klao village of Nifu in 1985. Samson Tiklo, a native of Nifu,
and I conducted interviews with elderly Krumen. Four of these interviews,
plus one that Tiklo had conducted in Monrovia in 1980 with a Nifu man,
form the corpus for the present study.[6]

The five speakers are the following: Explorer, Gangwayman, Headman, Pipefitter, and Steward. (An individual speaker is designated by a
pseudonym that represents one of the occupations that he has held during
his life. For example, Explorer participated in a European-led expedition to
what is now Zaire in search of pygmies.) As Table 1 indicates, the five have
lived extensively outside of their home village.

Table 1. The Five Speakers in the Corpus

	Age in 1985	First Trip	Number of years worked in			Ever worked on ship
			Ghana	Nigeria	Monrovia	
Explorer	84	1925	4	6	0	Yes
Gangwayman	78	1929	4	6	7	Yes
Headman	75	1939	21	0	0	No
Pipefitter	65	1939	13	0	2	Yes
Steward	65	1936	27	0	3	Yes

Many of the figures for length of tenure are approximations;
ages for everyone except Steward are approximations.

These five worked at the panoply of jobs that were part of the Kruman
experience. All five spent time as cocoa plantation laborers, and four of the
five worked on board ships. Steward and Pipefitter and, briefly,
Gangwayman worked as domestic servants for the English plantation man-
agers. The men held other jobs for a time as well, among them
mineworker, messenger, and warehouse worker. In terms of principal occupation for each, i.e. the job at which each worked longest, Explorer, Head-

man, and Gangwayman were cocoa plantation workers while Steward and
Pipefitter were domestic servants.

These social facts are presented to illustrate the range of experiences of
the Krumen under study. At the same time, there is a general — but by no
means exceptionless — correlation between speaker's principal occupation
and extent of decreolization in the speaker's corpus. The two domestic servants are the ones whose jobs would have entailed the greatest amount of
contact with native speakers of English, and it is these two, Steward and
Pipefitter, whose speech displays the greatest degree of decreolization.[7]

1.3. *The Bickertonian Prototype and Kru Pidgin English*

As outlined by Bickerton (1974), the classical TMA system includes
one preverbal AUX to mark anterior tense (simple past for states and past-
before-past for actions), one to mark irrealis mood ("future" and conditional) and one to mark nonpunctual aspect (progressive and habitual). As
discussed below in Section 4, KPE departs dramatically from the prototype
with regard to tense. However, in the fundamentals of its treatment of
mood and aspect, KPE conforms to the classic model. It has the irrealis
AUX *go* and the nonpunctual AUX *de*, as illustrated in (1)-(4). (IRR
stands for "irrealis" and NONP for "nonpunctual".)[8]

(1)　"Future"
　　　　*a **go** gev yu   twEni-fav.*
　　　　I   IRR give you twenty-five
　　　　"I'll give you twenty-five (lashes)".　　　　　　　　　(Explorer)

(2)　Conditional
　　　　*ef yu gE peken, ma ne   **go** go ha.*
　　　　if you get child my name IRR go high
　　　　"If you have children, then my name will go far".　　(Steward)

(3)　Habitual
　　　　*hOngri ma no **de**   set dan   wOn ples.*
　　　　hungry man NEG NONP sit down one   place
　　　　"A hungry man doesn't sit down in one place".　　(Headman)

(4)　Progressive
　　　　*i se, "pipo **de**   **wet** yu On di yad".*
　　　　he say people NONP wait you on the yard
　　　　"He said, 'People are waiting for you in the yard'".
　　　　　　　　　　　　　　　　　　　　　　　　　　(Gangwayman)

At the same time that *go* and *de* follow the creole pattern in their distribution and meaning, decreolization has entered the KPE system and has affected the marking of aspect and mood. The AUX *we* (<*will*) is in variation with *go*, while the AUX *kEn* (<*can*) and the verb suffix *-en* (<*-ing*) are in variation with *de*.

2. Mood

The present discussion of mood will concern itself only with irrealis. Modality in the broader sense — encompassing, for example, deontic and epistemic modality — is the focus of Singler (1989).

KPE uses both *go* and *we* as true irrealis markers. That is, each marks conditionals as well as "futures". (2) above illustrates *go*'s occurrence in the consequent clause of a conditional; (5) does the same for *we*:[9]

(5)　*so efi hem mOda no　de　na,*
　　　so if　his　mother NEG COP now
　　　"If his mother hadn't been there",
　　　*a **we** **dra**　ma han　fO pawa.*
　　　I IRR draw my hand for power
　　　"I would have slapped him".　　　　　　　　　　(Headman)

Future means "subsequent to the moment of speech". In KPE, however, the "future" is more accurately termed **posterior**. That is, an event occurring subsequent to a discourse-determined reference point is marked by the irrealis. This is so in KPE even when that reference point is in the past, as (6) and (7) indicate. Note that no other marking is present.

(6)　*so, hi kOl O di o　o　bO*
　　　so　he call all the old old boy
　　　"So, he called all the old laborers"
　　　*wE i　　**go**　**kOm** bak　tu nifu.*
　　　REL they IRR come back　to Nifu
　　　"who were going to come back to Nifu".　　　(Gangwayman)

(7)　*bikOz　a no　　da ma kes　e **we** **fOwad**.*
　　　because I know that my case it IRR forward
　　　"Because I knew that my trunk was going to be forwarded".
　　　　　　　　　　　　　　　　　　　　　　　　　　　　(Headman)

For these examples, if one changes the time reference of the higher verb to make it nonpast rather than past, that does not change the marking of the irrealis clause. Irrealis is a mood rather than a tense, but the posterior sense of the irrealis is grounded in a system of "pure" relative rather than absolute tense (cf. Comrie 1985). This point is further supported by the fact that the past counterfactual in (5) carries no indication of pastness.

3. Aspect

KPE is like most other pidgins and creoles and like Kru languages in being aspect-prominent rather than tense-prominent. (The terms come from Salone 1979.) In KPE, as a consequence of this, the marking of aspect is itself tense-free. Thus, when the sentence in (8) is divorced from context, it is not possible to know whether the action it refers to is past or nonpast.

(8) *e bi   so wi* **de   du**.
     it COP so we NONP do
     "That's what we do/used to do/are doing/were doing".

(Headman)

(An additional indicator of KPE's aspect prominence is the fact that the primary aspect marker, *de*, is by far the most frequently occurring preverbal marker in the corpus.)[10]

In Liberian English more generally, *de* (both as nonpunctual AUX and as locative copula) seems to be one of the more highly stigmatized cues of basilectal speech. The impact of this stigmatization is that in the mesolect — and even in the upper basilect — *de* is replaced by *kEn* for habitual actions and the verb suffix *-en* for progressive ones. The entry of these markers into KPE is discussed below. A preliminary point about them is that aspect marking with them (as with *de*) is independent of (and seemingly indifferent to) tense. Thus, the co-occurrence of a tensed variant of *bi* with *V-en* is uncommon. There are only ten instances where a tensed variant co-occurs with *-en* in a past environment, and of these half are **non**past forms, as in (9).

(9) **am wOken** *as e shep bO*.
     I'm working as a ship boy
     "I was working on a ship".   (Gangwayman)

Similarly, *kEn* is not tense-specific, occurring as readily in past (or anterior) contexts as in nonpast (or non-anterior) ones.

The distribution of *de*, *kEn*, and *-en* is given in Table 2. Locative-copula tokens of *de* have not been included, nor have instances where *-en* marks a nominal. All tokens of *kEn* and its negative analogue *kÉn* have been included. (The difference between the affirmative and negative forms of *kEn* is one of pitch; cf. Singler 1981b.)

Table 2. Distribution of Nonpunctual Markers

	de	*kEn*	*-en*
Headman	212	0	15
Explorer	90	4	5
Gangwayman	60	10	17
Steward	20	50	172
Pipefitter	11	56	15

Several comments are in order with regard to Table 2. To begin with, it should be noted that the table counts number of occurrences of each form as an AUX or verb suffix, not necessarily number of **nonpunctual** occurrences. For *de* this is not an issue; for *-en* and *kEn* it is. These markers are discussed further below.

The first column of the table, the number of occurrences of *de*, illustrates the greater degree of decreolization in the speech of the two domestic servants. While *de* is the dominant marker for the other three speakers, Steward and Pipefitter use it only infrequently.

The entry of *kEn* into the continuum comes first (most basilectally) as an indicator of ability and then subsequently as a habitual marker. The negative form occurs first. Thus, Explorer and Gangwayman use only the negative form, both of them using it to signal inability more often than habitual non-action. Steward uses the affirmative form more often than the negative, but he too uses it to signal ability (or permission) far more frequently than habit. Only Pipefitter uses *kEn* regularly and predominantly to signal habitual/iterative.

While the distribution of *kEn* is restricted, its meaning is generally clear. This is not the case for *-en*. For Headman, Gangwayman, and Explorer (the three whose speech tends to be less decreolized), the presence of *-en* marks nonpunctual only about half the time. (When it is nonpunctual, it is almost always progressive rather than habitual.) The rest of the time, *V-en* is apparently in variation with the stem form. It can occur not only in sharply punctual contexts (as in [10]) but also in imperatives (as in [11]) and infinitives ([12]) and can co-occur with AUX's.

(10) *dEn di ka rish   ibadan.*
      then the car reach Ibadan
      "Then the car got to Ibadan".
      de   pOt mi dan.
      they put me down
      "I got out".
      *a **rish-en**   en yad.*
      I reach-NONP in yard
      "I went to the yard".
      a kOl tia   En   wlE.
      I call Tiah and Wleh
      "I called Tiah and Wleh".   (Gangwayman)

(11) *hi se, **"kOm-en**   dan".*   *a gEt dan.*
      he say come-NONP down   I get down
      "He said, 'Get out (of the car)'. I got out".   (Gangwayman)

(12) *so de   kOm fO di pipo   fO **kE-en***
      so they come for the people for carry-NONP
      "So they came to get the people to take them"
      fO di go   kos.
      for the Gold Coast
      "to the Gold Coast".   (Headman)

Steward accounts for three times as many tokens of *-en* as the other four speakers put together. He uses it primarily (140 times out of 172) with three verbs: *wOk* "work", *go*, and *kOm* "come". However, Steward's use of *-en* is like that of the three speakers mentioned above: that is, particularly in the case of *go-en* and *kOm-en*, the action being described is often perfective (and, by extension, punctual) rather than imperfective (and nonpunctual). Indeed, among the speakers in the corpus, only Pipefitter confines his use of *-en* to nonpunctual verbs. (Note, however, that Pipefitter uses *-en* in habitual contexts as well as progressive ones.)

In sum, the entry of *kEn* and *-en* into the KPE aspect system represents decreolization at work. However, for all but one of the speakers under study, the stage of decreolization at hand is a very early one.[11]

While a single AUX, *de*, can be shown to express the full range of nonpunctual aspect, a second strategy exists, one that does not seem to be a consequence of decreolization. This involves the use of irrealis AUX's, i.e. *go* and *we*, to mark habituals.[12] This use of "irrealis" AUX's to mark habituals occurs most often in the consequent clause of *wEn*-marked "conditionals", as in (13) and (14).

(13) *wEn   a   set   dan   sOn   ples,   asi   a   set   dan   ya,*
    when I   sit   down some place as   I   sit   down here
    "When I used to sit down some place the way I'm sitting down here",
    wEn   yu   breng   fitija   fO   mi,
    when you bring   disrespect for me
    "when you showed disrespect to me",
    wEn   a   no   se   a   hav   mOni   fO   ma pakE,
    when I   know COMP I   have money for my pocket
    "when I knew that I had money in my pocket",
    *a   **go**   **tel**   yu   se,   "a   fat   yu".*
    I   IRR   tell you COMP   I   fight you
    "I would tell you, 'I'll fight you'".   (Gangwayman)

(14) *wEn   dE   tan   En   tu kOm   hom   de   **we**   **mek**   dans.*
    when their time end to come home they IRR   make   dance
    "When their (a work gang's) time was up and it was time for them to come home, they would hold a dance".   (Pipefitter)

In both of these examples, it is clear from context that the events described are past and are habitual. In (13), Gangwayman's remark comes in response to the interviewer's question, *bO na yu yustu du krokroji ten?*, "But did you use to misbehave?" Work gangs no longer exist among the Kru, so (14) is necessarily past as well.

While the habitual conditional construction is almost always the site for this use of *go* and *we*, it sometimes happens that the use of *go* or *we* to express the habitual moves outside the conditional. This is the case with (15).

(15) *das   hem wOk hi   **we**   **du**.*
    that-COP his work he   IRR do
    "That's the work that he (a tailor) does".   (Explorer)

This convergence of the habitual with irrealis is not unknown among creoles. Taylor (1971) identifies the merging of habitual with future as a feature of Negerhollands, Capeverdean Crioulo, and the Portuguese-lexifier creoles of the Gulf of Guinea. Indeed, Bickerton (1981) discusses the convergence of habitual/iterative and irrealis, noting that

> we could claim that . . . [a habitual/iterative predication] does not refer at
> all to any specific events, but rather to a generalized concept which may be
> based on one or more such events (1981: 257).

At present, the use of *go* and, like it, *we* to signal habitual aspect seems secondary; that is, *de* is the dominant marker of all nonpunctual aspect. Still,
questions arise about the history of KPE (and about the extent to which its
TMA system has undergone change during the last century). *Go* seems to
be the old KPE irrealis AUX, but Grade (1892) in a description of what is
apparently an earlier form of KPE indicates the existence of **two** future
AUX's. (Grade deals only with the future and does not consider conditionals.) In a description of the tenses of "Neger-Englisch", he identifies *go* as
the future AUX (1892:384). In a subsequent section on AUX's, however,
he says that Standard English *will* and *shall* can be "replaced" by *can*, and
he provides the following example:

(16) *him* **can die**.
　　　"He will die".   (Grade 1892:384)

An example from the corpus of the use of *kEn* to mark irrealis — and not
simply to express possibility or habit — is given in (17). In it Steward is telling about the time he was in the Ghanaian port city of Sekondi and went to
apply for work on a Danish ship that was in the harbor. When the job offer
was extended, Steward accepted.

(17) *di   ma   se, "yEs, a lak des bO tu go tu ma bot".*
　　　the man   say yes   I like this boy to go to my boat
　　　"The man said, 'Yes, I'd like this boy to go to my boat'".
　　　a se, "oke. a **kEn go** *dE. pO ma ne   dan".*
　　　I say OK I IRR go there put my   name down
　　　"I said, 'OK. I'll go there. Put my name down'".   (Steward)

However, apart from this example and one ambiguous example from
Pipefitter, there are no occurrences of *kEn* to express irrealis in the corpus.
On the other hand, one of the Nifu elders not included in the present study
(see fn. 6) — a Kruman who had lived in Nigeria but had never been in a
work gang — uses *kEn* to mark irrealis with some regularity; (18) provides
an example.

(18) *dEn de   nO   wOn kE   mi en di kOna,*
　　　then they NEG want carry me in the corner
　　　"After that, they no longer wished to take me into the corner
　　　(and say)".

*"wi **kEn bit** otwE"*.

we IRR beat Otueh

"'We're gonna beat Otueh'".   (Gunsmith)

Further, as discussed in Singler (1987a, 1989c), *kEn* is an irrealis AUX in Liberian Interior English, the variety posited as being a repidginized version of KPE.

The relevance of the discussion of *kEn* as an irrealis marker is simply to point out the history in KPE of the confluence of irrealis and habitual. The convergence of the two semantic ranges in contemporary KPE may be an innovation but it may also be part of an ongoing tradition within the language. The two *kEn*'s, the irrealis *kEn* reported upon by Grade that has all but disappeared and the habitual *kEn* of the modern mesolect, seem to be distinct; establishing whether that is the case or whether the new *kEn* is actually a modern manifestation of the old one requires further study into the history of KPE.

4. Tense

In creole languages generally and in Bickerton's prototypical system specifically, the tense locus (cf. Chung and Timberlake 1985) is a discourse-determined reference point. For an event, the presence of the creole anterior tense marker indicates that the event took place prior to some reference point that is itself located in the past.[13]

Viewed another way, a marker of anteriority can be said to mark the **disruption** of temporal order. In a narrative about the past, for example, the reference point is ordinarily moving forward as the narrative progresses; the only actions that then need to be marked are those which disrupt the sequence by moving backwards (making reference to an event prior to the reference point).

KPE does not mark anteriority. There is the occasional marking of simple past, but it is sporadic rather than systematic. Quite simply, KPE is tenseless. In order to demonstrate this, I will work through putative markers of tense, going into some detail in order to make the following two points:

1) the tense marking that is present is almost all the result of decreolization; and

2) even when tense marking introduced by decreolization is considered, tense is not signalled in KPE in any pervasive or systemic way.

4.1 *Bin* and *dOn*

In the English-lexifier pidgins and creoles spoken in West Africa outside of Liberia, *bin* and *dOn* are the principal markers of tense.[14] In the KPE corpus, there is a single preverbal use of *bin*, in a excerpt from Gangwayman's description of an episode that occurred in the harbor at Accra:

(19) *frOn ya   e go so.*
from here it go so
"From here it went in that direction".
de   kOnEk tu   bot.
they connect two boat
"They tied the two boats".
frOn so kOm.
from so come
"They came from the other side".
*de   **bin kOl** mi.*
they   call me
"They summoned me".
i se, "Eniwe, a go standi yu bak.
he say anyway I IRR stand you back
"He said, 'Anyway I'll keep you back'".
a wOn yu lod   des dan".
I want you load this down
"'I want you to unload this'".   (Gangwayman)

It's not clear what *bin* accomplishes in (19). The action in question is not anterior (or perfect); in no way does it disrupt the temporal sequence. In fact, as far as I can tell, removing *bin* has no impact on the passage whatsoever.[15]

With regard to *dOn*: elsewhere in Liberian English there is the completive AUX *na/nO*; Singler (1987b) argues that this AUX evolved from the *dOn* found more generally in West Africa.[16] Just as there is but a single use of *bin* as an AUX, so there is but a single use of *na/nO*:

(20) *fav hOndrE pipo   na   di   **nO kEsh**.*
five hundred people now they   catch
"They took five hundred people off the boat".   (Headman)

The sole example of *na/nO* in the corpus, like the sole example of *bin*, is presumably to be explained by contact with varieties of pidgin that use these AUX's. Their all-but-total absence from the present corpus makes clear that they are not now KPE AUX's. The question that arises is whether they were KPE AUX's in the past. It would be most unusual for tense markers simply to have faded away. A more likely pattern involves the replacement of particular tense markers by other ones. In decreolization generally (as instantiated for Guyanese in Bickerton 1975), a distinction must be made between creole forms and the creole system, i.e. the set of semantic oppositions that obtain in the creole. Typically, the first stage of decreolization involves the replacement of creole forms by forms from the lexifier language. However, while the forms have changed, the system has not: thus, at this stage forms from the lexifier language express the creole semantic oppositions. Subsequently, the creole system gives way to that of the lexifier language. At that point, forms from the lexifier language now express that language's system. If that is the usual pattern, the next consideration for KPE, then, is to determine whether English forms that mark tense (and possibly the English tense system itself) have entered KPE. Sections 4.2 and 4.3 assess this, as reflected in the KPE use of inflected verbs and tense-marked copulas.

4.2 Tense Inflection

In the corpus there is but a single instance where a weak verb is marked for the past (Explorer's inflection of *fenesh* "finish"). Strong verbs are sometimes inflected for past tense but not very often and not very many of them. Specifically, inflection is largely limited to four verbs: *brOt* "brought", *ken* "came", *tol* "told", and *wEn* "went". Other than these four verbs (and Pipefitter's five tokens of *den* "didn't"), fewer than five past-tense forms of strong verbs occur in the entire corpus. Even with these four, the distribution varies sharply from speaker to speaker. Table 3 illustrates this. As the table shows, each verb has its "champion", a speaker who accounts for more than half the total number of occurrences of that verb in the corpus.

It is worth noting that the inflected forms are restricted in domain. In an overwhelming number of cases, their presence is restricted to actions that are [+Punctual]. Bickerton (1975) shows that in Guyanese Creole [+Punctual] strong verbs are the first to be inflected along the continuum

Table 3. Number of Occurrences of Strong Verbs in Past Contexts

	ken	brOt	wEn	tol
Steward	14	5	4	12
Gangwayman	5	11	0	0
Pipefitter	1	0	12	0
˙Explorer	1	2	2	3
Headman	1	2	0	2

(where **first** means "least acrolectal"). Singler (1984) finds the same correlation holding in Liberian English. In the present case, this link supports the expected: that is, the presence of inflection is a manifestation of decreolization. The significance of decreolization as an explanation is reinforced by the fact that one of the two domestic servants, Steward, is the principal user of past-tense forms (and the only speaker to use all four). Still more evidence for decreolization comes from the examination of individual speakers' use of the strong verbs. When Steward is reporting conversation involving a European (either as speaker or listener), he uses *brOt* "brought" in [+Punctual] past contexts half the time (5/10, 50%); in any other [+Punctual] past context, i.e. reported speech not involving a European or non-reported speech, Steward uses the uninflected form, *breng* "bring", categorically (16/16).

However, even when the focus is restricted to past events that are [+Punctual], the strong forms of verbs simply are not used very much. (With particular reference to anteriority, the only one of the inflected strong verbs that occurs more than once in an anterior context in the corpus is *brOt*.) The decreolizing impulse has introduced strong verbs; however, the occasional presence of inflection in four verbs, even four frequently occurring ones, is insufficient to constitute a system of tense.

4.3 Copulas and Tense Marking

The basic KPE and pan-West African copula system has *bi* as the equational copula, *de* as the locative, and *0* as the attributive. While this system accounts for the overwhelming majority of the instances of copula use in the corpus, tense-marked copulas are sometimes present, both nonpast and past. The nonpast forms are sometimes used in past contexts, as in (21) and (22).

(21) *a ste fO sEkOndi nantinfOtitu, fOtitri.*
I stay for Sekondi 1942   43
"I stayed in Sekondi 1942, '43".
frOn dE, dEn di wa es   strOn.
from there then the war COP strong
"After that, then the war was heavy".   (Steward)

(22) *hi kE   wi. wi a fefti mE. wi de   fO sanwan.*
he carry we we COP fifty men we COP for Sanwan
"He took us. There were fifty of us. We were there in Sanwan".
(Gangwayman)

The past copula forms are used only in past contexts; even here, however, they are in variation with other copulas, as (23) illustrates.[17]

(23) *ba di tan a bi   lebras.*
by the time I COP laborer
"At that time I was a laborer".
wEn a waz   lebras, a du lebra wOk . . .
when I PAST-COP laborer I do laborer work
"When I was a laborer, I did laborer work . . ."   (Steward)

Once again, the explanation for the presence of tense-marked copulas
lies in decreolization.[18] Here, the difference between speakers is pronounced. At one end is Pipefitter, who usually uses *waz* in past-tense contexts. At the other end is Headman, who never uses *waz*. The remaining
three speakers fall somewhere in between these two, none of them using
waz very often. The occasional marking of copulas for tense, even when
combined with the occasional use of the past-tense form of some strong
verbs, cannot be said to constitute a **system** of tense.

4.4 **Waz** as a Preverbal Auxiliary

It is my claim that the tense markers found in other English-lexifier
pidgins and creoles of West Africa are not found in KPE and that the
expressions of tense introduced by decreolization are insufficiently regular
and pervasive to have provided KPE with a tense system. There remains a
final possibility, the preverbal AUX *waz*. It is illustrated in (24).

(24) *kOmne kE   mi dE, nO ma on   mOni. yu si.*
company carry me there not my own money you see
"The company used to take me there (to Ghana), not my own
money. You see".

so   di   tan   a **waz kOm** *bak,*
so   the   time   I   come   back
"So when I would come home",
a **waz kOm** *bak   ba   di   sem   kOmne.*
I   come   back   by   the   same   company
"it was the company that brought me back".   (Pipefitter)

In all, there are 63 occurrences of preverbal *waz* in the corpus. Fifty-nine of them are *waz V* and four the acrolectal *waz V-en*. However, the overwhelming number of these tokens come from a single speaker: 55 of the 59 occurrences of *waz V* come from Explorer. The eight tokens that do not come from Explorer — four *waz V* and four *waz V-en* — come from Pipefitter and Gangwayman. For these two speakers, in every instance but one, the *waz*-marked verb, whether bare or suffixed, is nonpunctual. This suggests that their target is Standard English *waz V-en*. These cases will not be discussed further.

In the remaining cases — Explorer's 55 tokens — *waz* signals completive aspect; pastness is implied. Any event that is past or anterior (depending upon the language's system of temporal reference) is the potential site for completive marking. This raises the question as to why some events get marked with the completive while others do not. Elsewhere in Liberian English (but not in KPE), there is the completive AUX *feni*.[19] Singler (to appear) shows that in basilectal speech it functions to **reinforce** (rather than disrupt) temporal order.

In Explorer's speech, four of the occurrences of *waz* show up when he is reporting the speech of Europeans (who seem to have tense). Of the remaining 51 tokens, 45 occur in temporal clauses, 41 of which are *wEn*-initial. Only in three of the 45 instances do these clauses involve a disruption of temporal sequencing. Indeed, the usual function of these clauses is like that of *feni*: to reinforce temporal sequencing. Further, these clauses are frequently recapitulative. In fact, in 18 of the 42 cases, the *wEn* clause repeats the verb of the preceding clause. (25) contains two examples of this.

(25)   *wi* **go.** *wEn   i* **waz go**,
we   go   when   we   go
"We went. When we went",
wi   go Op   tu   di   siria   ma   ples.
we   go up   to   the   Syria   man   place
"we went up to the Syrian's place".

*debre   wi **go** en di   bush.*
daybreak we go in the bush
"The next morning we went into the bush".
*wEn   i   **waz go** tru   dE,   frOn ya   tu rish   tu bEtu.*
when we   go through there from here to reach to Betu
"When we went through the bush, (we walked) as far as from here to Betu".   (Explorer)

The usual sequence of clauses where *waz* appears is the following:

$$V_i\text{-} waz\ V_i\text{-} V_j$$
$$V_i\text{-} waz\ V_j\text{-} V_k$$

The order of the clauses matches the chronological order of the events they describe. The first of these sequences is illustrated by (25).

For Explorer's use of *waz* and for *feni*, a substratal model exists. Marchese (1978, 1984) shows that narratives — and also procedurals — in Kru languages are rich with cues that reinforce the obvious temporal order. Recapitulative clauses in particular — like those in (25) — recur with remarkable frequency. The gloss of a procedural text in Marchese (1978), given in (26), illustrates this.

(26)   "And then you build a shelter. If you have built a shelter, then you and your wife, you will pull out the grass. If you have finished pulling out the grass, then the rice will sprout. If the rice has sprouted . . ." (1978:71)

All the speakers in the KPE corpus recapitulate constantly, particularly with *wEn* clauses; however, Explorer is alone among them in introducing preverbal *waz* into those clauses.

The possibility exists that *waz* in Explorer's speech also signals the perfect. This proves to be unlikely: there are many instances like (27) where the events are in sequence but the *waz*-marked verb seems clearly not to mark the perfect.

(27)   *a bi   di ma   waz ple   yuphoniOm.*
       I COP the man   play euphonium
       "I was the man who played the euphonium".
       *wEn a **waz ple** yuphoniOm, we Eri   wat   ma   sE,*
       when I   play euphonium   with every white man self
       "When I played the euphonium, even all the white people",

i   ma   kÉn luk   Eniten,   yu · luk   mi.
you mind NEG look anything you look me
"their minds couldn't go elsewhere; they had to notice me".
(Explorer)

Waz's function — as distinct from its core meaning and as evidenced by its
pattern of occurrence — seems to be the reinforcement of temporal
sequencing. Or, it can be said, its presence helps to advance the point of
reference (in, for example, a narrative). If this is so, the question that follows from it is whether this usage is wholly idiosyncratic or whether
Explorer, the earliest learner of KPE among the group, is representative of
an older order within KPE. If one considers the marking of the reinforcement of temporal order (rather than the marking of its disruption) to be a
legitimate example of "tense", i.e. temporal sequencing, is Explorer's
speech to be considered evidence that KPE used to mark tense? That is, did
KPE have tense marking and then lose it, or did it never have it? Certainly
Labov (elsewhere in this volume) argues that tense is not **necessary** for
communication, linking its evolution to the development of style rather
than to grammatical or communicative necessity. On the other hand, there
is cross-linguistic support for the use of *waz* as a tense marker, particularly
in decreolizing varieties: Holm (1988) notes that such varieties of Creole
English often replace the basilectal tense marker *bin* with "forms derived
from *did*, *had*, or *was*; these are frequently less deviant from standard usage
and thus less stigmatized" (1988:152).[20]

The evidence for KPE's having had tense in the past is, apart from
Explorer's use of *waz*, largely secondary, coming from other varieties of
Liberian English. *Bin* is nowhere to be found in contemporary Liberian
English and there is no evidence concerning it, but there is evidence relating both to *dOn* and to *waz*. Tonkin, quoted above, refers to the Krumen
as "important diffusers and standardizers of Pidgin English" (1971b:143).
The historical evidence strongly suggests that their diffusing and standardiz-
ing started at home. That is, the first Liberian speakers of the West African
English-lexifier pidgin were predominantly the coastal Kru (Klao, Grebo,
and also Bassa). There is ample evidence that the Liberianization of the
pidgin consisted primarily of the incorporation of Kru substratal features.
One instance of this — at least as argued for in Singler (1987b) — involves
the transformation of *dOn* to *nO* (and on to *na* subsequently in much of the
country), a change that seems to have been impelled by pressure from Kru-
specific phonotactics. The imprint of Kru phonotactics on *na* and the his-

tory of pidgin in Liberia, taken together, suggest that *dOn/na* was part of an earlier stage of KPE even if it is not present now.

Distinct from the broader relation of KPE to Liberian English more generally is the specific relation of KPE to the other Liberian basilect, Liberian Interior English (LIE). LIE evolved in the early part of this century on rubber plantations and in the Frontier Force, settings where initial Kru dominance was soon overwhelmed by the preponderance of speakers of Mande languages from the Liberian interior. In some cases, the new Mande-dominated pidgin has retained KPE features that have disappeared — or are now disappearing — from KPE itself. The irrealis AUX *kEn*, discussed above, is a case in point. LIE's first-person plural possessive *wia* (as in *wia fada* "our father") is another. It is found in the KPE corpus only in the speech of the oldest speakers, Explorer and Gangwayman.

The point of the discussion of older KPE features that show up in modern LIE is that LIE has the AUX *waz* (ordinarily pronounced [wə]): there it is a past nonpunctual marker, marking both actions and states, as in (28) and (29).

(28) *Owe   hi **waz keli**.*
     always he   kill
     "He just kept killing (the animals)".

(29) *bikO,   yu   no,   a **waz ha**   hanwash.*
     because you   know   I   have wristwatch
     "Because, you know, I had a wristwatch".

(examples from Singler 1987a)

The presence of preverbal *waz* in LIE raises the possibility that it was a feature of earlier KPE. At the same time, LIE's use of *waz* is drastically different from Explorer's use of it. *Waz* is a past nonpunctual AUX in LIE but a completive that signals the preservation of temporal order in Explorer's KPE. (While *waz* is not exclusively punctual in Explorer's speech, it is punctual more often than not.) It is possible, then, that the presence of *waz* in LIE and in Explorer's speech is little more than co-incidence.

Even if it is not, a problem persists. If an earlier stage of KPE had *dOn/na* and/or *waz*, where did the AUX's go? Tense forms get replaced through decreolization, and so do the semantic oppositions that govern them. But tense forms and semantic oppositions rarely give way to nothingness. Washabaugh's (1977) argument that the strongest impetus for moving "up" the continuum is the desire to avoid stigmatized forms seems inapplicable here. The "shedding" of tense by KPE, if that is what happened, is baffling.

However, the alternative, that KPE never had tense, is also unlikely. The tenseless Hawaiian Pidgin that Labov (this volume) describes is far more rudimentary than KPE. Labov states:

> When pidgins become creoles, and acquire native speakers, they are spoken with much greater speed and fluency. The speech of O-san [a pidgin speaker] is slow and deliberate; the creole used by native Hawaiians is very fast. (this volume)

KPE has achieved the speed, the range, and the elaboration of a creole without ever undergoing nativization. (For an alternative to the view that ascribes central importance to nativization, see Gilman 1979, Hancock 1980, and Singler 1988a.) KPE has the kind of rules of stylistic variation that Labov describes; it is just that they do not appear in the tense component of the grammar.

To return to modern KPE: the use of *waz* is largely confined to a single speaker who uses it primarily in a single syntactic environment. Given the restricted domain of this tense marker, it is appropriate to conclude that, for the most part, KPE does not mark tense. Decreolization has brought in the occasional use of tense-marked forms from English, specifically the occasional use of a tensed variant of *bi* or of a past-tense form of a strong verb in [+Punctual] settings. However, apart from these and Explorer's use of *waz*, there is no overt indication of tense within the VP in KPE. It seems legitimate to speak of tenselessness in contemporary KPE.

In the TMA system outlined by Bickerton for creoles, verbs expressing action in the past are ordinarily not marked. Only verbs expressing anterior action — most often past-before-past — would be marked. In KPE, however, it is not just the simple past that is not consistently or systematically marked: neither is the anterior. The examples in (30)-(32) illustrate the nonmarking of anteriority. In each one, there are no cues within the VP of a particular verb's anteriority. Each of the passages comes from a narrative about the past, and in each of them the material set off by brackets involves actions that are anterior to the time line of the narrative.

> (30) *di tan de bre, [ha di wuma trit wi,*
>   the time day break how the woman treat us
>   "The next morning, the way the woman had treated us (the day before)"

i   se di haws i   no   gEt am],
she say the house she NEG get it
"by saying that that the house wasn't hers",
wi tu wi go lEf awa ne   ya.
we too we IRR leave our   name here
"we too we had to get our revenge by leaving our mark".

(Headman)

(31) *dEn a liv   di   keshEn wOk. wi wOk en di mEs*
then I leave the kitchen work we work in   the mess
"Then I was transferred from the kitchen to the mess".
[bikOz   wEn de   kOm frOn yurop,
because when they come from Europe
"Because when they had come from Europe",
de   breng sOn bO, wOk en di   keshEn.
they bring some boy work in the kitchen
"they had brought someone to work in the kitchen".
bO des bO, wEn wi liv   en di afrika,
but this boy when we leave in the Africa
"But this man, while we were in Africa",
wi de   en di afrika, dEn i   fili hOt].
we COP in the Africa then he feel hot
"we were there in Africa, he had felt hot. (Now he returned to
work, and I was transferred from the kitchen.)"   (Steward)

(32) *di tan a kOm, [a liv   tu wuma dE],*
the time I come   I leave two woman there
"When I came home, I had left two wives there at home",
wEn   a waz kOm, a breng plEni klo.
when I   come I bring plenty clothes
"when I came back, I brought them a lot of clothes".

(Explorer)

There is — or used to be — a claim that particular pidgins and creoles
marked the past by the use of adverbial time-markers. Indeed, Bickerton
calls the claim "a hardy perennial in pidgin and creole studies" (1975:50).
But note that KPE speakers do not even use adverbial time markers to signal anteriority. In the three examples given above, there are no temporal
cues whatsoever.[21]

5. Conclusion

Inasmuch as decreolization is a fact about contemporary KPE, a study of KPE tense-mood-aspect is necessarily a study of decreolization. In some cases, it is possible to extrapolate the "pre"-decreolization system, the pidgin system. This is so, for example, for mood and aspect. In these areas, a fundamental congruence can be seen between KPE and the prototypical TMA system proposed by Bickerton. One AUX expresses irrealis mood and another nonpunctual aspect. The principal departure from Bickerton's model in this realm involves the use of the irrealis marker to signal habitual/iterative actions. For mood and aspect, the process of decreolization has operated along predictable lines: *go*, the irrealis AUX, gives way to *we* (from English *will*), but the system (future/posterior **plus** conditional) remains that of the pidgin. Nonpunctual aspect splits into habitual and progressive, with the progressive represented by the verb suffix *-en*. The basic pidgin aspectual AUX *de* is then replaced in habitual contexts by an AUX that is recognizably English, the mesolectal AUX *kEn*. Though the acquisition of the progressive marker, the verb suffix *-en*, seems somewhat problematic for speakers, the effect of its introduction on the system is straightforward enough.

If the treatment of mood and aspect in KPE conforms to the creole prototype and if the impact of decreolization upon them is unremarkable, this is not so for tense. Apart from the occasional use of the past-tense form of one of four strong verbs and the occasional use of a tensed copula, decreolization has had no obvious impact upon tense. At the same time, however, there is but scant evidence as to what the "pre"-decreolization tense system was. (And that evidence is largely the repeated use of a preverbal AUX by a single speaker in a single kind of clause.) Decreolization may have eliminated the pidgin tense system without replacing it, but this seems unlikely. Perhaps KPE never had a tense system, but this too is unlikely. Whatever the history of KPE and whatever further studies of the history of KPE will determine, the present reality is a decreolizing pidgin that does not mark tense.

Notes

1.   A preliminary version of this study was presented at the 1986 meeting of the Linguistic Society of America held in New York City. The research on which this article is based was made possible by a Research Challenge Fund grant from New York University.

I am grateful to Samson Tiklo and Beth Craig for their expert assistance. I am also grateful to those who shared their stories of the Coast with me: Matthew Saawon Wiah, A. B. Kantee, Matthew Knonya, Amos Sewlu, and Packson Sleweon. Finally, I am grateful to the people of Nifu, Grand Kru County, Liberia, for their kind hospitality.

2. Gilman (1979) asserts that the difference between extended pidgins and creoles is essentially sociohistorical rather than linguistic. In Singler (1988a) I argue that, while the basis for the difference between the two types is sociohistorical, there is in principle a linguistic difference between them: ordinarily, a pidgin continues to have direct and ongoing contact with its original substrate languages, while a creole does not. This difference, however, does not seem to motivate any clearcut difference in linguistic behavior.

3. Greenberg (1963:39fn.) places Kru within Kwa, but says that this affiliation "is to be considered tentative". Several linguists working independently in the 1970's concluded that Kru should be separated from Kwa within Niger-Congo.

    In Singler (1988a) and elsewhere (e.g. 1981a, 1984), I follow Hancock (1971) in identifying KPE as a dialect of Liberian English. However, Hancock and I are alike in asserting rather than demonstrating this relationship; that is a task for future research.

    Hancock (1986:83) states: "My own work in Sierra Leone indicates that some of the notionally 'deepest' Krio is spoken in Kroo Town by the Kru . . ." Individual Klao and Grebo villages tended to be identified with particular locations and types of labor; among the people whom Tiklo and I interviewed in the town of Nifu, there were none who had ever worked in Freetown, and the KPE data that I obtained in Nifu do not represent a form of Krio.

4. For the most part, the description of the Krumen given here follows from that presented in Ludlam (1825). The principal adjustment subsequent to 1825 involves the shift of the bulk of the Kru laborers from ships and Sierra Leone to Nigeria and then, in the early part of this century, to the Gold Coast (and the enormous increase in the number of Krumen). Further discussion of the Krumen is to be found in Brooks (1972) and Martin (1982).

5. A question that arises is the extent to which there are "dialects" of KPE: for example, are there significant differences between the KPE of those who went to Ghana and those who went to Nigeria? The evidence at hand is inconclusive. A second question is whether the KPE of Krumen who went to Nigeria is more properly considered a variety of KPE or a variety of Nigerian Pidgin English (and likewise for the other countries). The KPE that I have heard and studied, whether the speakers lived primarily in Ghana or Nigeria, is fundamentally KPE. Thus, the KPE of speakers who lived in Kru enclaves in Nigeria is clearly distinct from the Nigerian Pidgin English described in Agheyisi (1971), Faraclas (1987), and elsewhere. Admittedly, the relationship of KPE to, for example, an earlier variety of Nigerian Pidgin English has not been considered.

6. Tiklo and I conducted seven interviews in Nifu. Two of the three interviews removed from present consideration are with men who served in the British West Africa Forces in World War II in, among other places, India and Burma. Although wandering the globe is very much a part of the Kruman tradition, these two speakers have been excluded because of the limited contact that they would have had with the KPE speech community. Similarly, an elder who had lived in Nigeria but had never been part of a work gang was also excluded.

    In this century, Kru women sometimes went to the Kru enclaves. There were, for example, women present in Nifu who had lived in the Gold Coast. However, none of the women consented to be interviewed in English, i.e. KPE.

The 1980 interview with Steward and the interview with Headman are ninety minutes each; the others are sixty minutes each.

7.   Steward and Pipefitter are both ten years younger than any of the other three Krumen. It is possible that this difference in age further contributes to the greater decreolization that characterizes these two men's speech.

8.   The orthography is that used by Fyle and Jones (1980) and Todd (1979) for Krio and Cameroonian, respectively. *O* is [ɔ], and *E* is [ɛ]. *Ch* is [č] and *sh* is [š]. *Vn* indicates [Ṽ] (except in the sequence [VnV], in which case the nasal consonant is pronounced). The word-final consonants that I have indicated, while present phonemically, are frequently not pronounced.

9.   There is extensive inter-speaker variation regarding the distribution of *we* and *go*, ranging from a strong preference for *go* by Gangwayman to a virtually categorical preference for *we* by Pipefitter.

10. Though they are not numerous, there are instances in the corpus where *de* marks states. This goes against Bickerton's prediction in this regard. Two such examples are given in (i) and (ii):

    (i)   *tu hEdma de se i de   hOngri.*
          two headman they say i NONP hungry
          "Two headmen said they were hungry".   (Gangwayman)
    (ii) *we de   kOl pEpa fangbadE.*
          we NONP call pepper
          "We call pepper 'fangbadeh'".   (Headman)

11. Further evidence of the extent to which Pipefitter's speech has undergone decreolization is his use of *yustu* (<*used to*), a marker that signals past habitual, i.e. both tense and aspect. Apart from a single use by Steward, Pipefitter is the only speaker in the corpus to use it; there are six tokens of it in his speech, including the example in (i):

    (i)   *spEshali di ples wE   kru pipo En kana pipo*
          especially the place where Kru people and Ghana people
          "The Kru and the Ghanaians especially"
          de yustu   fat es   tu go drawi wata.
          they PAST-HABIT fight COP to go draw water
          "used to fight when they were drawing water".   (Pipefitter)

M. E. Kropp-Dakubu (p.c.) reports that in popular Ghanaian English *yustu* is a non-tense-specific habitual AUX; that is, it can occur in nonpast environments. It is possible — but not likely — that Pipefitter is using it in this way as well.

12. The pattern whereby decreolization first replaces creole forms without altering the creole strategy or system can be argued for here. The basilectal irrealis marker, *go*, gives way to the standard one, *we*, but the basilectal strategy of using the irrealis to mark habituals persists.

    Gangwayman uses *go* to mark habituals in 9 instances, Explorer in 8. Pipefitter uses *we* in this way 17 times, Headman 15, and Explorer 5.

13. There are some uses of, for example, the Guyanese anterior marker *bin* with actions where the action is not past-before-past. Bickerton's characterization of such cases (cf. 1975:46) comes quite close to Li et al.'s (1982) definition of perfect aspect, suggesting that

at times *bin* signals simple perfect rather than pluperfect. For present purposes, the rough definition — "past-before-past for actions and past for stative verbs" — is entirely adequate.

My focus is on events rather than states. In KPE, past states are never marked for the past; like nonpast states, they carry no marking for tense.

14. In some varieties, *dOn* is best characterized as a completive marker. Comrie (1976) iden-
    fies **completive** as an aspect (because it is concerned with the internal temporal consti-
    tuency of an event or state) rather than a tense. Still, it frequently functions — by implica-
    ture — to signal tense. It is this function that is relevant to the present discussion.

15. In addition, Gangwayman and Headman both use *bin* as a main verb, meaning "to have
    gone somewhere and to have returned", in opposition to *gOn*, which means "to have
    gone somewhere and to have remained there". There are no tokens of *bin*, either as
    AUX or main verb, in the speech of the other three speakers.

16. *nO* is the variant found in southeastern Liberia among more mesolectal speakers (cf.
    Hancock and Kobbah 1975). The Kru Coast is part of the southeastern region.

17. As will be seen below, Steward's use of a tenseless form in a main clause, followed by *waz*
    in the *wEn* clause of the next sentence, strictly parallels Explorer's use of *waz* as a prever-
    bal AUX. However, there are no other occurrences of copulas in this configuration in
    Steward's speech or anywhere else in the corpus.

18. With regard to the use of nonpast copulas in past contexts, this would seem to be another
    instance where the standard language's **forms** express the creole (here, pidgin) **system**.

19. *Feni* does show up twice in Steward's speech, post-clausally as in (i):

    (i)   *a go tu ma rum, a lOk ma rum, pOt ma drEs,*
          I go to my room, I lock my room put my uniform
          "I went to my room and locked the door. After I had put on my uniform"
          pOt *ma ta* **feni**, *go shO.*
          put my tie   go shore
          "and tied my tie, I went ashore".   (Steward)

20. On the other hand, the use of *was* is a feature of the eighteenth-century Nigerian Pidgin
    Diary of Antera Duke (Fayer, this volume), apparently to mark anteriority. This raises
    the possibility that *was/waz* is a West African Pidgin tense marker of long standing.

21. My focus in this study has been on TMA as expressed by the presence (and absence) of
    preverbal AUX's and verbal suffixes. Elsewhere (Singler 1988b) I have argued for treat-
    ing sentence-final *o* as a marker of perfect aspect in sentences like (i):

    (i)   *so di ma wEn hi go dan   na,   Eribadi   rOn fO hem.*
          so the man when he go down now, everybody run for him
          "So when the man went down now, everybody ran to him".
          "E! E! jlakrun kOm o!   jlakrun kOm o!"
          eh eh jlakrun come PERF jlakrun come PERF
          "'Eh! Eh! Jlakrun has come! Jlakrun has come'"!   (Headman)

That analysis extends to KPE; however, space limitations preclude further discussion
here.

228   JOHN VICTOR SINGLER

References

Agheyisi, Rebecca Nogieru. 1971. "West African Pidgin English: Simplification and simplicity", Ph.D. dissertation, Stanford University.
Bickerton, Derek. 1974. "Creolization, Linguistic Universals, Natural Semantax and the Brain". *University of Hawaii Working Papers in Linguistics* 6(3).125-41. (Reprinted in *Issues in English Creoles: Papers from the 1975 Hawaii conference* ed. by Richard Day, 1-18. Heidelberg: Groos.)
————. 1975. *Dynamics of a Creole System*. Cambridge: University Press.
————. 1981. *Roots of Language*. Ann Arbor: Karoma.
Brooks, George E., Jr. 1972. *The Kru Mariner in the Nineteenth Century: An historical compendium*. (Liberian Studies Monograph Series Number 1). Newark, DL: University of Delaware, Department of Anthropology.
Chung, Sandra, and Alan Timberlake. 1985. "Tense, Aspect, and Mood". *Grammatical Categories and the Lexicon, Vol. 3: Language typology and syntactic description* ed. by Timothy Shopen, 202-58. Cambridge: University Press.
Comrie, Bernard. 1976. *Aspect: An introduction to the study of verbal aspect and related problems*. Cambridge: University Press.
————. 1985. *Tense*. Cambridge: University Press.
DeCamp, David. 1971. "Toward a Generative Analysis of a Post-Creole Speech Community". *Pidginization and Creolization of Languages* ed. by Dell Hymes, 349-70. Cambridge: University Press.
Faraclas, Nicholas. 1987. "Creolization and the Tense-Aspect-Modality System of Nigerian Pidgin". *Journal of African Languages and Linguistics* 9.45-59.
Fayer, Joan M. this volume. "Nigerian Pidgin English in Old Calabar in the Eighteenth and Nineteenth Centuries".
Fyle, Clifford N., and Eldred D. Jones. 1980. *A Krio-English Dictionary*. London: Oxford University Press.
Gilman, Charles. 1979. "Cameroonian Pidgin English: A neo-African language". *Readings in Creole Studies* ed. by Ian F. Hancock, 269-280. Ghent: Story-Scientia.
Grade, P. 1892. "Das Neger-Englisch an der Westküste von Afrika". *Anglia* 14.362-93.
Greenberg, Joseph H. 1963. *The Languages of Africa* (= *Indiana University Research Center in Anthropology, Folklore, and Linguistics*, 25; also

International Journal of American Linguistics 29:1, part 2.) Bloomington: Indiana University.

Hancock, Ian F. 1971. "Some Aspects of English in Liberia". *Liberian Studies Journal* 3.207-13.

————. 1980. "Lexical Expansion in Creole Languages". *Theoretical Orientations in Creole Studies* ed. by Albert Valdman and Arnold Highfield, 63-88. New York: Academic Press.

————. 1986. "The Domestic Hypothesis, Diffusion and Componentiality: An account of Atlantic anglophone creole origins". *Substrata Versus Universals in Creole Genesis: Papers from the Amsterdam Creole Workshop, April 1985* ed. by Pieter Muysken and Norval Smith, 71-102. Amsterdam and Philadelphia: John Benjamins.

Hancock, Ian F., and Piayon E. Kobbah. 1975. "Liberian English of Cape Palmas". *Perspectives on Black English* ed. by J. L. Dillard, 256-271. The Hague: Mouton.

Holm, John. 1988. *Pidgins and Creoles. Vol. 1, Theory and structure*. Cambridge: University Press.

Labov, William. this volume. "On the Adequacy of Natural Languages: I. The development of tense".

Li, Charles N., Sandra A. Thompson, and R. McMillan Thompson. 1982. "The Discourse Motivation for the Perfect Aspect: The Mandarin particle *le*". *Tense-aspect: Between semantics and pragmatics* ed. by Paul J. Hopper, 19-44. Amsterdam and Philadelphia: John Benjamins.

Ludlam, Thomas. 1825. "Report on the Kroo". *African Repository* 1, April: 43-54.

Marchese, Lynell. 1978. "Time Reference in Godié". *Papers on Discourse* ed. by J. E. Grimes, 63-75. Dallas: SIL.

————. 1984. "On the Role of Conditionals in Godie Procedural Discourse". Paper presented at the Symposium on Discourse Relations and Cognitive Units, Eugene, Oregon.

Martin, Jane J. 1982. *Krumen "Down the Coast": Liberian migrants on the West African coast in the 19th century* (= *African Studies Center Working Papers*, 64.) Boston: Boston University.

Salone, Sukari. 1979. "Typology of Conditionals and Conditionals in Haya". *Studies in African Linguistics* 10.65-80.

Singler, John Victor. 1981a. *An Introduction to Liberian English*. with J. Gbehwalahyee Mason, David K. Peewee, Lucia T. Massalee, and J. Boima Barclay, Jr. East Lansing: Michigan State University, African

Studies Center.

————. 1981b. "Tone and Intonation in Liberian English Negation". *Studies in African Linguistics, Supplement 8: Précis from the 12th Conference on African Linguistics* 124-128.

————. 1984. "Variation in Tense-Aspect-Modality in Liberian English", Ph.D. dissertation, UCLA.

————. 1987a. "Tense-Mood-Aspect (TMA) in Liberian Interior English (LIE)". Paper presented at the Nineteenth Conference on African Linguistics, Université du Québec à Montréal.

————. 1987b. "Where Did Liberian English *Na* Come From?" *English World-Wide* 8.69-95.

————. 1988a. "The Homogeneity of the Substrate as a Factor in Pidgin/Creole Genesis". *Lg* 64.27-51.

————. 1988b. "The Story of *O*". *Studies in Language* 12.123-144.

————. 1989. "Topics in Liberian English Modality". *Current Approaches to African Linguistics, Vol. 5* ed. by Robert Botne and Paul Newman, 253-266. Dordrecht: Foris.

————. to appear. "On the Marking of Temporal Sequencing in Liberian English". *Proceedings from the Thirteenth NWAVE Meeting* ed. by Sharon Ash.

Taylor, Douglas. 1971. "Grammatical and Lexical Affinities of Creoles". *Pidginization and Creolization of Languages* ed. by Dell Hymes, 293-296. Cambridge: University Press.

Todd, Loreto. 1974. *Pidgins and Creoles*. London: Routledge and Kegan Paul.

————. 1979. "Cameroonian: A consideration of 'what's in a name?'" *Reading in Creole Studies* ed. by Ian F. Hancock, 281-94. Ghent: Story-Scientia.

Tonkin, Elizabeth. 1971a. "Some Aspects of Language from the Viewpoint of Social Anthropology, with Particular Reference to Multilingual Situations in Nigeria", D.Phil. dissertation, Oxford University.

————. 1971b. "Some Coastal Pidgins of West Africa". *Social Anthropology and Language* ed. by Edwin Ardener, 129-55. London: Tavistock.

Washabaugh, William. 1977. "Constraining Variation in Decreolization". *Lg* 53.329-52.

Author Index

Adekunle, Mobolaji A. 187
Agheyisi, Rebecca Nogieru 187, 225
Aksu, Ayhan A. 128
Alatis, James E. 2
Alleyne, Mervyn C. ix, 159
Almada, Dulce 144
Andersen, Roger W. xi, 59-96, 165
Anderson, Lloyd B. 100, 175
d'Ans, André-Marcel 125, 134, 137, 140
Bailey, Beryl Loftman 25, 53, 111, 115
Bailey, Charles-James 55
Barbag-Stoll, Anna 187
Bereiter, Carl 2
Bernstein, Basil 5
Bickerton, Derek viii-xiii, xiv, 53, 60,
   61, 63, 70, 72, 89-90, 92, 100, 122-
   123, 124, 125, 129, 134, 135, 137, 138,
   139, 143, 144, 146, 148-149, 150, 157-
   163, 174, 177, 178, 179, 192-193, 203,
   204, 206-207, 211-212, 213, 215-216,
   222, 223-224, 226
Bierwisch, Manfred 111
Bishop, Isabella 12
Bloom, Lois 3, 4, 31
Boggs, Steve 51
Bokamba, Eyamba G. 111
Brito, Antonio de Paula 144
Bronckart, J. P. 161
Brooks, George E. Jr. 225
Carreira, Antonio 159-160
Carter, Hazel 115
Cassidy, Frederic G. 18, 52
Chaudenson, Robert ix
Chung, Sandra xiii-xiv, 98, 99, 100, 111,
   115, 213
Coelho, Francisco Adolfo 144
Cohen, Paul 53-54

Comrie, Bernard xi, xii, xiii, xv, 62, 63,
   83, 92, 98, 100, 101, 112, 123, 129,
   134, 135, 140, 144, 187, 208, 227
Corne, Chris 136-137, 140
Costa, Joaquim Vieira Botelho 144
Dahl, Östen 98, 100, 102, 111, 112, 113
Day, Richard viii
DeCamp, David 51, 203
Déchaine, Rose-Marie 119
Duarte, Abílio 144, 155, 156
Duarte, Custodio José 144
Engelmann, Siegfried 2
Ervin-Tripp, Susan 7
Faine, Jules 38
Faraclas, Nicholas 225
Fayer, Joan M. xi, 185-202, 227
Fehderau, Harold W. 18, 51, 52, 97,
   106
Ferguson, Charles A. 51
Forde, Daryll 185, 188-195, 196, 197,
   200, 201
Frota, Silvia Nagem 93
Fyle, Clifford N. 226
Gilman, Charles 222, 225
Goilo, E. R. 60, 68, 83, 88, 89, 93
Goldie, Hugh 186
Gomes, Adriano 144
Goodman, Morris F. 40, 91, 110
Grade, P. 187, 212, 213
Greenbaum, Sidney 143
Greenberg, Joseph H. 225
Gumperz, John J. 7
Hall, Robert A., Jr. 125, 134
Hancock, Ian F. 222, 225, 227
Herzfeld, Anita 144
Herzog, Marvin 26
Holm, John 220

Holman, James 186, 197
Hooper, Joan B. 128
Hutchison, John 164
Jakobson, Roman 127
Jones, Eldred D. 226
Joos, Martin 52
Juliana, Elis 71
Kobbah, Piayon E. 227
Koopman, Hilda 119, 123
Kouwenberg, Silvia 170, 173
Kropp-Dakubu, M. E. 226
Labov, William vii, viii, xi, xiv, 1-58, 220, 222
Lambert, W. E. 50
Lawton, Denis 5-6
Leech, Geoffrey 150
Lefebvre, Claire 119, 123, 134
Lenz, Rodolfo 42-43
Lewis, John 53-54
Li, Charles N. 226
Lopes da Silva, Baltasar 144
Ludlam, Thomas 225
Lyons, John 171, 175
Macedo, Donaldo P. 144, 150, 151, 153, 154, 155, 156, 164
Maduro, Antoine 93
Mafeni, Bernard 186, 187
Magloire-Holly, Hélène 119, 137
Marchese, Lynell 187, 219
Martin, Jane J. 225
Martin, Robert 115
Marwick, William 186
Maurer, Philippe 60, 72, 83, 88, 92, 93, 114
McFarlan, Donald M. 186, 197
Meintel, Deirdre 144
Meisel, Jürgen 63
Mendonce, João Gomes 144
Mihalic, Francis 18, 52
Morais-Barbosa, J. 144, 162
Mourelatos, Alexander P. 63, 64, 65, 66
Moverly, A. W. 22-23, 52
Mufwene, Salikoko S. xi, xiv, 97-117
Muller, Enrique 92, 93, 94
Murphy, John J. 17, 52

Muysken, Pieter vii, ix
Naro, Anthony 60
Ngalasso, Mwatha M. 106
Nida, Eugene 18, 51, 52
Nwoye, Onuigbo Gregory 187
Odo, Carol 54
Palmer, F. R. 129
Parsons, Elsie Clews 144, 149, 150, 154, 156
Piou, Nanie 119
Quirk, Randolph 143
Rameh, Cléa 165
Reichenbach, Hans 99
Reinecke, John E. 9, 12-13, 15-16, 43, 51, 53
Rickford, John 92
Robertson, Ian E. xi, xiii, xiv, 169-184
Robins, Clarence 53-54
Rosenthal, Robert 50
Ross, Alan S. C. 22-23, 52
Sag, Ivan 135, 146
Salone, Sukari 208
Samarin, William J. 97
Sankoff, David 8, 19-22, 51
Sankoff, Gillian 8, 19-22
Santos, Rosine 144
Scantamburlo, Luigi 144, 162
Schmidt, Richard W. 93
Schuchardt, Hugo vii, 17
Seligman, C. R. 50
Shnukal, Anna 187
Silva, Izione S. xi, xiv, 93, 143-168
Sinclair, H. 161
Singier, John Victor vii-xvi, 113, 115, 149, 177, 192, 203-230
Slobin, Dan I. 128
Smith, Carlota S. 141
Smith, Norval xiv, 169-170, 183
Spears, Arthur K. x, xi, xiii, xv, 119-142
Stewart, William 92
Sylvain, Suzanne 121, 123, 125-126, 134
Taylor, Douglas R. vii, viii, 60, 94, 177, 211
Thompson, R. McMillan 226
Thompson, Roger W. vii, viii, 60

Thompson, Sandra A. 226
Timberlake, Alan xiii-xiv, 98, 99, 100, 111, 115, 213
Todd, Loreto 203, 226
Tonkin, Elizabeth 186, 187, 203, 204, 220
Torrey, Jane 4-5
Tsuzaki, Stanley 26, 27, 51
Tucker, G. R. 50
Twaddell, W. F. 191
Ultan, Russell 146
Valdman, Albert 123, 125, 131, 134
Valkhoff, Marius F. 45, 144, 162
van Buren, Hamilton 9-11, 51
Van Name, Addison vii
Veiga, Manuel 144, 164
Vendler, Zeno 64,65

Vendryes, J. 43-44 ·
Voorhoeve, Jan 115, 144
Waddell, Hope Masterton 186, 197, 199
Washabaugh, William 221
Watanabe, Ruth 54
Weinreich, Uriel 26
Welmers, Beatrice viii
Welmers, William E. viii, 194, 200-201
Whinnom, Keith 52, 60
Whorf, Benjamin 3
Williams, Frederick 2
Williams, Gomer 185, 195, 196
Williamson, Kay xiv, 169-170, 183
Wilson, Robert J. 7
Wilson, W. A. A. 40-41, 144, 159, 162
Wurm, Stephen A. 52
Youssef, Valerie 109, 112, 113

Language Index

Antillean Creole French 38
Bantu languages xi, 97, 105, 106, 109, 111
Bassa 220
Beach-la-Mar 18
Berbice Dutch xi, xii, xiii, xiv, 169-184
Bisayan 9
Black English 1-6, 8, 18, 39, 46-47, 48-49, 50, 53-54
Brazilian Portuguese 165
Buang 14-15
Cameroonian Pidgin English 225
Capeverdean Crioulo xi, xii, xiv, 91, 143-168
Chinese 9, 11, 12-13, 17, 111
Chinese Pidgin English 13
Dutch xi, 8, 51, 68, 84, 90, 91, 92, 178, 180
Dutch-lexifier creoles 169
Efik 194, 200-201
English xi, xv, 1-6, 8, 10-12, 13, 16, 17, 18, 21, 22, 23, 24, 25, 26, 28, 29, 30, 31, 32, 36, 38-39, 40, 41, 45, 46-50, 51, 52, 54, 55, 63, 68, 69, 73, 78, 84, 93, 103, 112, 114, 115, 123, 129, 130, 135, 136, 139, 140, 141, 144, 150, 158, 165, 182, 186, 191, 192, 194, 196, 197, 198, 199, 201, 206, 212, 215, 218, 222, 224
English-lexifier creoles 40, 45, 61, 90, 92, 101, 102, 144, 158, 161, 171, 203, 214, 217, 220
English-lexifier pidgins 203, 214, 217
Français Populaire d'Abidjan 113
French xi, 8, 16, 43, 51, 112, 113, 126, 136
French-lexifier creoles 17, 40, 43, 45,

90, 101, 102, 119
German 6
Ghanaian English 226
Grebo xiv, 204, 220
Guinea-Bissau Crioulo 40-41, 52, 53, 91, 157, 158-161, 162-163
Guinean Crioulo, see Guinea-Bissau Crioulo
Gullah 100, 102, 113
Guyanese Creole viii, 61, 100, 114, 122, 150, 160, 170, 174, 177, 178, 179, 181, 182, 183, 215, 226
Haitian Creole viii, x, xi, xii, xiii, 38, 119-142
Hawaiian 10, 12, 35
Hawaiian Creole viii, xi, xv, 8, 11, 12, 13, 14, 18, 23-24, 25-26, 27-38, 39, 40, 41, 42, 43, 45, 46, 51, 53, 54, 61, 122, 158, 159
Hawaiian English 10, 11, 13, 14, 26, 27, 34, 53, 54
Hawaiian Pidgin 8, 9-14, 15, 16-17, 23, 26, 27, 31, 38, 51, 53, 159, 222
Hebrew 63
Hopi 6
Ijo, Eastern xiv, 170, 173, 178, 180
Ile-de-France Creole 136-137
Ilocano 9, 11, 16
Indian Ocean Creole 158
Indo-European languages ix
Jamaican Creole 18, 25, 38, 51, 53, 61, 92, 100, 102-103, 113
Jamaican English 25, 92
Japanese 9, 10-11, 13, 14
Kannada 7
Kikongo ("Ethnic" Kikongo) xi, 97, 100, 114, 115

Kikongo-Kiladi 114
Kikongo-Kintandu 106, 115
Kikongo-Kituba, see Kituba
Kituba xi, xii, xiv, 97-117
Klao xiv, 204, 220
Krio 225
Kru languages xiv, 203, 204, 208, 219, 220, 221, 225
Kru Pidgin English xi, xii, xiv, 192, 203-230
Liberian English 113, 177, 192, 203, 208, 214, 215, 218, 220, 225
Liberian Interior English 203, 213, 221
Lingala 105, 111
Macanese 52
Mande languages 203, 221
Marathi 7
Mauricien Creole, see Mauritian Creole
Mauritian Creole 38
Negerhollands 211
Neo-Melanesian xi, xv, 8, 14-15, 17, 18-22, 38, 40, 42, 44-45, 52
Niger-Congo languages 170, 225
Nigerian Pidgin English xi, xii, 113, 185-202, 225, 227
Papiamentu xi, xii, 42-43, 59-96, 114, 158, 161, 163, 165

Palenquero 91
Pidgin French, see Tây Bồi
Pidgin Portuguese 60, 186
Pitcairnese 18, 22-23, 52
Police Motu 51
Portuguese xi, 8, 9, 11, 40, 51, 52, 91, 92, 93, 94, 158, 160, 161, 163, 165
Portuguese-lexifier creoles 45, 60, 91, 93, 144, 158, 161, 162, 163, 211
Punti 13, 17
São Tomé Crioulo, see São Tomense
São Tomense 161, 162, 163
Saramaccan 122
Seychelles Creole 160-161
Spanish xi, 6, 8, 9, 42, 51, 60, 61, 63, 68, 84, 91, 92, 93, 94, 140
Spanish-lexifier creoles 60, 91, 93
Sranan viii, 18, 122, 158, 161, 163, 177
Swahili 51
Tagalog 9
Tây Bồi 17-18, 43
Tex-Mex 51
Tok Pisin, see Neo-Melanesian
Trinidadian Creole English 112, 113
West African Pidgin English 186, 204, 220, 227
Yoruba 178

Subject Index

absolute tense xi, 61, 62, 68, 69, 72, 92, 208
absolute-relative tense xii, 83
accomplishments 64-65, 92
achievements 64-65
acrolect 92, 196, 216-217, 218
action verbs viii, xii, 11, 29, 41, 63-66, 69-70, 74-75, 122, 125-126, 138, 146, 154, 156, 173, 175, 178, 180, 188, 194, 197-199, 206, 208, 209, 210, 213-215, 221-223, 226
activities 64-65, 76, 85, 92
actual mood xiii
adverbs, temporal vii, 10, 14, 16, 17-18, 18-19, 21-22, 31, 40, 42, 44, 49, 52, 67, 78, 81, 98, 101, 104, 111, 112, 113, 115, 165, 169, 189-191, 197-198, 223
anterior viii, xi-xiii, 60, 62, 70, 78, 89, 91, 92, 98-102, 104-108, 111, 112, 114, 115, 120-122, 124, 127, 133, 137-139, 145, 146, 154-155, 157-161, 162-163, 164, 192-193, 206, 208, 213-214, 216, 218, 222-223, 226, 227
aorist 138-139
aspect vii, viii, xii, xiii-xiv, xv, 17, 18, 21, 42, 45, 59-83, 85-87, 89-91, 92, 99-110, 111, 115, 119, 123, 134-138, 143-144, 146-147, 150-151, 153, 155, 157-158, 161, 163, 169-174, 177, 179, 182-183, 187-190, 194-195, 198, 199-200, 203, 206-213, 218, 223-224, 226, 227
    grammatical aspect 63, 66, 72, 92
    lexical aspect 63-66, 72
atelic 63-64, 92
auxiliaries xii, xiii, 11, 17, 18-24, 30-32, 35, 36-42, 44, 49, 52, 53, 54, 67, 71, 83-85, 89, 92, 93, 98, 109, 111, 114, 119-120, 144-147, 151, 158-159, 161-162, 164, 183, 191-199, 206-215, 217-224, 226, 227
    semi-auxiliaries 49, 119-120, 140
basilect 61-62, 68, 73, 78, 83, 89, 91, 92, 94, 143, 157, 170, 183, 193, 196, 197, 199, 203, 208, 209, 218, 220, 226
Bickerton's prototypical creole TMA system viii-xiv, 60-61, 72, 89, 122-139, 143-144, 153-163, 174, 203, 206-207, 213, 224, 226
clause-final position 144-145, 155-156, 158, 162, 177, 198, 227
clause-initial position 19-20, 144-145, 155-156, 162, 189, 191, 197-199
co-existent systems 26, 36
completive x, xii, xiv, 67, 100-101, 108-110, 112, 143, 155-158, 160-163, 165, 177, 194, 214, 218, 221, 227
concomitant 98, 100, 103-104, 106-110, 114, 115
conditionals xiii, 122-124, 127, 129-131, 133, 138-139, 140, 150, 155, 179, 183, 206-207, 211-212, 224
continuous xiii, 11, 66, 74, 75, 134-136, 138, 143, 147, 151, 153, 155, 157, 165, 174
contrary-to-fact 155
control 146-149
counterfactual 124, 128, 133, 208
creole continuum 7, 8, 61, 89, 92, 203, 209, 215-216, 221
créole endogène ix, xi, xiv
créole exogène ix, xi, xiv
creole genesis vii-x, xiv, 18, 52, 60, 183
    monogenesis vii
    social setting viii-x, 42-43, 51, 225

creoles, "radicalness" of viii-ix, 139
creoles, shared properties of vii-x, xiv
current relevance 100-101, 104-105, 107-108, 175
de dicto 108, 115
de re 108, 115
decreolization 97, 139, 163, 165, 206-207, 209-210, 213, 215-217, 220-224, 225, 226
deictic centre 92, 112
developments 65, 72
durative vii, xv, 38, 60, 63-66, 69, 72, 92, 98-99, 103-110, 111, 114, 115, 123, 135, 137, 152, 158, 163, 173-174
    transient duration 104, 107, 114
dynamic 63-65, 175
elaborated code 5-6
fort creoles ix
future xiii, 10, 16, 18-22, 23, 30-31, 38-39, 42, 44, 52, 60, 62, 69, 73, 74, 98-100, 104-105, 107, 110, 111, 122-127, 129, 133, 134, 136-139, 140, 146-147, 150-151, 153-155, 161, 163, 164, 165, 177-180, 189, 193-194, 196-199, 206-207, 211-212, 224
    immediate/imminent/near future 18, 104-105, 125-127
future-in-the-past 124-125, 127, 134, 138-139, 140
habitual xiii, xv, 20-21, 67, 69, 70, 76, 84-85, 86, 99, 102-103, 104-110, 114, 123, 134-138, 139, 143, 150-151, 153-155, 158, 161, 163, 165, 174, 199, 206, 208-213, 224, 226
    universal habitual 99, 105-106, 114
imperfect 40, 42, 161
imperfective xii, xiii, 60, 62-63, 66-83, 85-88, 89, 92, 93, 108, 134-136, 173-174, 180, 210
incompletive xiv
indicative xiii, 128-130, 133-134, 136-138, 140, 141
inflection 11, 14, 15, 16, 18, 22, 98, 102, 105, 107-109, 111, 196-199, 216-217
intelligence 1-3

irrealis viii, xiii, 60-61, 67, 82-83, 89, 110, 115, 120-124, 129, 158-159, 161, 178-180, 182, 206-208, 210-213, 221, 224, 226
iterative xv, 11, 69, 123, 135, 137, 143, 150-151, 153-154, 158, 161, 163, 164, 165, 173-174, 209-211, 224
language and thought, relation between 3-9
language bioprogram hypothesis, the viii-x, 60, 61, 72, 89-90, 92
lexifier languages viii, x, xi, xiv, 8, 51, 59, 92, 161, 215; see also superstrate
logic 1-3
mesolect 92, 203, 208, 213, 224, 227
modality xiii, 59, 60-61, 91, 195, 208; see also mood
modals 22, 67, 83-89, 92, 93, 102, 111, 123, 128, 144, 150, 161, 170, 181-183, 195-197, 199-200; see also mood
mood vii, viii, xiii-xiv, 61, 66-67, 90, 91, 98, 109, 111, 115, 119, 122, 125-134, 140, 141, 179, 182-183, 200, 203, 206-208, 223-224
narrative tense 99, 102-104, 106-110, 113, 115
nativization xii, 7, 14, 17, 18, 159-160, 222
non-anterior 62, 122, 124, 133, 208
nonconcomitant 105
nondurative 105-108
nonfuture xiii, 110, 126
non-indicative 141
nonpast viii, 62, 110, 146, 148-150, 155-156, 173, 177, 207-208, 216-217, 226, 227
nonpresent 73
nonprogressive xiii, 124, 136
nonpunctual viii, xiii, 60, 63, 72, 92, 120-124, 127, 137-139, 158, 161, 163, 173-174, 200, 206, 208-210, 212, 218, 221, 224
nonstate verbs, see nonstative
nonstative xii, xiii, 29, 41, 63, 101-102, 104-106, 110, 112, 113, 115, 122, 135,

136, 146-150, 153-154, 156-157, 171, 177, 199
nonsubsequent 107
passé composé 112, 115
past vii, viii, xi, xii, xiii-xiv, 4, 10, 12, 16-17, 22-24, 29-37, 40-42, 44, 46-50, 52, 53, 54, 55, 60, 62, 66-69, 71-76, 78-83, 84-87, 92, 93, 97, 99-100, 106, 110, 113, 122, 124-125, 127, 134, 138-139, 140, 146-150, 154-156, 161, 165, 173-174, 176-177, 179-182, 188-192, 194, 196-199, 200-201, 206-208, 211, 213, 215-218, 220-224, 226, 227
  remote past 122
  simple past viii, xii, 40, 69, 146, 154, 177, 192, 206, 213, 222
past-before-past viii, xii, 122, 154, 156, 192, 206, 222, 226
perfect xii, 4, 24, 31, 40, 42-43, 45, 50, 53, 63, 79, 98-101, 104-105, 107-110, 112, 113, 115, 140, 156, 165, 174-177, 181, 183, 194, 196, 199, 214, 219, 226, 227
  future perfect 31
  near perfect 98, 101, 104, 109, 113
  past perfect 24, 31, 40, 50, 53, 165, 196
  present perfect 156, 165, 196
  remote perfect 99, 101, 107, 109, 113
perfective xii, xiii, 23, 40, 41-42, 53, 60, 62, 63, 67-69, 72-73, 75-77, 85-87, 89, 92, 93, 98, 100-104, 106-109, 111, 112, 115, 165, 210
plantation creoles ix
pluperfect 227
post-creole continuum, see creole continuum
posterior 207-208, 224
potential vii, xiii
present xiii-xiv, 4, 12, 16, 22-23, 29, 30, 33, 40, 42, 52, 60, 62, 66, 68-69, 73-74, 78, 81-87, 90, 92, 100, 113, 114, 115, 122, 125, 136, 138, 146, 150-151, 155-156, 175, 189, 191, 194, 195-199, 200

historical present 25, 28, 30, 46, 113
preterit 24, 28, 35, 40, 42-43, 44, 52, 53
preverbal markers vii, viii, xii-xiii, 11, 19-20, 59-60, 91, 100, 107, 119-124, 127, 137, 139, 144-145, 150-154, 161, 170, 174, 177, 182, 183, 194-199, 206, 208, 214, 217-219, 221, 224, 227
processes xi, 64-66, 72, 136-137, 140, 152
progressive xii, xv, 4, 11, 32, 41, 42, 45, 63, 68-69, 75, 103-104, 114, 123-124, 134-138, 139, 147, 151, 153-155, 158, 163, 189, 195-199, 206, 208-210, 224
punctual xiii, 41, 63-66, 76, 77-78, 85, 124, 135, 157, 158, 161, 209-210, 215-216, 221-222
punctual occurrences 64-66
quasi-modals 21, 23, 29, 67
realis 102, 108, 110, 115, 124, 129, 161
relative tense xi, xii, 62, 83, 89, 92, 93, 99-100, 107, 108, 110, 112, 114, 208
restricted code 5-6
resultative 105
situation xi-xii, xiii, 62-66, 75, 77, 83, 92, 122-123, 125, 128-130, 133, 134-138, 144, 146, 187, 189
state verbs, see stative
stative viii, xi, xiii, 32, 63-66, 71-72, 93, 101, 103-108, 110, 113, 114, 122-123, 134-138, 140, 146-150, 152-158, 170-171, 174-175, 180, 188, 196, 199, 206, 221, 226
subjunctive xiii, 67, 82-83, 92, 99, 102, 106, 114, 122-123, 127-133, 138
subsequent 99, 104, 106-109, 114, 115
substrate languages ix, x, xiv, 59, 170-171, 194, 200-201, 203-204, 219-220, 225
suffixes, verb xii, 30-31, 48-50, 53, 55, 102, 106-108, 111, 114, 115, 144-145, 154-155, 161, 170, 173-174, 180-183, 198-199, 207, 208, 218, 224, 227
  semi-suffixes 52
superstrate languages ix, x, 59, 163; see also lexifier languages

telic 63-65, 92

tense vii, viii, ix, x, xi-xiv, 10, 16-18, 18-24, 26-43, 44-50, 53, 54, 55, 59-63, 66-73, 78, 83, 85, 89-91, 92, 93, 99-110, 111, 112, 113, 114, 115, 119, 122, 125-126, 133, 136, 138-139, 143-144, 146-150, 155, 157-159, 161, 163, 165, 170-173, 176-177, 179-183, 187, 188-191, 193-200, 203, 206, 208, 212, 213-224, 226, 227

tense locus 99, 223

universals vii, viii, x, 8, 18, 59, 89, 97, 129

verbal deprivation 1-3

In the CREOLE LANGUAGE LIBRARY series the following volumes have been published and will be published during 1990:

1. MUYSKEN, Pieter & Norval SMITH: *Substrata versus Universals in Creole Genesis. Papers from the Amsterdam Creole Workshop, April 1985.* Amsterdam, 1986.
2. SEBBA, Mark: *The Syntax of Serial Verbs: an Investigation into Serialisation in Sranan and other Languages.* Amsterdam, 1987.
3. BYRNE, Frank: *Grammatical Relations in a Radical Creole: Verb Complementation in Saramaccan.* Amsterdam, 1987.
4. LIPSKI, John M.: *The Speech of the Negros Congos of Panama.* Amsterdam/ Philadelphia, 1989.
5. JACKSON, Kenneth David: *Sing Without Shame. Oral traditions in Indo-Portuguese Creole verse.* Amsterdam/Philadelphia, 1990.
6. SINGLER, John: *Pidgin and Creole Tense-Mood-Aspect Systems.* Amsterdam/ Philadelphia, 1990.
7. FABIAN, Johannes: *History from Below.* Amsterdam/Philadelphia, 1990.